ARCHITECTS' SKETCHBOOKS

ARCHITECTS' SKETCHBOOKS

Will Jones

METROPOLIS BOOKS

CONTENTS

FOREWORD

Narinder Sagoo

Occasionally there is someone or something that brings my daily practice of creating and designing to a halt by questioning not what I am doing, but how I am doing it. For me, the process is often more fascinating than the end result, and at the heart of architecture, which is part of the process of building worlds, lies the language of drawing.

I have been drawing since the age of three. In my adult life and professional career, I have drawn thousands of conversations and ideas, relating to many hundreds of projects. I have been able to share the passion of design through my ability to draw and, over time, like any draughtsman, I have developed an extensive vocabulary for visualizing design. I use drawing to tell stories about the spaces and places that we intend to create; how a building can interact with history, culture and events; and how it will behave at different times of day and seasons of the year. I can use this storytelling to give instructions, observe and record, capture a discussion or even just make note of a mid-afternoon thought. It provides me with a tool to communicate often very complex ideas in the simplest possible way.

When we consider drawing literally as a language, we can recognize it as a fluid, ever-evolving means by which to express, discuss and state ideas or tell anecdotes with a multitude of accents and mannerisms and even with wit. You can say what you want in whatever way you want. A drawing can be a snapshot of a distinct thought, sometimes an unfinished idea or something not yet useful. It is a medium that does not require a conclusion, but gives us the means to discuss possibilities. In such a provisional form a drawing is referred to as a sketch — it is the embodiment of a free conversation. All the architects featured in this book reveal through their sketches their individual energy of thought, their own stories, and, if we look a little further, their personalities.

There is a misconception that all architects think through drawing, and it is astonishing how widely held this spurious belief is. Drawing is such a personal endeavour that many people never try it, but, for those who do, it can be the most liberating way of communicating. I believe that everyone can draw but some of us just need to be reminded that it is okay to draw. The humble drawing runs the risk of being overlooked, as a mere stepping stone between idea and computer realization, or a minor contribution to the early shaping of a building; and it is often technology that then gets the glory. This makes the investigative journey in *Architects' Sketchbooks* all the more pertinent to the question of where the role of the architect sits between those of artist and builder. There are many sources that provide us with the end product from the architects' drawing board, but few that explore and celebrate the sketchbook, and the liberating processes that lead to the finished work.

Architects' Sketchbooks celebrates drawing as a 21st-century medium for architects. It gives a much-needed overview of the way we think about and invent our built environment through the sketches and drawings of an extraordinary collection of architectural creators and thinkers, some of whom I am proud to have met, studied and worked with. This book offers a unique opportunity to eavesdrop on their creative graphical conversations, and it is a powerful reminder that the mind-to-hand process of drawing prevails, even for the most technologically advanced minds in architecture.

NARINDER SAGOO
PARTNER, FOSTER + PARTNERS

BLOOD, SWEAT AND PENCIL LEAD.

Will Jones

Where do architects get their inspiration? What does that first stroke of pencil on paper look like? And how do they embark on the monumental task of turning a sketch into a skyscraper? *Architects' Sketchbooks* provides the reader, or perhaps we should say viewer, with a rare glimpse of the first inklings of the individual creative processes—the blood, sweat and pencil lead—that go into designing the world we live in.

Sketches are presented alongside paintings and models by eighty-five architects from around the world, showing how they think, draw and archive the results in their sketchbooks. The sketches range from simple doodles to intricate and beautiful masterpieces, executed in a mixture of styles and media that exhibit the individual traits and nuances associated with each architect's background and working practice. Every page is the graphic record of one step in a long journey that began with a few lines in a notebook, and ends, potentially, with a structure of landscape-changing proportions. The images are set alongside illuminating texts that quote, wherever possible, the words of the architects themselves.

Architects' Sketchbooks includes the work of world-renowned architects such as Norman Foster and Rafael Viñoly, radical thinkers like the architecture practice Smout Allen and Junya Ishigami, recognized artists such as Will Alsop and C. Errol Barron and young architects such as Kristofer Kelly and Luke Pearson. All unveil their conceptual designs, revealing the unusual, stimulating and sometimes unstructured ways in which they find their inspiration and set down their creative thoughts. Despite the diverse range of individuals and approaches featured, every architect would concur with Austrian practice DMAA that

  FREEDOM OF IMAGINATION IS THE
  CORNERSTONE OF EVERY DESIGN.

Although these works are not the finished articles, they assume an aesthetic value in their own right. American architect Michael Lehrer explains his lifelong fascination with Lloyd Wright's drawings, which he reveres as others do Picasso's or Rembrandt's

  IT ALL STARTED WITH FRANK LLOYD WRIGHT
  FOR ME. FROM THE AGE OF TEN, I WOULD STARE
  AT HIS DRAWINGS, HIS SINUOUS LINES MELDING
  FIGURE AND GROUND, LANDSCAPE AND BUILDING,
  PAPER AND IMAGE. I FOUND THEM, AND STILL DO,
  RAVISHING AND COMPLETELY SEDUCTIVE. FOR ME,
  THEY ARE PARADIGMS OF BEAUTY.

Unlike art, architecture is often considered a precise activity, a science, undertaken solely to create the essential built environment that accommodates society. And, to some extent, it is. There are swathes of laws, rules and regulations to abide by when designing even the simplest building, and there are social implications and practicalities to be considered as the scale of construction gets larger. Architecture is not something merely to be admired and to be pontificated over, but something to be *used*. The same cannot be said of art. Australian architect Sean Godsell agrees that

  ARCHITECTURE IS ULTIMATELY A BUILT THING;
  A SKETCH IS EVERYTHING AND THEN NOTHING.
  BUT THE ABILITY TO IMBUE A SIMPLE SKETCH
  WITH COMPLEXITY, TO INSTILL THE NUANCES
  OF A RESOLVED PLAN INTO A SIMPLE DIAGRAM,
  THIS IS WHERE ARCHITECTURE BEGINS AND A
  SKETCH CAPTURES THAT MOMENT FOREVER.

Godsell sums up the agony and ecstasy of an architect's work. A sketch is ultimately throwaway, and yet it has the potential to capture a moment in time and an instant of pure inspiration. It is the ability to absorb and record this moment of inspiration that reveals the artist, painter, sculptor or poet within the architect. Architects see themselves as 'creatives', working towards something beyond a specified, determinate end. They see more to a building than four walls and a roof, as Louis Kahn explains simply and concisely:

◊◊ A GREAT BUILDING MUST BEGIN WITH THE UNMEASURABLE, MUST GO THROUGH MEASURABLE MEANS WHEN IT IS BEING DESIGNED, AND YET IN THE END MUST BE UNMEASURABLE.

When complete, a building, which begins in the imagination and passes into reality, should transcend the mere bricks and mortar from which it is built. Architects do not thrive on the mundanity of regulations or form filling but on the challenge, the excitement of creating a new design, seeing it realized in built form, and watching how it stimulates those who go on to use and experience it.

Henri Matisse once said:

◊◊ DRAWING IS NOT AN EXERCISE OF PARTICULAR DEXTERITY, BUT ABOVE ALL A MEANS OF EXPRESSING INTIMATE FEELINGS AND MOODS.

Cennino Cennini encouraged fellow artists:

◊◊ DO NOT FAIL, AS YOU GO ON, TO DRAW SOMETHING EVERY DAY, FOR NO MATTER HOW LITTLE IT IS, IT WILL BE WELL·WORTHWHILE, AND IT WILL DO YOU A WORLD OF GOOD.

These are wise words that probably ring true for all the contributors to *Architects' Sketchbooks*. While masters of their craft such as Rafael Viñoly and Norman Foster understand the benefits of CAD (computer-aided design) and other digital techniques, and employ them in their practices, both worry about a new generation of designers who may not possess skill or interest in using pencil and paper. Foster says:

◊◊ I WORRY ABOUT STUDENTS WHO MIGHT FEEL THAT THE POWER OF SOPHISTICATED COMPUTER EQUIPMENT HAS SOMEHOW RENDERED THE HUMBLE PENCIL IF NOT OBSOLETE, THEN CERTAINLY SECOND RATE. THE PENCIL AND COMPUTER ARE VERY SIMILAR IN THAT THEY ARE ONLY AS GOOD AS THE PERSON DRIVING THEM.

Viñoly adds:

◊◊ I DRAW ALL THE TIME, WHEREVER I AM, BECAUSE TO ME IT IS A WAY OF EXERCISING MY MIND AND SEARCHING FOR THE NEXT THOUGHT THAT WILL BECOME A DESIGN. YOU CANNOT DO THIS WITH A COMPUTER—THERE IS NOT THE FREEDOM.

Similarly, radical thinkers such as Penelope Haralambidou and Ana Rocha bemoan the contemporary preference for designing on-screen instead of hands-on, stating that digital design has neither the soul nor the spirit of work that has been handcrafted.

So, do the architects in this book sketch, paint and model because they need to? Overwhelmingly so—such drafting and redrafting remains the lifeblood and backbone of an entire industry. Do these architects sketch because they like to? Of course they do. In a professional world that is laden with costs, constraints and client pressure, the chance to escape reality even for a few moments is priceless. Will Alsop explains:

◊◊ I CAN SIT IN MY STUDIO ON A SATURDAY MORNING AND FIND SOMETHING ON A LARGE PIECE OF PAPER. THE FEELING THAT YOU GET IS ALMOST AS GOOD AS HAVING FINISHED A BUILDING. IT'S NOT ABOUT DESIGNING SOMETHING, IT'S ABOUT DISCOVERING WHAT SOMETHING COULD BE.

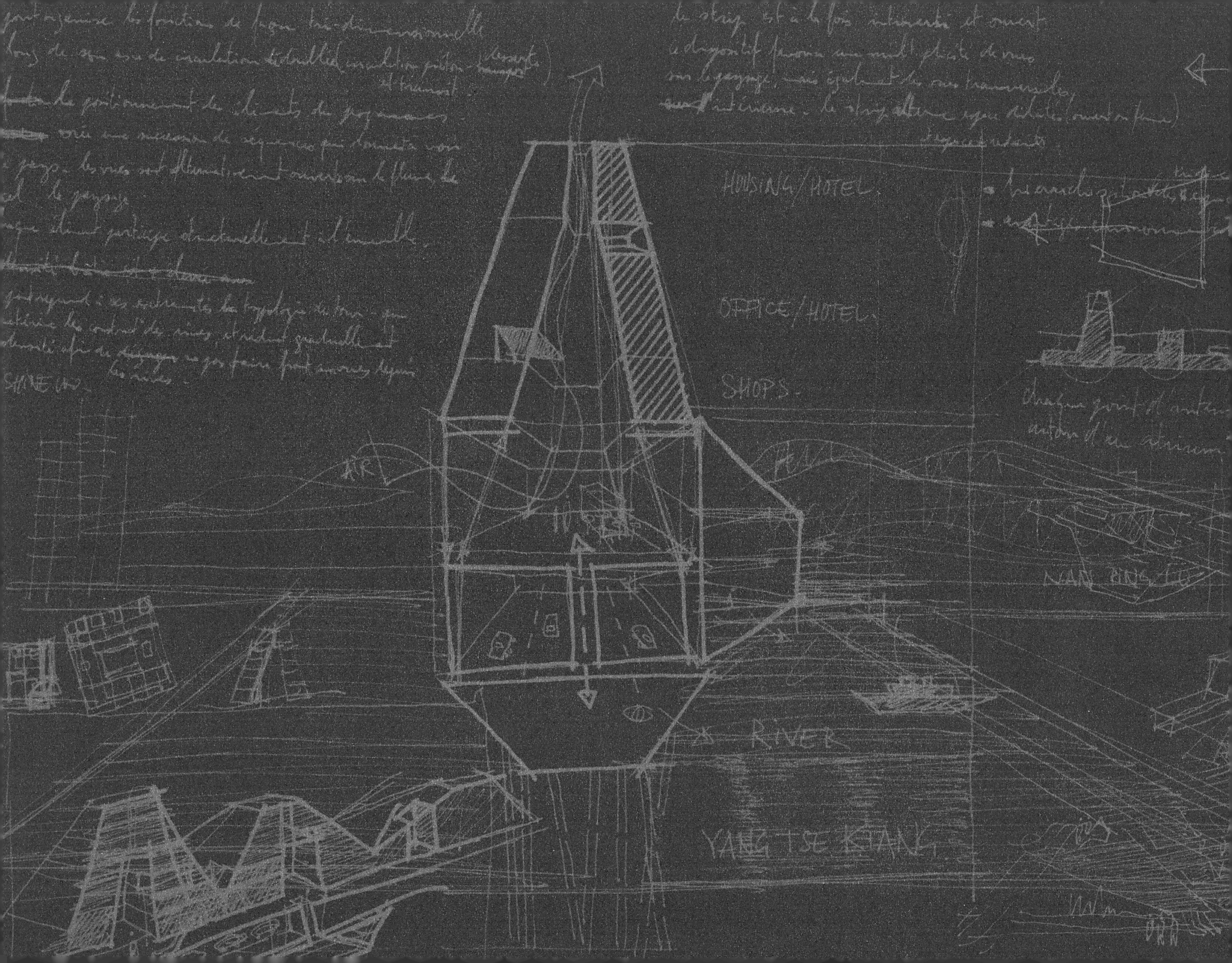

HOUSING/HOTEL.

OFFICE/HOTEL

SHOPS.

AIR

NAN PING

RIVER

YANG TSE KIANG

This enjoyment—wonder, even—is a gift that few people experience in their job. And so, these sketches, half-conscious musings played out on paper, in so many cases forgotten or lost on the tortuous journey that ends in the construction a building, deserve to be seen as works of art in progress. So then, why is it that the important sketches and drawings of countless talented architects, whose buildings affect our lives in so many ways, are never aired in public?

Perhaps the explanation lies in the function of the sketches—their reason for being. They are composed not as end products, but as the first step on the aforementioned journey towards a goal. As such, an overdependence or undue reverence for the ideas in the sketch has the potential to turn a creative outlet into a limiting factor. An extreme example of an artist's disregard for his own sketches concerns the sculptor Eduardo Chillida. His wife, when asked what Chillida did with drawings and preparatory images for his works, said that he threw everything into the fireplace to burn. The interviewer was horrified but Chillida's wife explained that he didn't see the need to save everything:

◐◐ HE IS AN EXPLORER AND EXPLORERS CANNOT
CARRY TOO MANY THINGS WITH THEM IF THEY
ARE TO HAVE STRENGTH THAT LASTS TILL THE END.

Spanish architect and professor Julio Barreno agrees with Chillida and his wife, using the analogy as a way of describing his own work:

◐◐ AN ARCHITECT MUST BE AN EXPLORER...
HE DOESN'T KNOW WHERE HIS DESIGNS WILL
ARRIVE AT. HE MUST TRAVEL WITH A BACKPACK
OF USEFUL TOOLS—KNOWLEDGE, EXPERIENCE,
COURAGE AND INTUITION—EVERYTHING
TO ENABLE HIM TO GET TO AN INTERESTING
NEW PLACE.

And this is the key to *Architects' Sketchbooks*: don't look for artistic beauty, though it can be found in many of the sketches here, but search for the inspiration—the architect's personal quest—that lies a pencil line's thickness behind the marks seen on paper. Don't look *at* the sketches, models, painting and collages but *into* them and draw out the immeasurable, the magic that makes a great building.

These architects are not artists, and most do not profess to be; but their graphical and spatial thinking is exquisite. They seek inspiration in all manner of ways and record what they see in their mind's eye, using only paper and pencil. What they all achieve is more than an impersonal response to specific topographical or logistical challenges: they seek to unleash their imagination upon the world. With this in mind we delve into *Architects' Sketchbooks* and into the psyche of the individuals who make the marks, to attempt to understand how great and interesting buildings come to look as they do.

Images

ARCHITECTS' SKETCHBOOKS

3DELUXE

'Sketching, both by hand and on to the computer, plays an important role right from the beginning' say the architects of 3deluxe. 'The drawings are created with different techniques, types of pencils and colours, and then further processed digitally.'

The practice develops designs mainly with 3D software because it is more efficient than model-making when handling complex organic shapes. Additionally, working models are built to experiment with structures or materials. Despite this, sketching is regarded as the pre-eminent and most immediate method of visualizing ideas. 'You are not tempted to gloss over a crude design with digital filters and effects, or to finalize the draft at too early a stage. Sketching brings out the essence of design.'

In this series of drawings the design can be seen to progress through initial sketch ideas, into colour drawings and on through digital manipulation. Each stage helps to move the concept a step closer to becoming a buildable structure.

Compared with 3D models, 2D sketches are vague and leave room for interpretation. The practicability of an initial sketch always has to be verified using a 3D representation. However, since many of the practice's hand drawings are scanned in and developed with the help of image-processing software, they have a great influence on the final design. 'After completion, we often rediscover sketches from a very early project phase that passed out of our minds—retrospectively it turns out that they largely anticipated the final shape.'

Recently, some of the practice's sketch sheets were printed as a limited edition by LUMAS, a leading supplier of art and photographs. A selection of their projects were also exhibited in a solo show in Berlin.

19

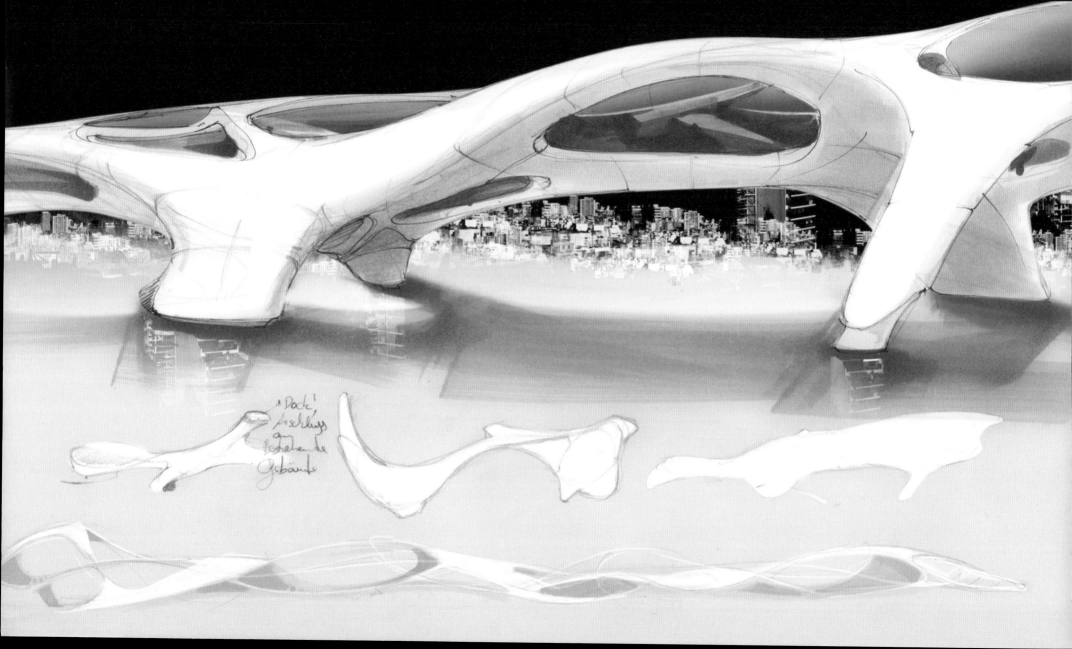

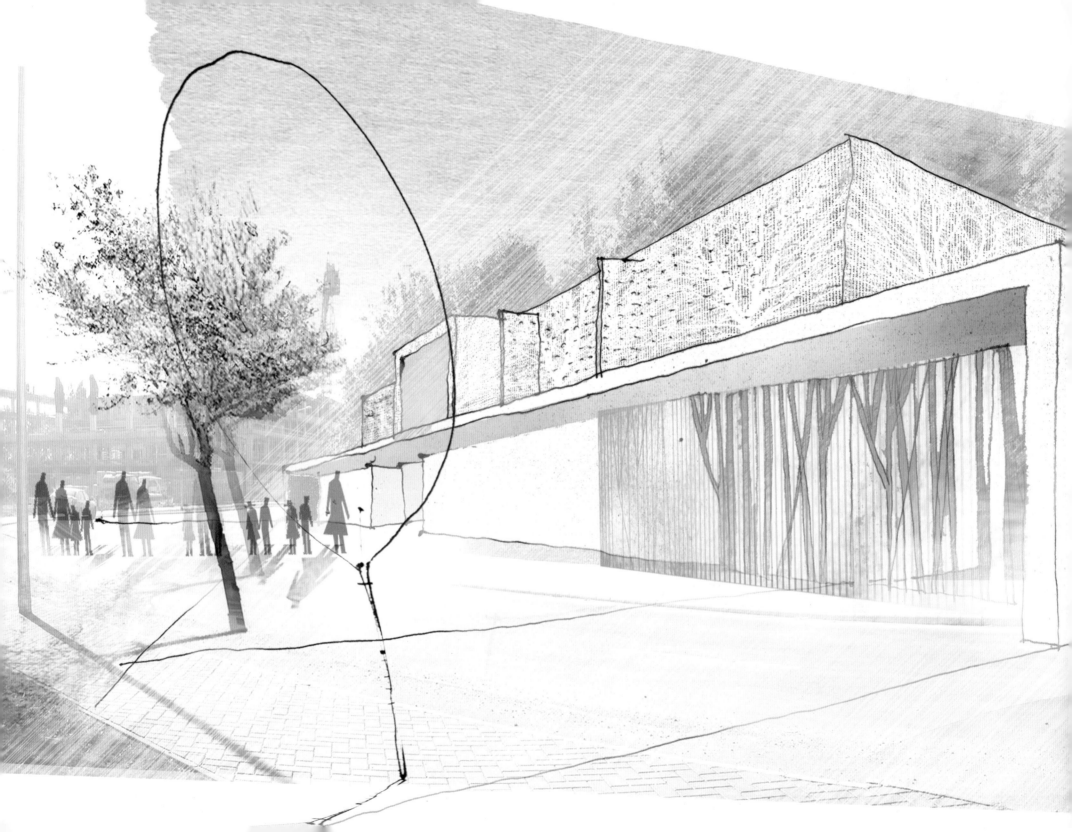

↑ 24–25
↑ 26–27
← 28–29

A4 STUDIO

This Hungarian practice uses a variety of media to create its initial architectural ideas. 'We prepare mock-ups and model on the computer simultaneously,' say the architects. 'This way we plan the outside mass and the inside spaces of the building at the same time. And then, based on these simple ideas, we take photos and sketch hand drawings that we then clothe with collages.'

The desired results are hyper-realistic pictures of the buildings at the earliest stages of planning. 'It is very important to check the plans with 3D simulation, though,' says A4, 'to see if the planned building is coming through in ground plan, in mass and in space too.'

However, the architects admit that without sketches they cannot start planning the process that leads to their unique images. 'The first sketches are fresh, simple expressions of the final draft.' Next, the cut-and-paste method that the practice employs overlays sketches with images of model buildings and photos of people. It creates an other-worldly feel to the image, but also helps clients understand the design from a user's perspective.

A4 believes that the majority of its initial design ideas make it through to the completed scheme, whether built or not. 'We are trying to amplify the graphic hand drawings that we use to visualize our works, not just for fellow professionals but also so they can be inspirational to contractors. This is very important if you want everyone to work as passionately as yourself on any project.'

25

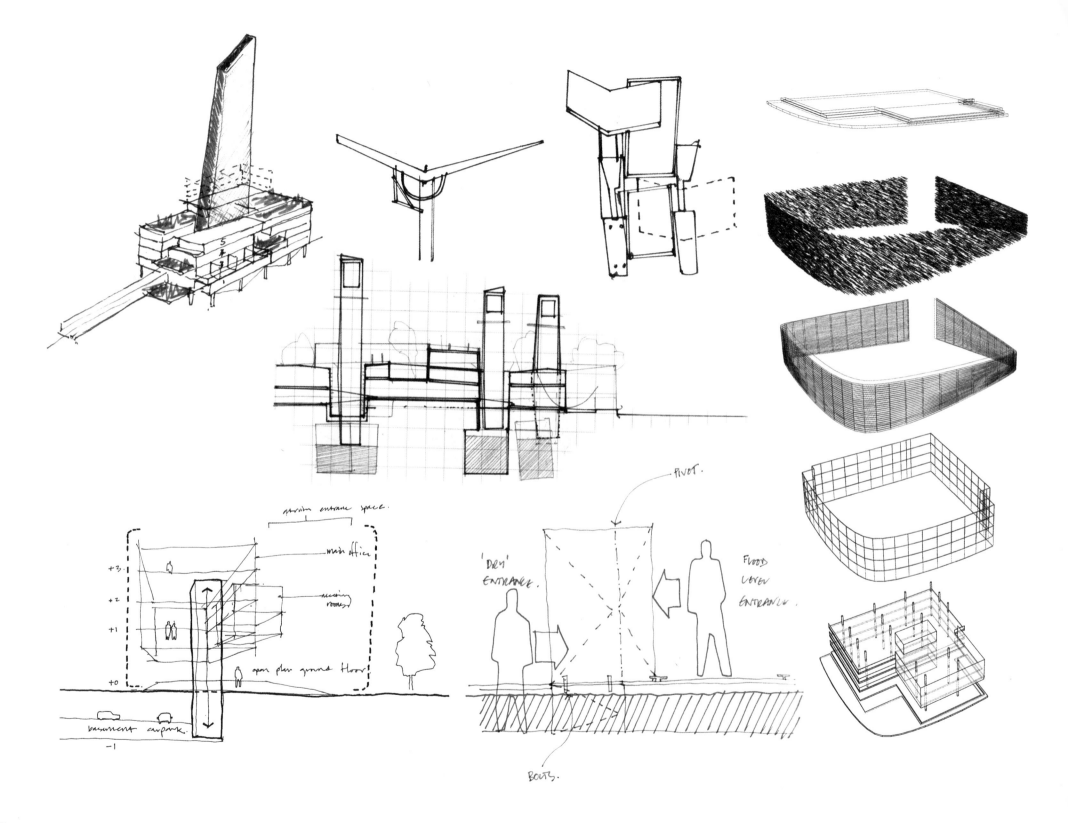

atrium entrance space.

main office

meeting rooms

+3.

+2.

+1.

open plan ground floor

+0.

basement carpark.

-1

PIVOT.

'DRY' ENTRANCE.

FLOOD LEVEL ENTRANCE.

BOLTS.

PROFILE OF BUILDING FEEDS INTO FACADE

open in morning.

open in evening.

shading from side.

never want lantern side sun. in heat

lan

low slated sun from side.

hot area.

3PM

when sun comes from these angles want facade blocked.

sun heals

BEN ADDY

'I always start with pen, pencil and paper,' says Ben Addy, principal of Moxon. 'Often at the first meeting with a client, during the discussion, ideas will be tabled in an unfussy and graphically unsophisticated way. So much so that the sketches later require explanation in order to be understandable. They are a "you had to be there" type moment.'

This rapid visualization can be plainly seen on these pages—doodles and rough sketches create solutions to numerous challenges [30–31]. However, Addy's designs also progress into wonderfully complex street-scapes [32–33], which can be read as a whole, rather than abstract parts.

Addy carries out a cyclical process of refinement and superimposition—still largely pen/paper but also with elements of 3D computer-based working. He sees no conflict between manual and digital processes. Indeed, Addy and his team use 'pens' on computers via graphics tablets, or they 'carve' into printouts from 3D with smudgy pencils.

'So many ideas are thrown up, modified and discarded in the initial stages that we find it impossible to work in any other way,' he says. 'The rapid discussion, dismissal and evolution of ideas is crucial, so direct and immediate expression is very important to ensure an open discussion, whether internally with oneself, with the team or with the client.'

Still in this mode of operation, but subsequent to the very first raw ideas, Addy finds working in 3D helps with scale and testing. 'We treat a lot of our digital models as "dirty tools" for getting the principles right. Iteration is essential and the more methods of describing and exploring that we use, the more ideas and possibilities are thrown up.'

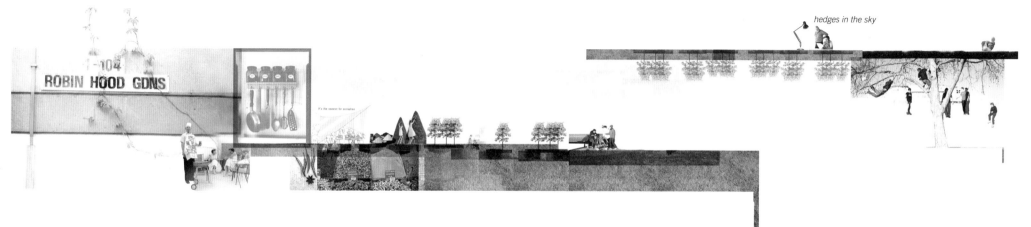

hedges in the sky

ROBIN HOOD GDNS

AGATHOM CO.

Agathom Co. believes that the first design steps in every project are individual, and as such each brief must be approached with an open mind. Even if the initial move is a mark made on paper, pretty soon this Canadian practice, run by Katja Aga Sachse Thom and Adam Thom, creates a sketch model.

'Our projects are born out of spatial ideas rather than graphic compositions,' says Adam Thom. 'The meat of each concept is tested by creating a 3D sketch. We learn from the sketch model more than the pencil sketch. We both come from a background of sculpture, so it is our natural approach. ...the finished project only can be spatially compelling as a result of constant spatial exploration throughout the design process.'

In the hands of Agathom Co., simple cardboard models transform into detailed, precisely scaled sculptures that are works of art in their own right. However, these are not considered the end product: they are used and then often forgotten as the design progresses. Here, spatial explorations of a residential project include whole building models [34, 36 left, and 37], as well as mock-ups of specific spaces and details such as stairways [35, 36 right]. Thom believes that these early models help to determine whether an idea has 'enough "nutrition" to continue', or whether it is time to start afresh.

'We feel that the successful sketch, be it a model or 2D drawing, must not be tripped-up by aesthetics of its own... The truly useful and beautiful sketches are not the least bit concerned with the selection of materials, methods of construction or level of finish. The best ones are fully focused on the spatial idea that they are exploring.'

35

↑
38–39

↑
40–41

↑
42–43

WILL ALSOP

Will Alsop is one of the most prominent architects in the UK, and his work brings a delight and playfulness to architecture that the discipline often lacks.

The inspiration for his multicoloured, outlandishly-shaped architectural offerings comes from Alsop's love of art and painting. 'Painting to me is a way of exploring architecture. It's all the same thing. I can sit in my studio, creating something on a piece of paper and the feeling that you get is almost as good as having finished a building. It's not about designing something, it's about discovering what something could be and I think that's a very important distinction.'

By attempting to bring art directly into architecture Alsop has abandoned the hegemony of acceptable style. He has rendered the whole process of architecture one of increasing fluidity and transparency—a new and refreshing position for such a concrete discipline.

'I don't see the point of architecture that simply blends in. I have done lots of work with the general public and what I hear over and over again is that people are looking for something that marks their spot on the earth's surface. Something that has an identity that is not shared with others,' says Alsop.

This parallel approach—as both architect and artist—is unusual, but Alsop feels that art is a discipline inseparable from architecture. His paintings and sketches have been presented alongside his architectural projects in numerous exhibitions.

39

ARCHITECTS
ATELIER RYO ABE

Ryo Abe is an avid collector of abstract imagery. 'I begin by collecting textures from fields or plains, salt flats or city streets. Then I make collages, often by taking photographs, to create new images of the space. This is done by printing them out, then manually cutting and pasting, even drawing directly on to the image.'

For Abe, accumulating these textures is 'like harvesting memories of feelings and emotions. I intend to design with these emotions, creating new spaces. I am always searching for different skills, another way to edit these emotions.'

But the architect is a perfectionist and many of the photos and collages he creates never get beyond the sketchbook. 'I tend to find disappointment most of the time,' says Abe, 'with 5% or less of my conceptual work translating into a built design. However, sometimes I feel the composed emotions from those collages. It is inspirational, similar to something like composing music, I guess. Once the "music" starts to flow it begins to form the spaces, to hint at contrast of light and dark, and to re-create the textures and emotions within the new space.'

For the mass of images, collages and sketches that don't immediately evolve into architecture, there beckons a future. Abe keeps them close to hand, piled around the desk as a potential source of inspiration for other projects.

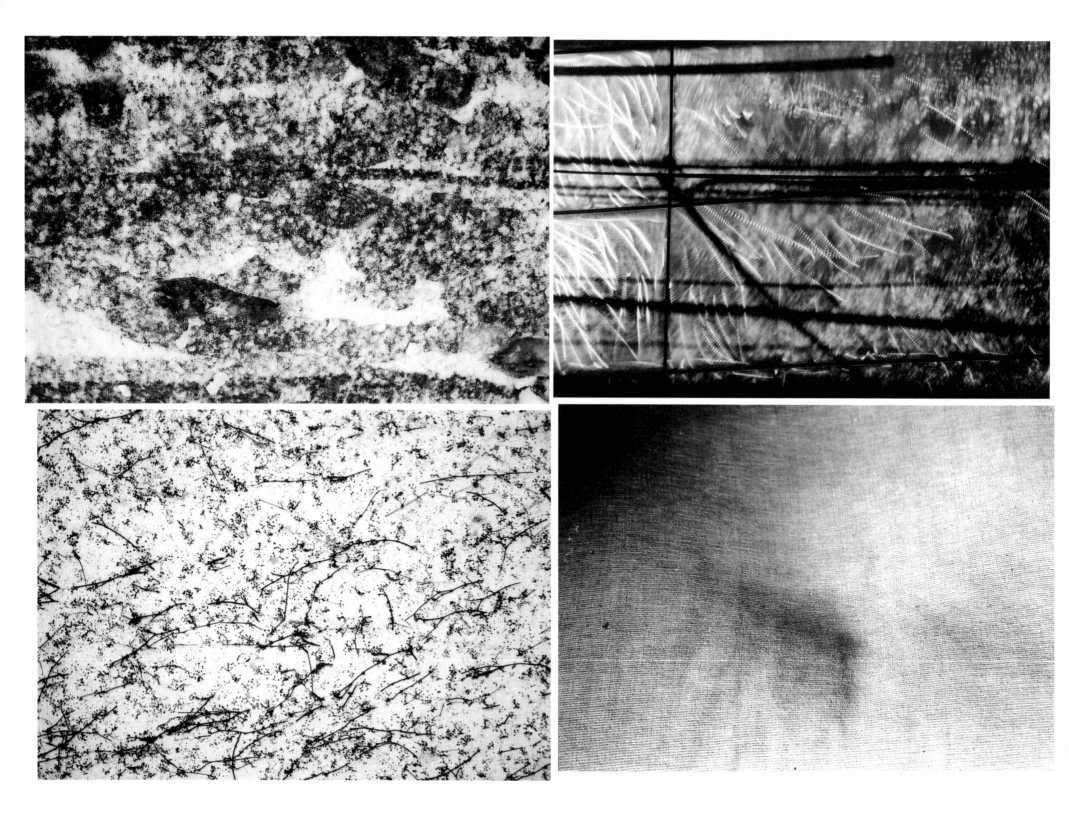

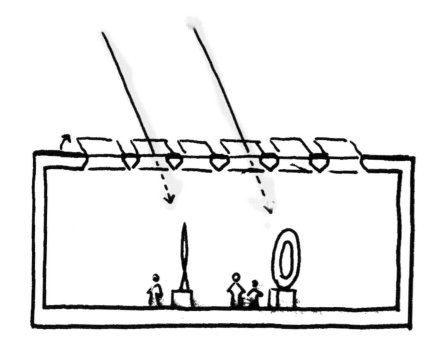
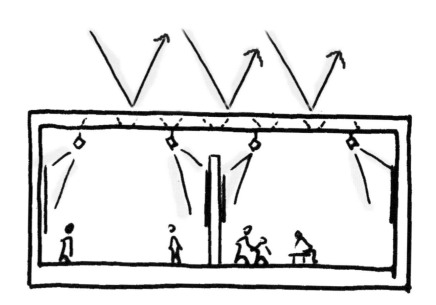
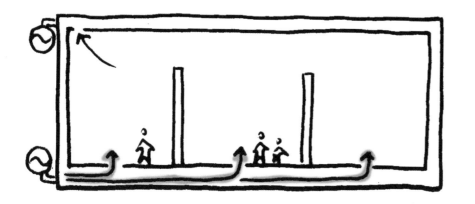

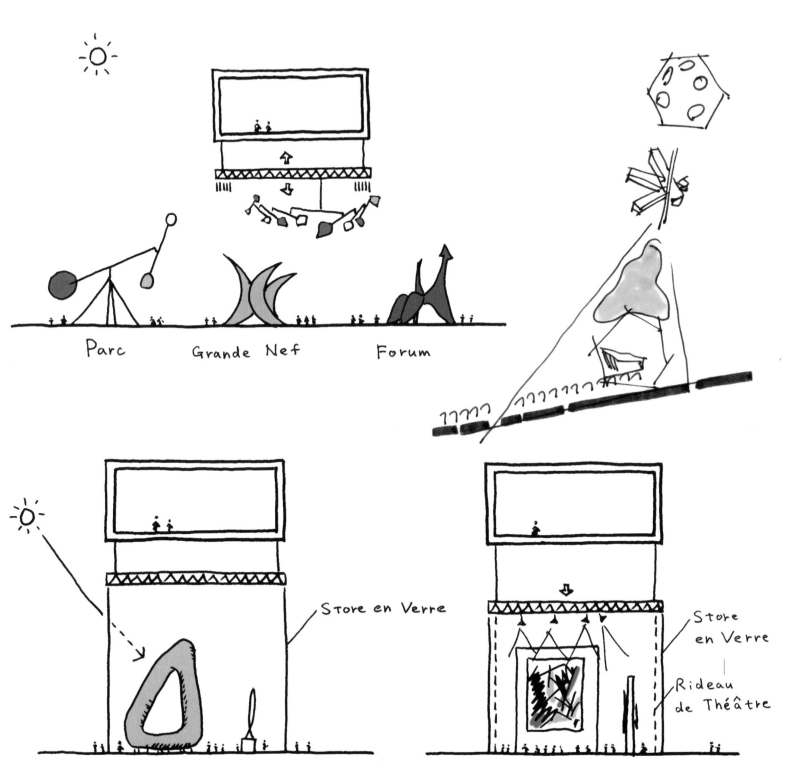

Parc   Grande Nef   Forum

Store en Verre

Store
en Verre

Rideau
de Théâtre

SHIGERU BAN

Born in Tokyo and educated in the USA, Shigeru Ban first worked for Arata Isozaki before setting up his own practice. Lauded for exciting design and admired for his use of unusual materials and techniques, one of Ban's latest projects is the Centre Pompidou-Metz in France [50–51].

Ban's sketches for the design are simple and instructive. They perhaps lack the finesse or artistic flair of some other architects' designs but instead focus on how the design will work—details such as the type of forms to be created, circulation of visitors, sight lines and sun paths.

The Centre Pompidou-Metz is enveloped by a gigantic lattice roof—an umbrella of hexagonal laminated timber, inspired by the woven bamboo of a Chinese hat. Ban's sketches, though, concentrate on the galleries, the overall site plan and how the weather—sun and wind—will influence the visitors' experience of the site. Three rectangular, cantilevered boxes [48–49] house parts of the Centre's permanent collection in a climate-controlled environment. Here, the sketches forgo artistic dedication in favour of a basic diagrammatic style that quickly delivers the desired message.

Ban and his team have reinforced the important relationship that the Centre has with the outdoors by encasing the entire complex within movable glass shutters, which can open to the surrounding gardens and park. They have also reduced what could have been a fiendishly complex project into bite-size chunks of pictorial information, making it simpler for everyone, from client to contractor, to understand.

49

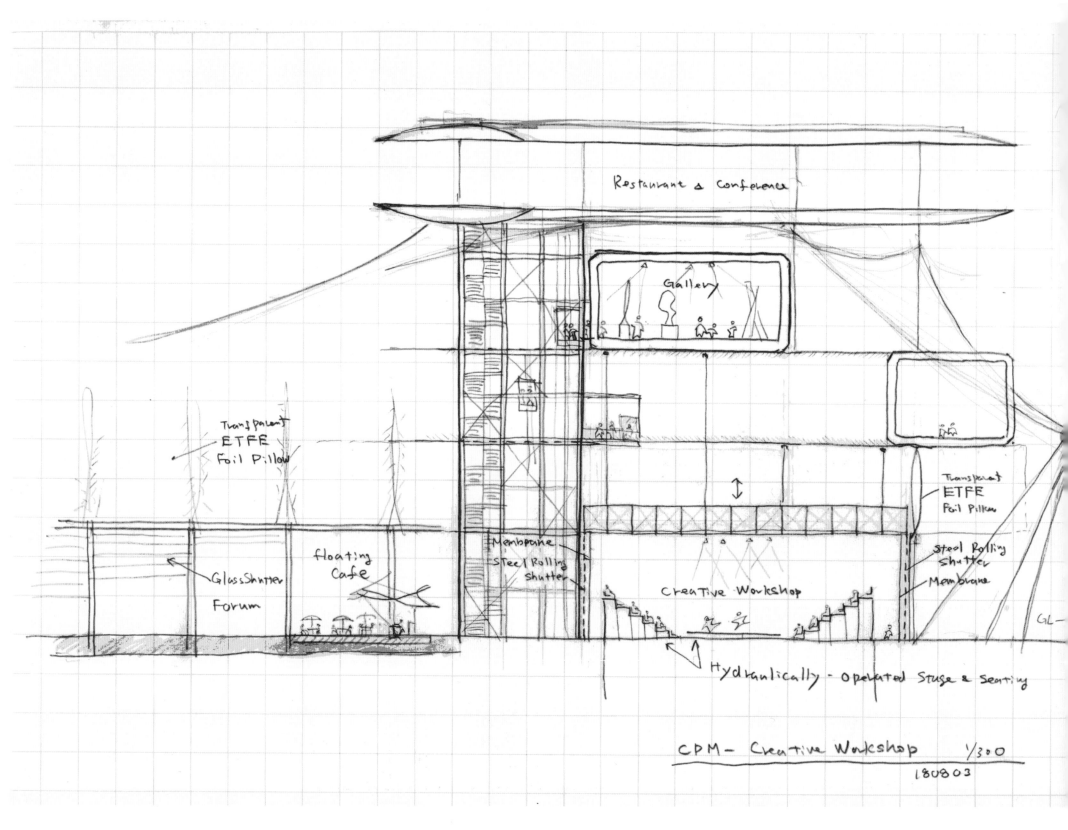

Restaurant & Conference

Gallery

Transparent
ETFE
Foil Pillow

Transparent
ETFE
Foil Pillow

floating
Cafe

GlassShutter
Forum

Membrane
Steel Rolling
Shutter

Creative Workshop

Steel Rolling
Shutter
Membrane

GL—

Hydraulically - Operated Stage & Seating

CPM — Creative Workshop   1/300

180803

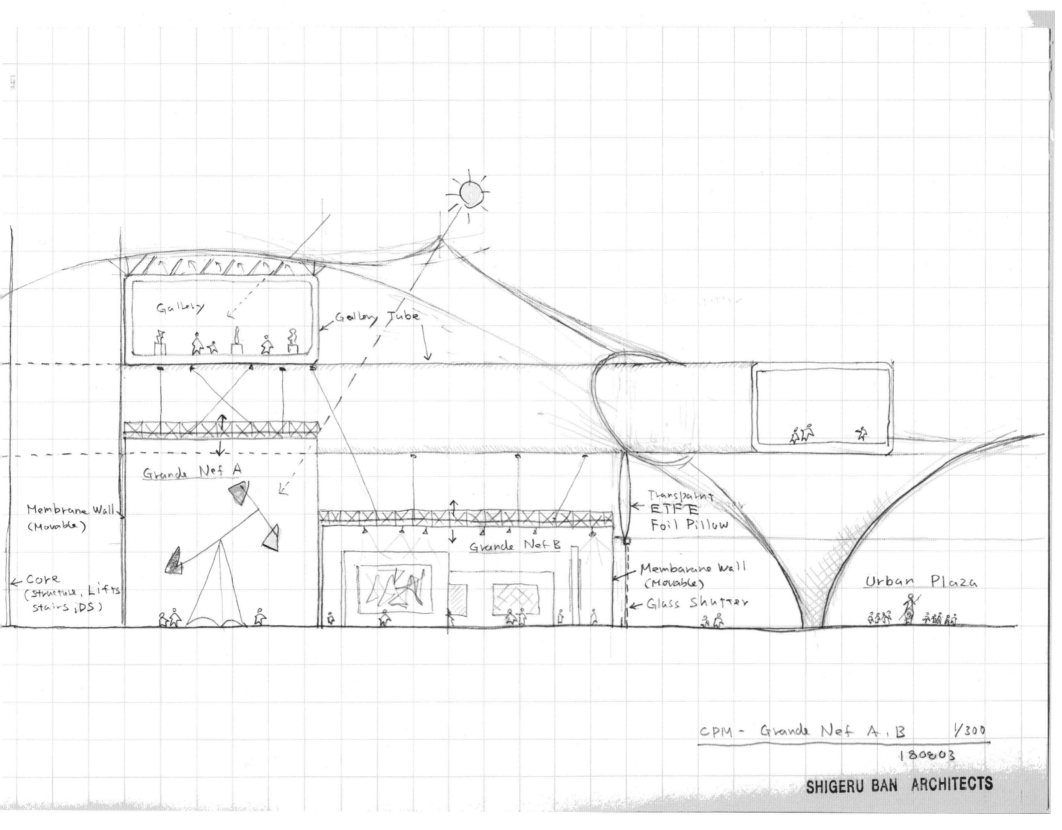

Gallery

Gallery Tube

Grande Nef A

Membrane Wall
(Movable)

Core
(Structure, Lifts
Stairs, DS)

Grande Nef B

Transparent
ETFE
Foil Pillow

Membrane Wall
(Movable)

Glass Shutter

Urban Plaza

CPM - Grande Nef A. B   1/300

180803

SHIGERU BAN ARCHITECTS

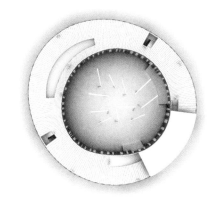
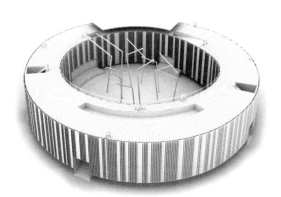

JULIO BARRENO

'An architect must be an explorer not a tourist guide,' says Julio Barreno. 'The architect doesn't know where his designs will arrive at. He must travel with a backpack of useful tools—knowledge, experience, courage and intuition—everything to enable him to get to an interesting new place. The tourist guide never goes to a new place.'

This Spanish architect and professor uses a mix of sketches and models to formulate his designs. He believes that each of the different media used says something different about the same work. 'A good way to work is to create using a range of sketches and models because among them you find interesting things to use in the final design,' he continues.

For example, a doughnut of string provides inspiration for Villafranca de los Barros, Badajoz, Spain [53]. While a paperclip is transformed into the circulation route in Viviendas en Huelva, Spain [52].

'However, above all, intuition is the best weapon to carry on this expedition,' he says. 'A deep observation of the empirical data can quickly suggest feasible courses of action. But in this process it is important to observe correctly everything at the site, to analyse properly, ...to know which option is the best one to be developed. In the case of the explorer, which is the good path to take...?'

Depending on which themes are more important for an architect, the journey and its destination can be totally different, Barreno believes. That's why he reiterates the importance of knowing how to observe and analyse carefully. 'Then the architect becomes a filter, able to sift all the information from the reality and convert it into a real design, a project and a building.'

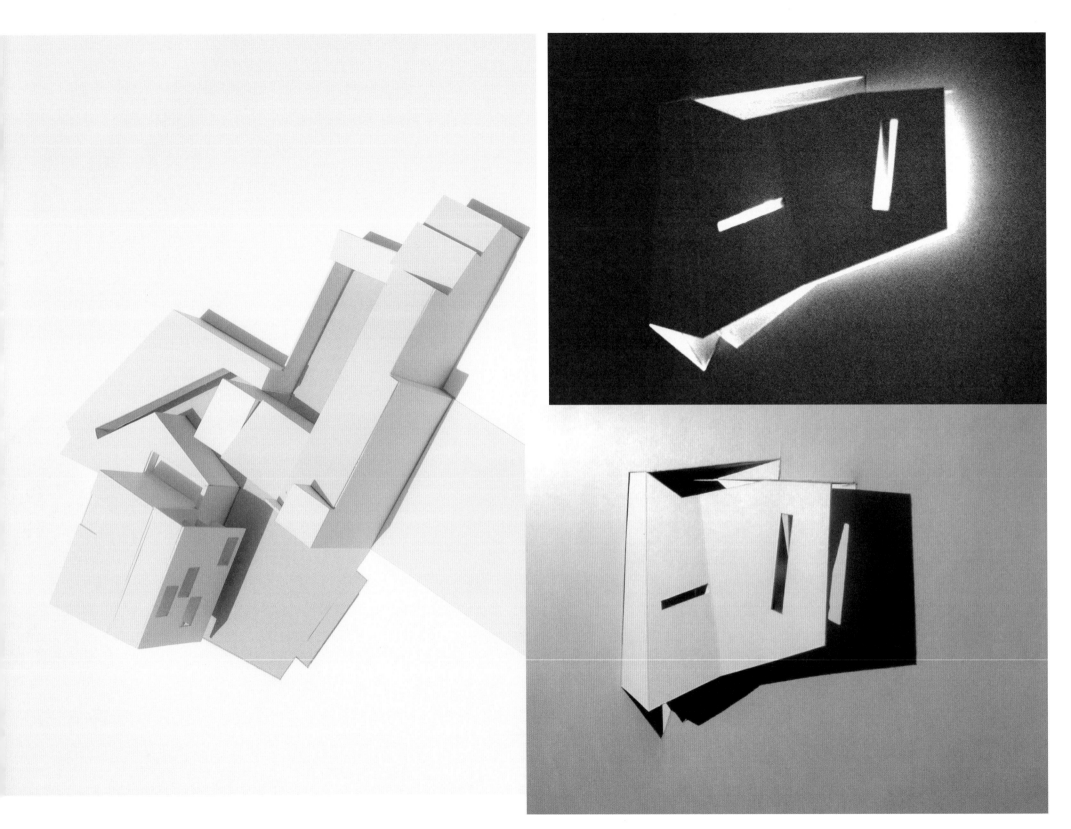

exposition blvd, ~ Audubon Park

C. ERROL BARRON

An architect, painter, professor and musician, C. Errol Barron has sketched and painted for more than 25 years to record ideas, events and observations from daily life. His classical style underlies all his work, both as architect and college professor, and he considers drawing to be one of the foundations of a good architectural education.

Barron's works record a variety of subjects—landscapes, buildings, objects and people—providing a unique perspective on the creative process itself, as well as the connection between painting and architecture.

Barron is a professor of architecture at Tulane University, New Orleans, and a partner in Errol Barron/Michael Toups Architects. He is also the author of Observation: Sketchbooks, Paintings and Architecture of Errol Barron, (2005). Recently, the Art and Architecture Building's Ewing Gallery at the University of Tennessee opened an exhibit dedicated to the work of Barron entitled 'Hand Drawing in the Digital Age'. Commenting on the exhibition, Barron said: 'It was good to be in these galleries, alone with the paintings—no one there. I was taken by the wonderful, clear values, so much so that they were as powerful way across the room as when close-by.'

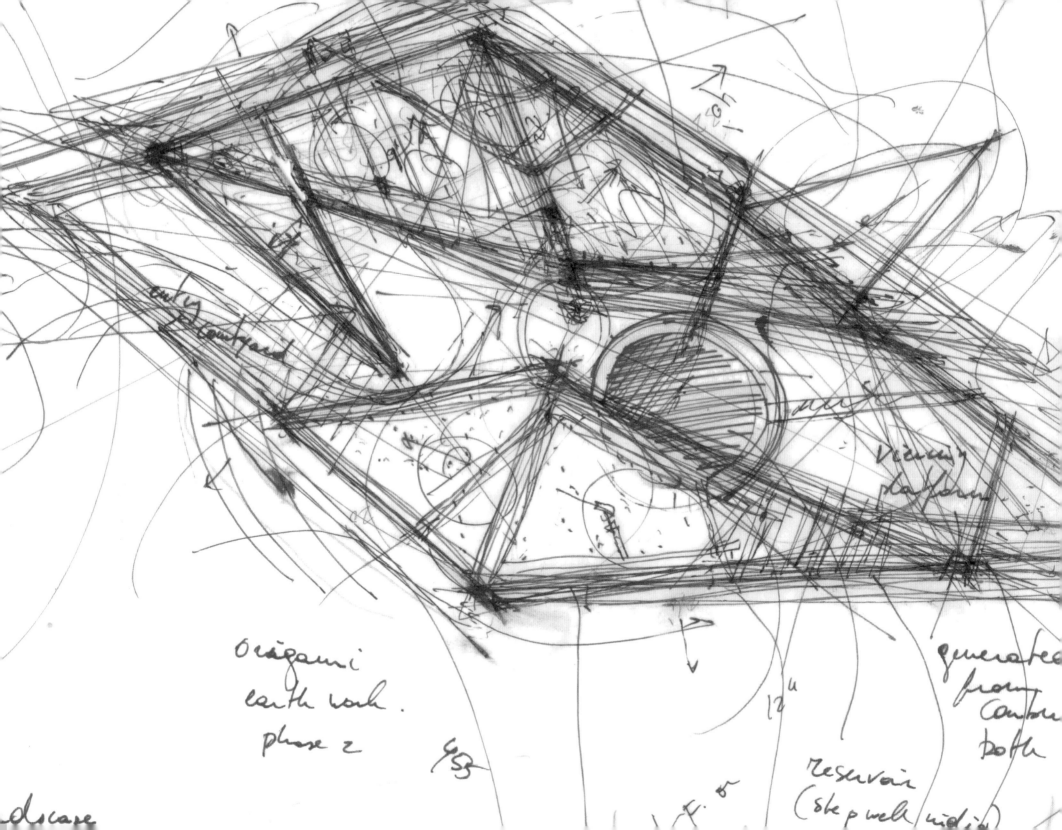

origami
earth work.
phase 2

reservoir
(step well india)

generated
from
contour
both

12"

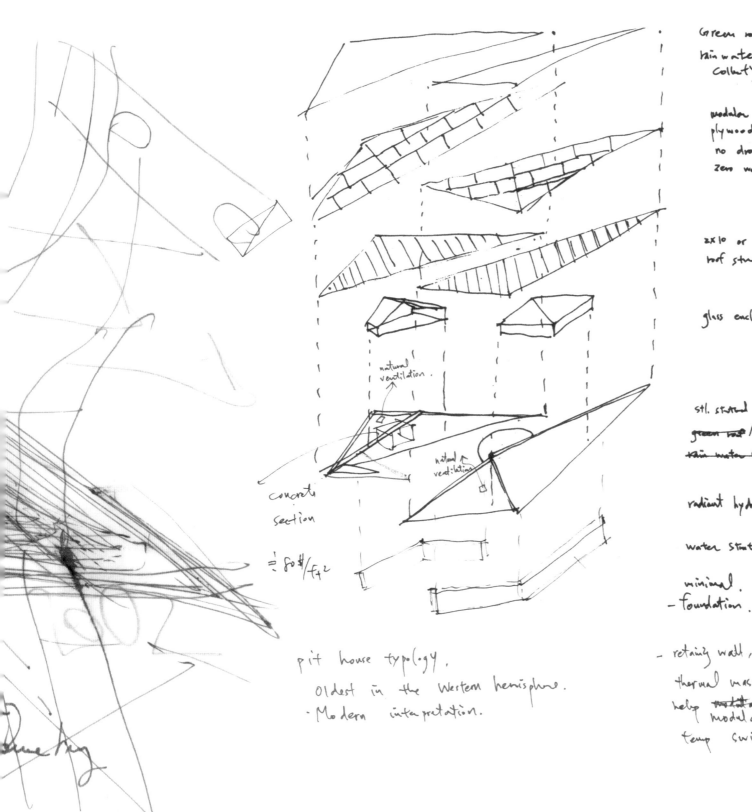

Green roof -
rain water
collecty

modular
plywood roof,
no drop,
zero waste.

2x10 or TGo
roof structure

glass enclosure

natural ventilation.

stl. stated frame
green roof /
rain water collecty

concrete section

natural
ventilation

radiant hydronic?

water strategy.

minimal.
- foundation.

$\dot{=} 80 \$/f+2$

pit house typology.
Oldest in the Western hemisphere.
- Modern interpretation.

- retaining wall.
thermal mass to
help modulate
temp swing.

BERCY CHEN STUDIO LP

Bercy Chen Studio LP is an architecture and urban planning firm founded by Thomas Bercy and Calvin Chen and based in Austin, Texas. The pair's European and Asian backgrounds (Bercy is Belgian, Chen is Taiwanese by way of Australia) give their work a rich multicultural feel and approach.

'Our office is unusual in that it is a design build office; we act as the general contractor on 70% of our projects,' explains Calvin Chen. 'The germination of an idea often occurs not in our office but rather on the site. Therefore, the impetus for a project can come from the direct experience of solving a problem during construction or an observation about the site. This feedback loop between the conceptual and the real has been extremely fruitful and stimulating.'

Bercy Chen Studio uses conceptual sketches to capture initial ideas and responses to the site. Thinking in three dimensions, the practice's first sketches are often perspectives. 'We will move back and forth between plans, elevations and 3D,' explains Chen. 'Often ideas about an appropriate structural system are also explored in this early stage.'

Here, and on the following pages, sketches of Red Bluff [60-61, 63], and the Gibbs Hollow Residence (both Texas) [62] show the detail and thinking that go into Bercy Chen's designs right from the outset. Materials, energy sources, circulation, all are included even in early designs.

Sketching in ink or pencil, the architects use colour pencils to quickly 'fill in' the designs, to denote materials, plants and spaces. The two partners will often sketch over each other's drawings too. 'There is an aspect of the Surrealists' idea of "exquisite corpse",' says Chen; 'we pick up where each other left off. This is an efficient way to explore many variations of an idea [so reducing] the risk of prematurely closing the door on a good concept.'

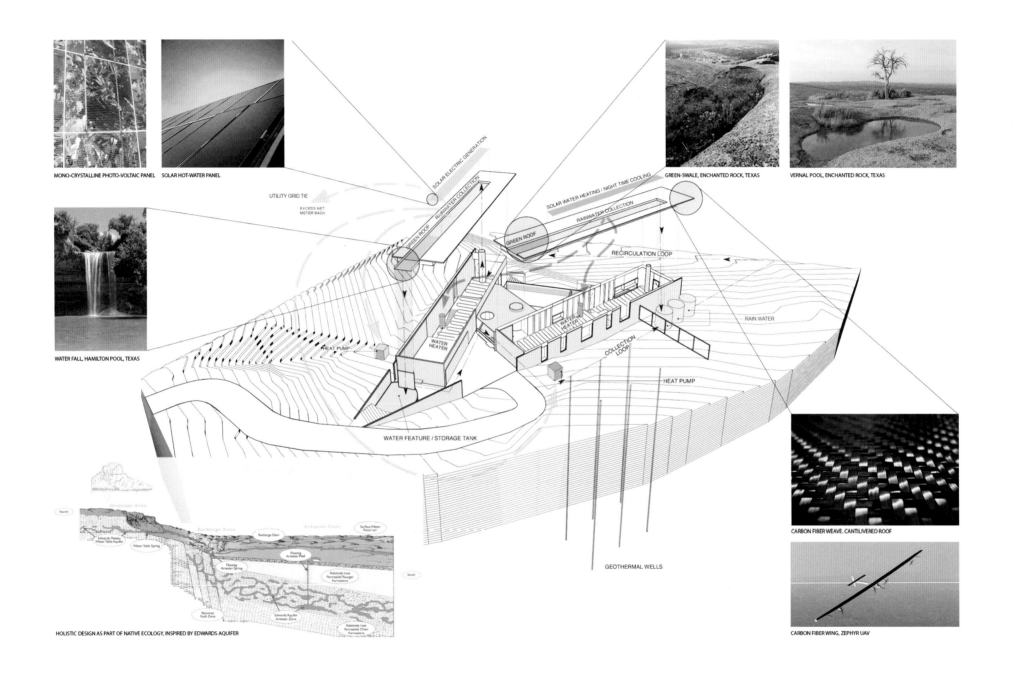

MONO-CRYSTALLINE PHOTO-VOLTAIC PANEL   SOLAR HOT-WATER PANEL

GREEN-SWALE, ENCHANTED ROCK, TEXAS

VERNAL POOL, ENCHANTED ROCK, TEXAS

UTILITY GRID TIE

EXCESS NET
METER BACK

SOLAR ELECTRIC GENERATION

GREEN ROOF / RAINWATER COLLECTION

SOLAR WATER HEATING / NIGHT TIME COOLING

RAINWATER COLLECTION

GREEN ROOF

RECIRCULATION LOOP

WATER FALL, HAMILTON POOL, TEXAS

RAIN WATER

HEAT PUMP

WATER
HEATER

WATER
HEATER

COLLECTION
LOOP

WATER
HEATER

HEAT PUMP

WATER FEATURE / STORAGE TANK

CARBON FIBER WEAVE. CANTILEVERED ROOF

GEOTHERMAL WELLS

HOLISTIC DESIGN AS PART OF NATIVE ECOLOGY, INSPIRED BY EDWARDS AQUIFER

CARBON FIBER WING, ZEPHYR UAV

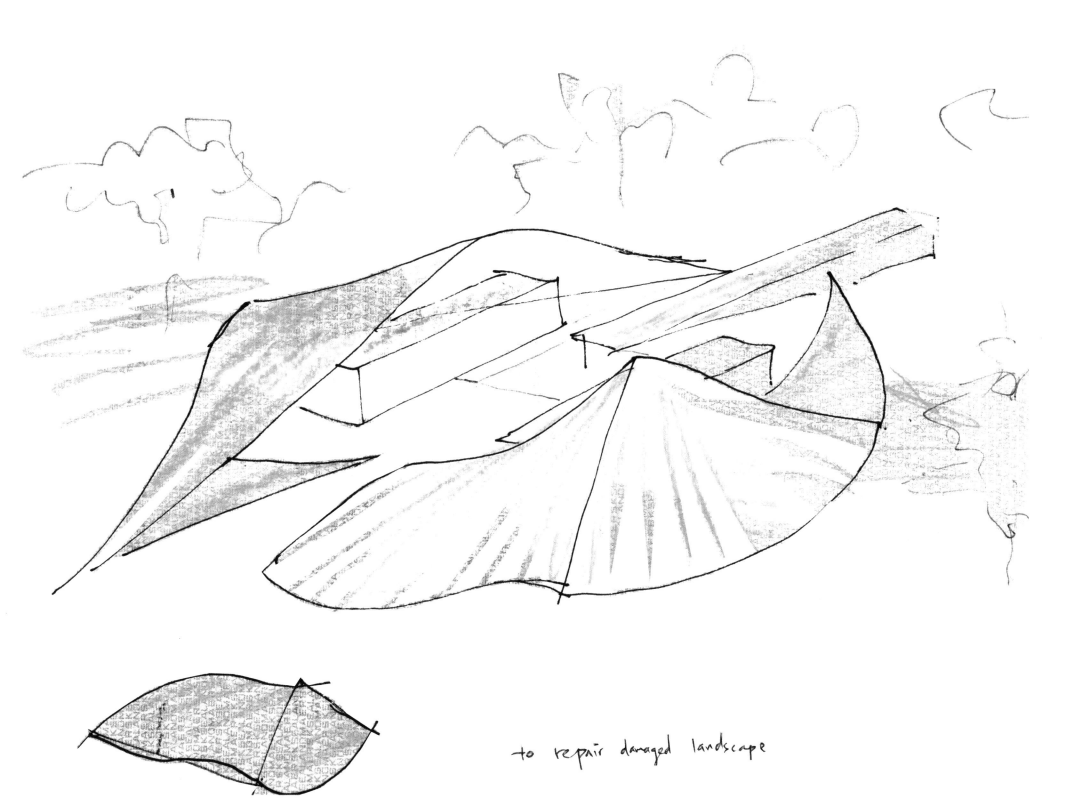

to repair damaged landscape

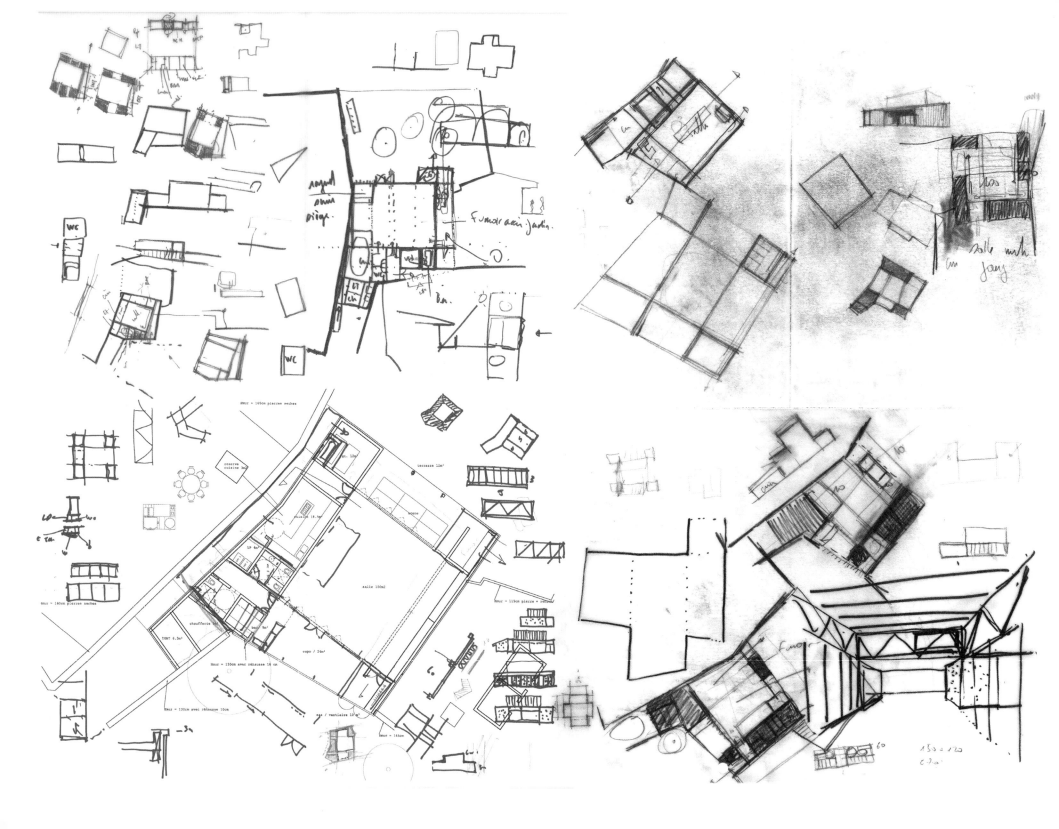

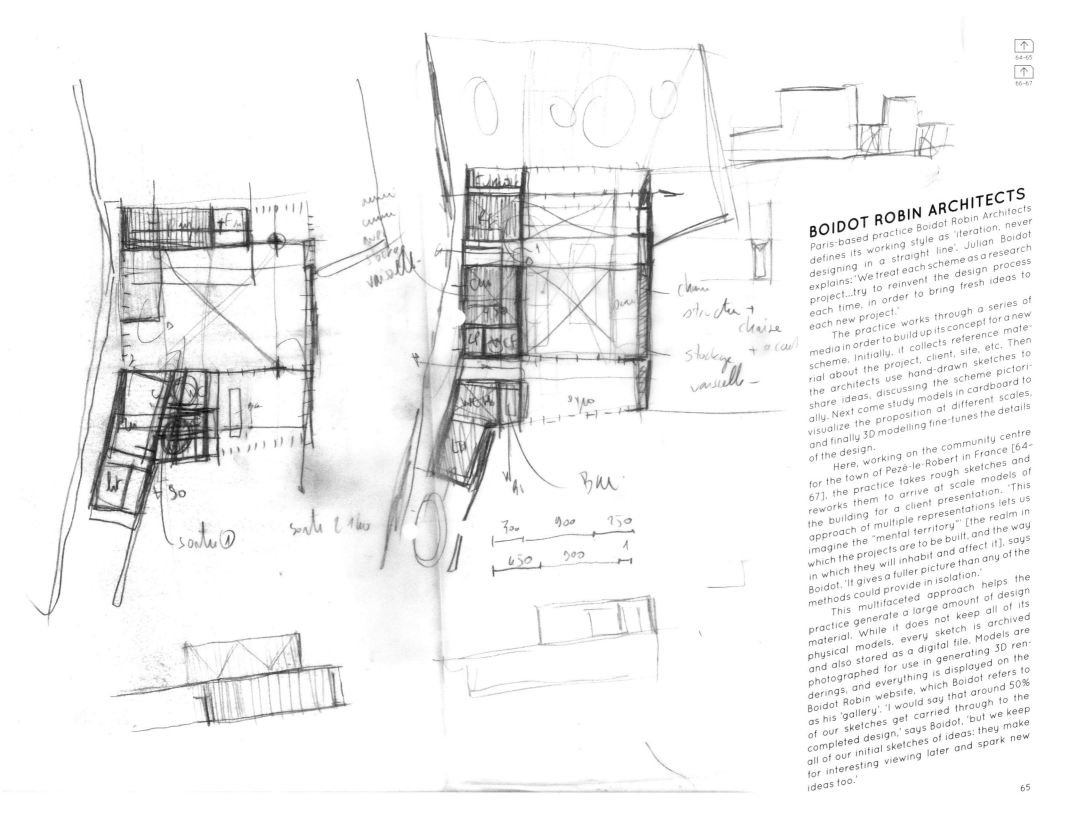

BOIDOT ROBIN ARCHITECTS

Paris-based practice Boidot Robin Architects defines its working style as 'iteration, never designing in a straight line'. Julian Boidot explains: 'We treat each scheme as a research project...try to reinvent the design process each time, in order to bring fresh ideas to each new project.'

The practice works through a series of media in order to build up its concept for a new scheme. Initially, it collects reference material about the project, client, site, etc. Then the architects use hand-drawn sketches to share ideas, discussing the scheme pictorially. Next come study models in cardboard to visualize the proposition at different scales, and finally 3D modelling fine-tunes the details of the design.

Here, working on the community centre for the town of Pezé-le-Robert in France [64–67], the practice takes rough sketches and reworks them to arrive at scale models of the building for a client presentation. 'This approach of multiple representations lets us imagine the "mental territory"' [the realm in which the projects are to be built, and the way in which they will inhabit and affect it], says Boidot. 'It gives a fuller picture than any of the methods could provide in isolation.'

This multifaceted approach helps the practice generate a large amount of design material. While it does not keep all of its physical models, every sketch is archived and also stored as a digital file. Models are photographed for use in generating 3D renderings, and everything is displayed on the Boidot Robin website, which Boidot refers to as his 'gallery'. 'I would say that around 50% of our sketches get carried through to the completed design,' says Boidot, 'but we keep all of our initial sketches of ideas: they make for interesting viewing later and spark new ideas too.'

65

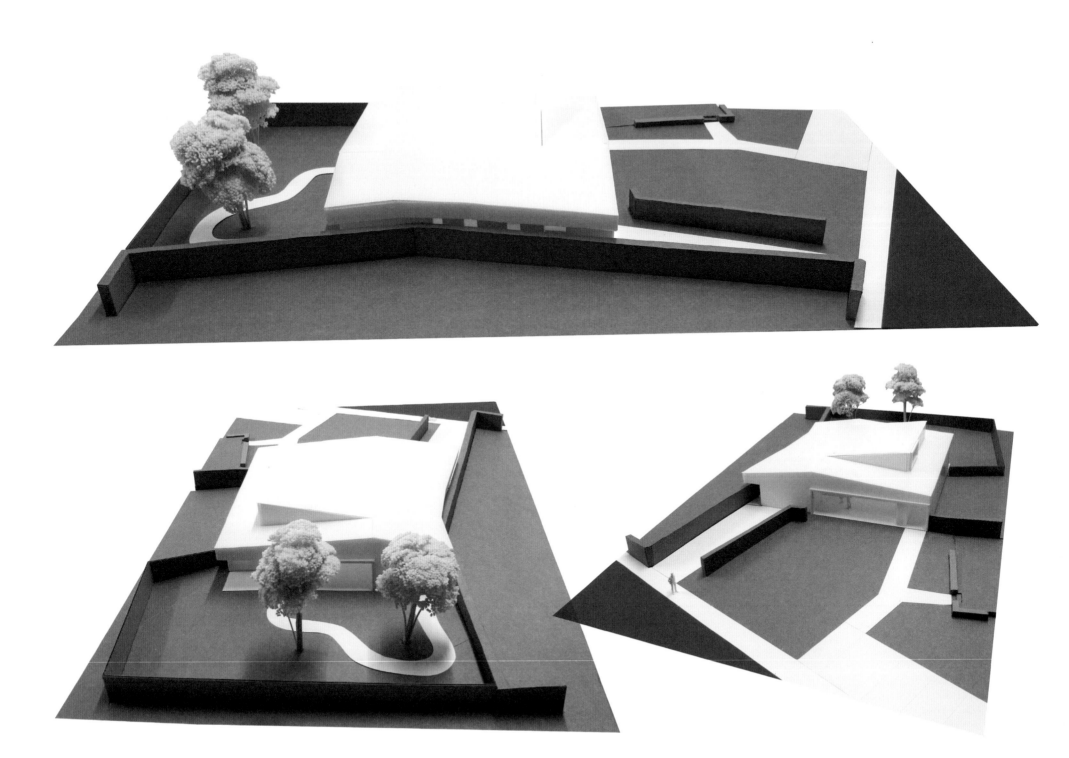

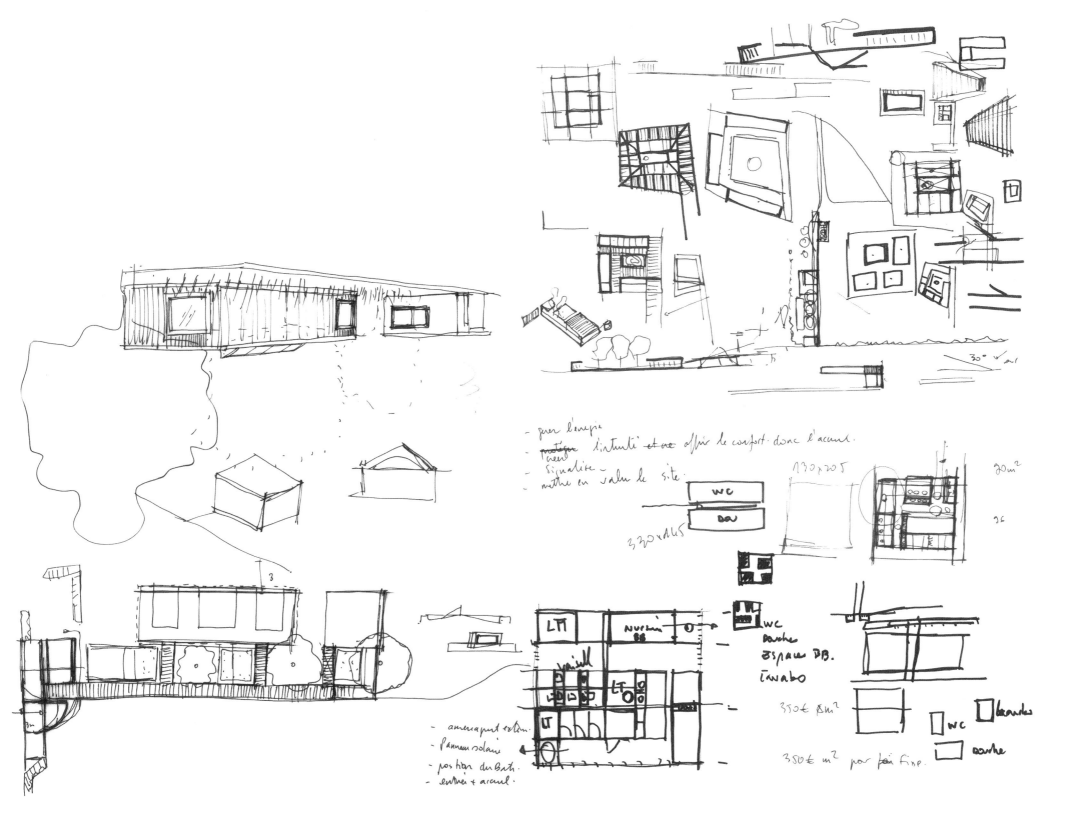

- fixer l'énergie
- ~~pratique~~ créer l'intimité et ~~en~~ offrir le confort. donc l'accueil.
- signalise~~r~~
- mettre en valeur le site.

WC
DOU

130×205
330×145

20 m²
26

WC
Douche
Espace DB.
Lavabo

350€ /m²

350€ m² por fini fixe.

WC   Lavabo
WC   Douche

LT   Nurserie BB   O

vaiss...
LT   O

LT

- aménagement exterieur.
- panneau solaire
- position du Bati.
- entrée + accueil.

3

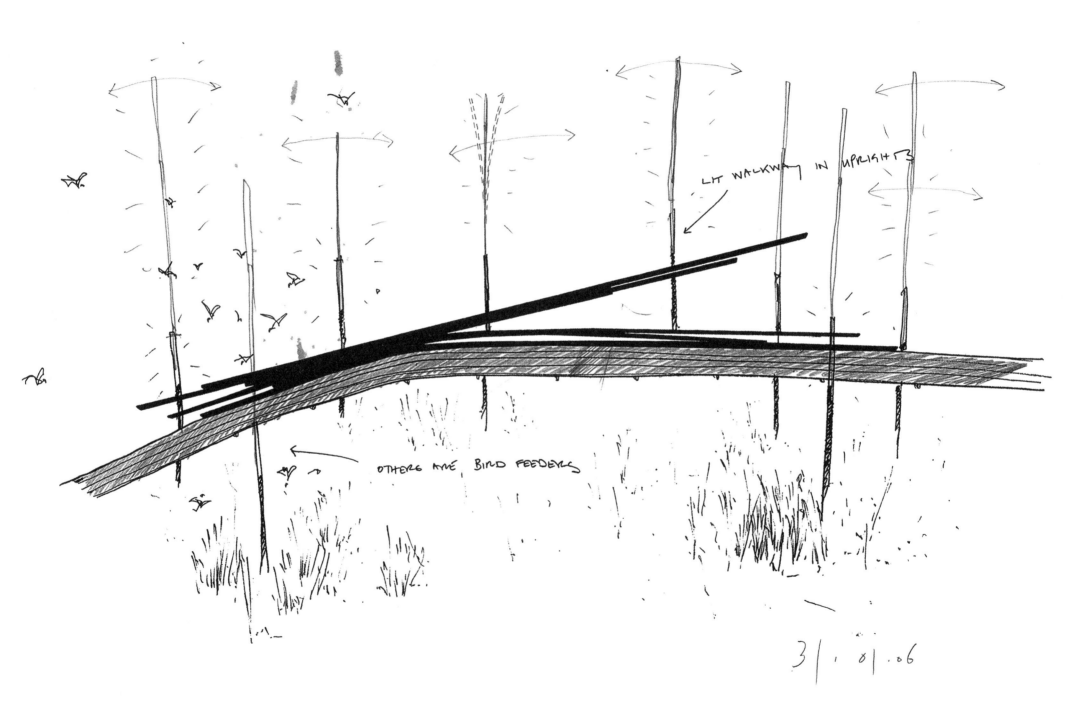

LIT WALKWAY IN UPRIGHTS

OTHERS ARE BIRD FEEDERS

31 . 01 . 06

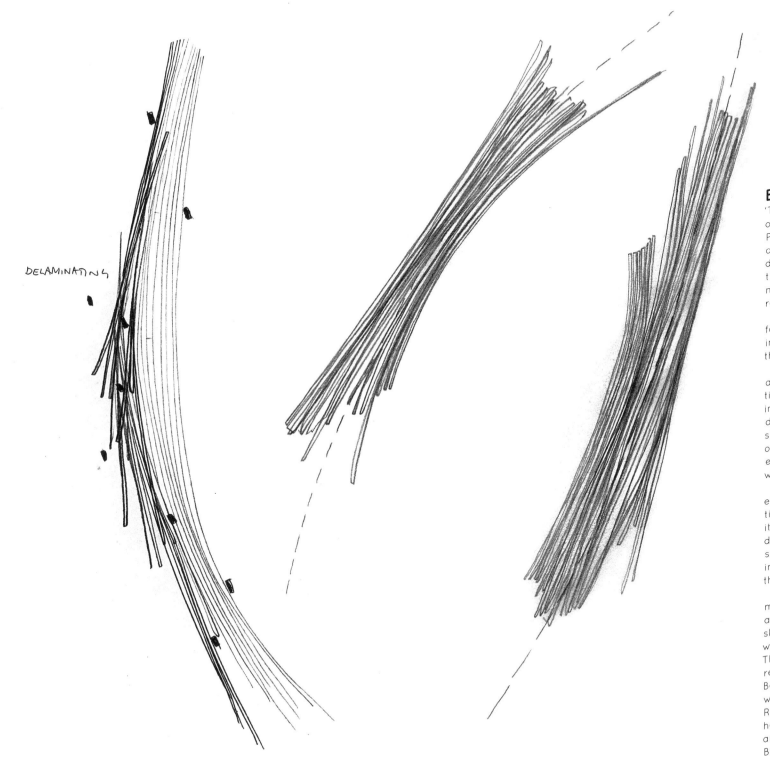

DELAMINATING

BPR

'The sketch diagram is key to the development of our designs,' says Mike Russum, of Birds Portchmouth Russum. 'Our work is developed through the key design stages by hand drawing. We work quickly and efficiently with this age-old technique to develop more and more refined designs that cut straight to the real essence of the issue.'

Abstract concepts, such as the designs for this pedestrian bridge [68–69], evolve into sketched details and photomontages, as the design progresses.

The three partners at BPR work in pen and ink or pencil, and often highlight contentious features with colour washes. Designs are initiated individually by the partners and then debated and appraised collectively. A decision is made to pursue either a single option, or, as is more probable, a hybrid solution that embraces a number of the positive ideas while also addressing their implications.

'Generally a concept sketch diagram emerges that is the distillation of our objectives for the design. If the sketch is robust it becomes a touchstone for the design's development. At a detail level we develop supporting drawings which explore and inform the design development and enrich the project.'

'Our office is in effect a gallery in which many of our models and original drawings are exhibited,' adds Russum. BPR keeps all sketches, models and collages: the practice's work has been exhibited throughout the world. Their drawings were the subject of a major retrospective at the Architekturmuseum in Basel in 2002. The practice has also exhibited work and lectured in Europe, the USA, India, Russia and Japan. Many architecture schools have welcomed the partners as visiting critics, and BPM have also taught a degree unit at the Bartlett School of Architecture, London.

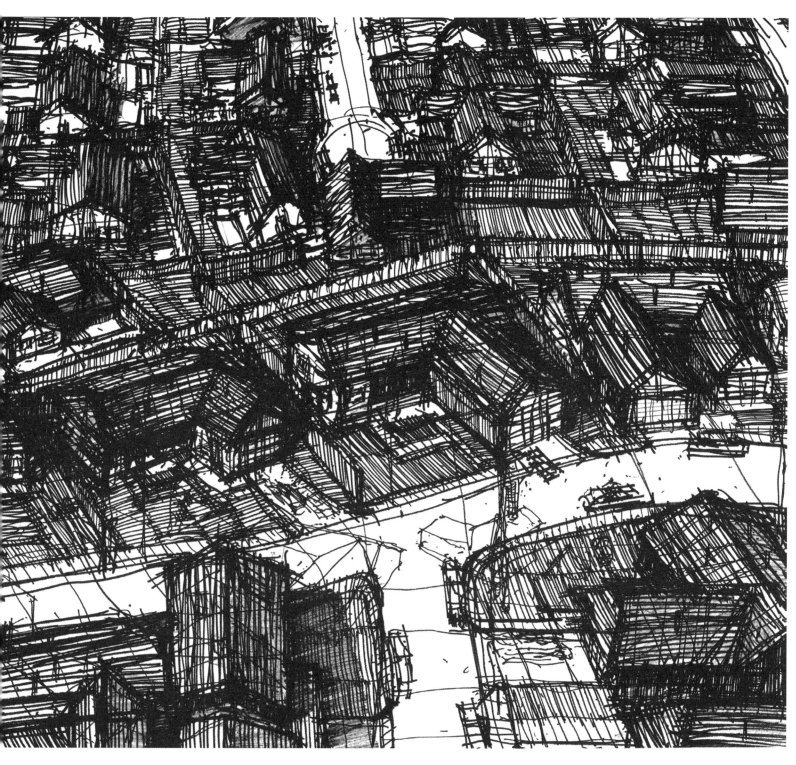

BRENT BUCK

'I heard about an architect who saved every sketch he did throughout the process of designing a house. He exhibited them in a gallery,' says Brent Buck, architect with TWBTA in New York. 'I imagine it was inspiring to see the design evolve from sketch to sketch—a great way to see inside the mind of an architect.'

Buck's stylized designs of American suburbia [70–73] evolve from black and white to colour, from freehand to measured drawing, but they never lose the hand-drawn quality.

'I find it most useful to illustrate ideas by hand. The scale of work is small, manageable and fluid,' he says. 'Concepts are flushed out using tracing paper, pens and a lot of white-out. I use a variety of colours to differentiate materials—a quick way to diagram that allows for easy visualization. This method of organizing a drawing brings about discovery—both strengths and weaknesses—and the drawing progresses, layer by layer.'

The process is quick and yet precise. Sketches are honest, displaying the benefits and drawbacks of details. Buck uses them as tools and learns from them how to push the design forwards. 'Initial sketches show hints of where the design may go. Details, dimensions, etc. are constantly re-examined, and none of the designs get carried through unchanged. I believe that if something is sketched early on in the process, I should be able to improve upon it: I believe each sketch should be allowed to wander.'

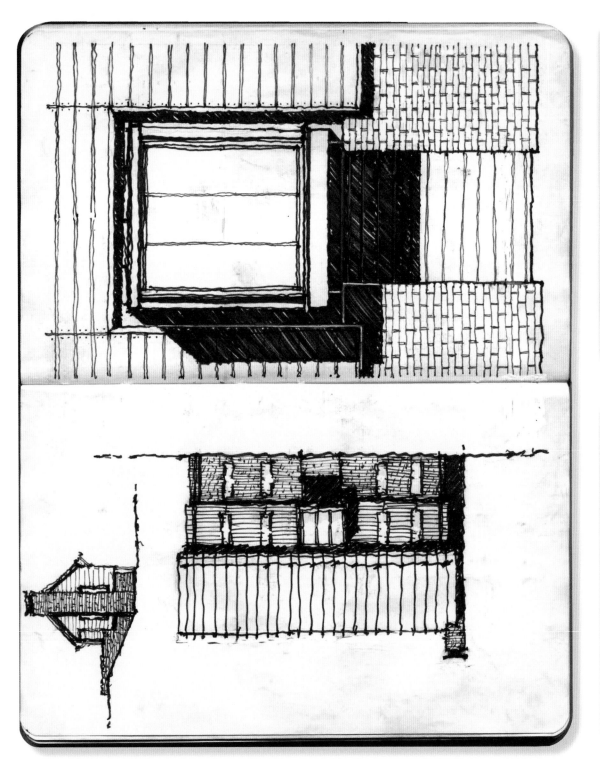
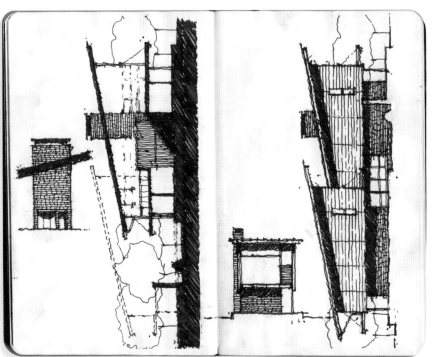
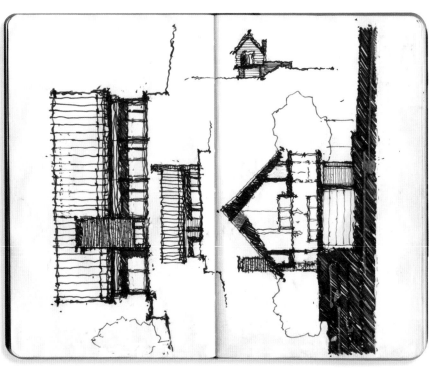

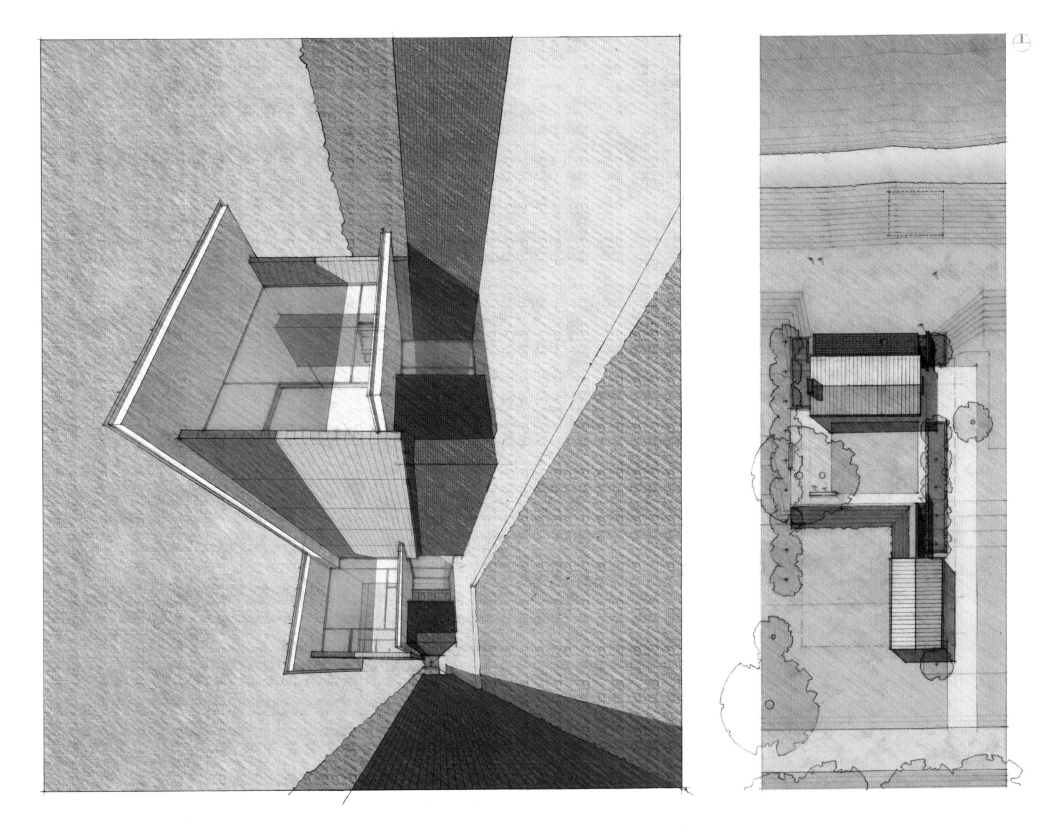

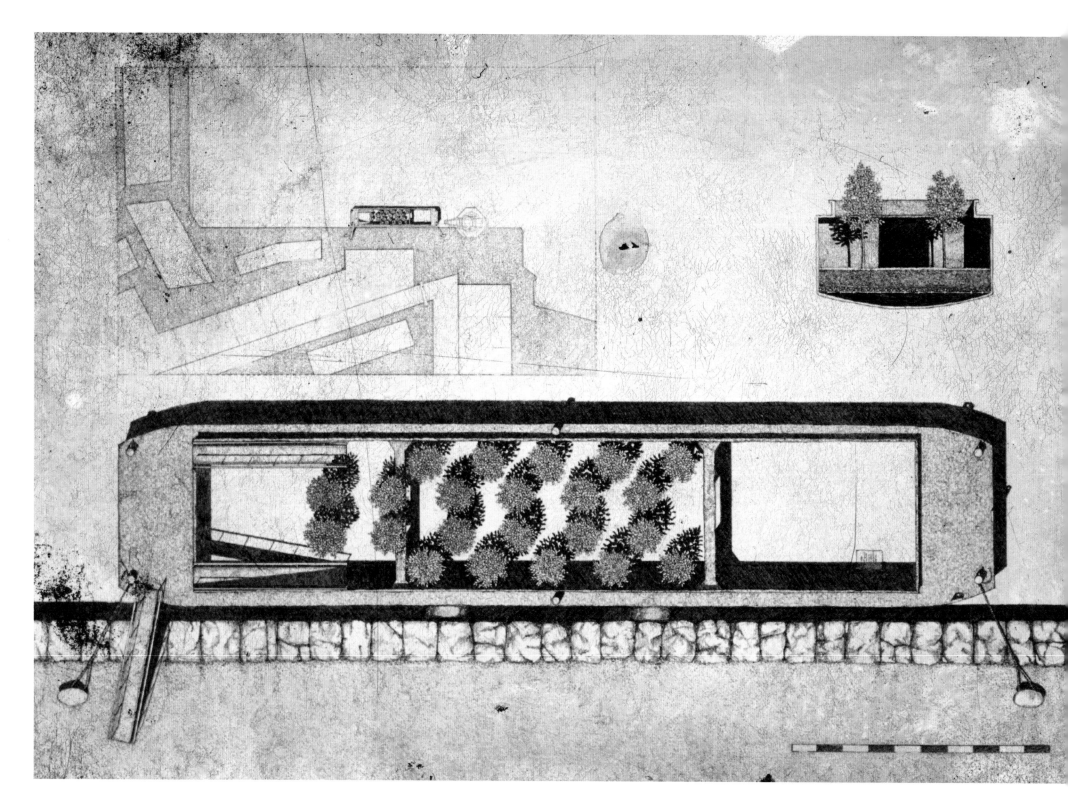

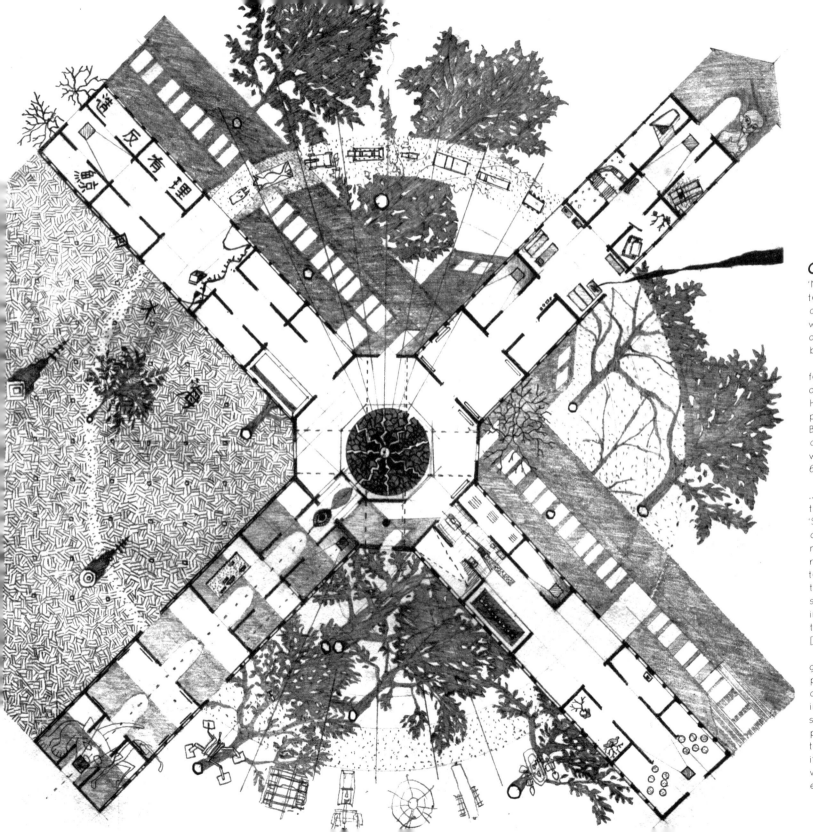

CASAGRANDE LABORATORY

'My design is organic. I don't control architecture, I grow it,' says Marco Casagrande, of Casagrande Laboratory. 'I need to find a way to be present in the situation where the architecture is growing from. Sketching helps, but to be present is the real key.'

This architectural maverick is renowned for finding rather unusual solutions to every-day problems, such as 60 Minute Man [74]. Here, an industrial barge was turned into a park planted with oak trees for the Venice Biennale, 2000 — the oaks were planted in and nourished by the composted human waste created by the city's inhabitants in just 60 minutes.

'Sketches are expressions of personality ...finding a way to understand space, structures, site and other things,' says Casagrande. 'Sketching is a kind of dreaming. First you dream you then build. And this way of working makes me site-specific. Architecture is not a remote-control art. To be present is the key to all art. I need to stay present through the whole process, from sketching to construction site.' Over the page Casagrande's imagination runs wild, with the Chamber of the Post-Urbanist [76] and CityZen Garden [77–79], both in Taiwan.

When asked what amount of his work gets built, Casagrande says it is not about a percentage amount in his projects. 'Attitude and the strength to be present is the most important thing for an architect.' And the secret ingredient? 'You have to have fire and protect that initial fire of creativity in architecture. You can not import this fire or borrow it. You must build it on site each time you work. It is all that there is in the end, a fire, an energy to succeed. Forget style, forget rules.'

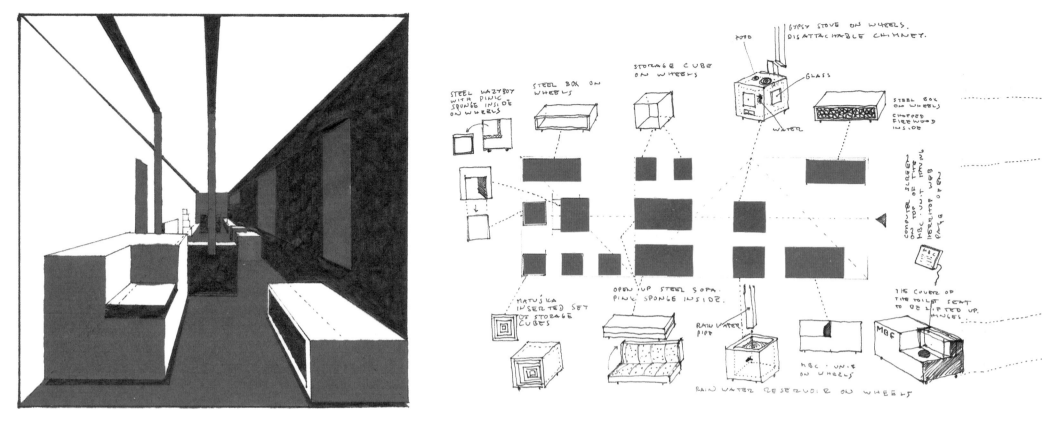

GYPSY STOVE ON WHEELS. DISATTACHABLE CHIMNEY.

FOOD

STEEL LAZYBOY WITH PINK SPONGE INSIDE ON WHEELS

STEEL BOX ON WHEELS

STORAGE CUBE ON WHEELS

GLASS

WATER

STEEL BOX ON WHEELS CHOPPED FIREWOOD INSIDE

COMPUTER SCREEN ON TOP OF THE MBC UNIT OF HAVING INTERNET/WEB INTERACTION

MATUSKA INSERTED SET OF STORAGE CUBES

OPEN UP STEEL SOFA. PINK SPONGE INSIDE.

RAIN WATER PIPE

THE COVER OF THE TOILET SEAT TO BE LIFTED UP. HINGES

MBC

MBC - UNIT ON WHEELS

RAIN WATER RESERVOIR ON WHEELS

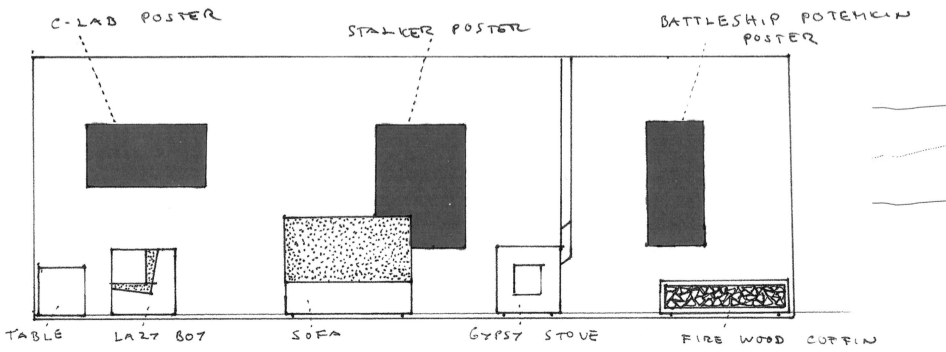

C-LAB POSTER   STALKER POSTER   BATTLESHIP POTEMKIN POSTER

TABLE   LAZY BOY   SOFA   GYPSY STOVE   FIRE WOOD COFFIN

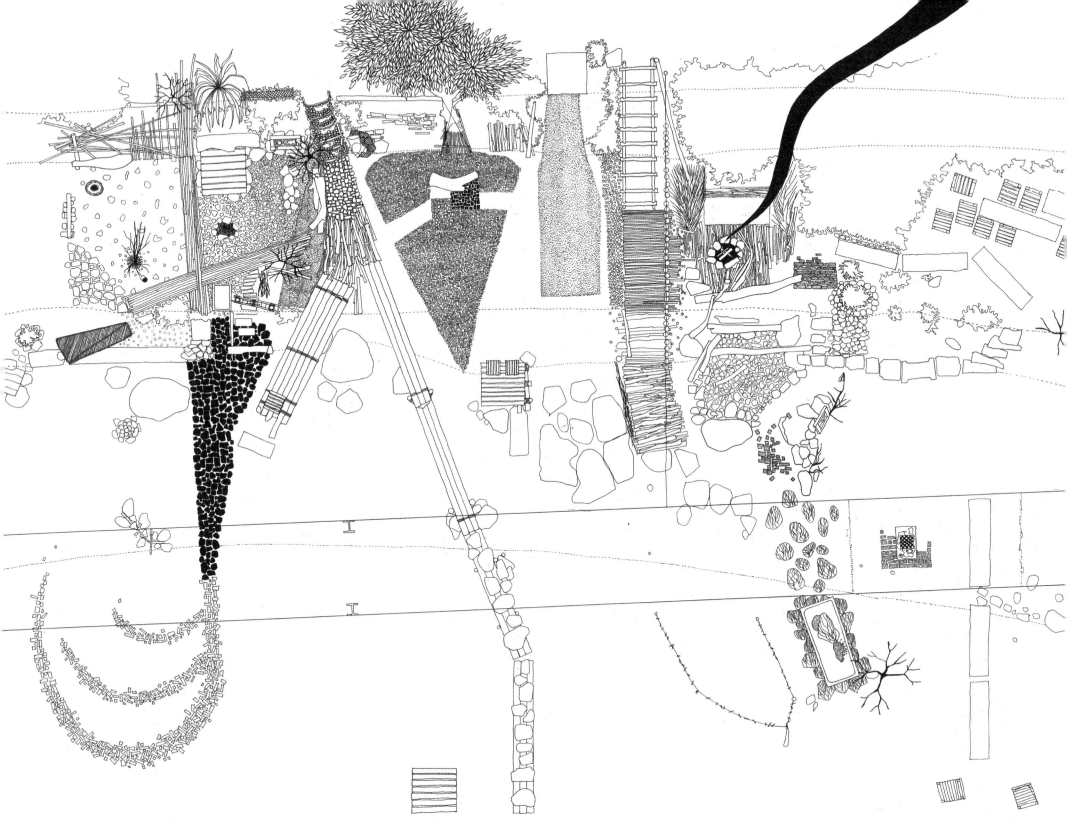

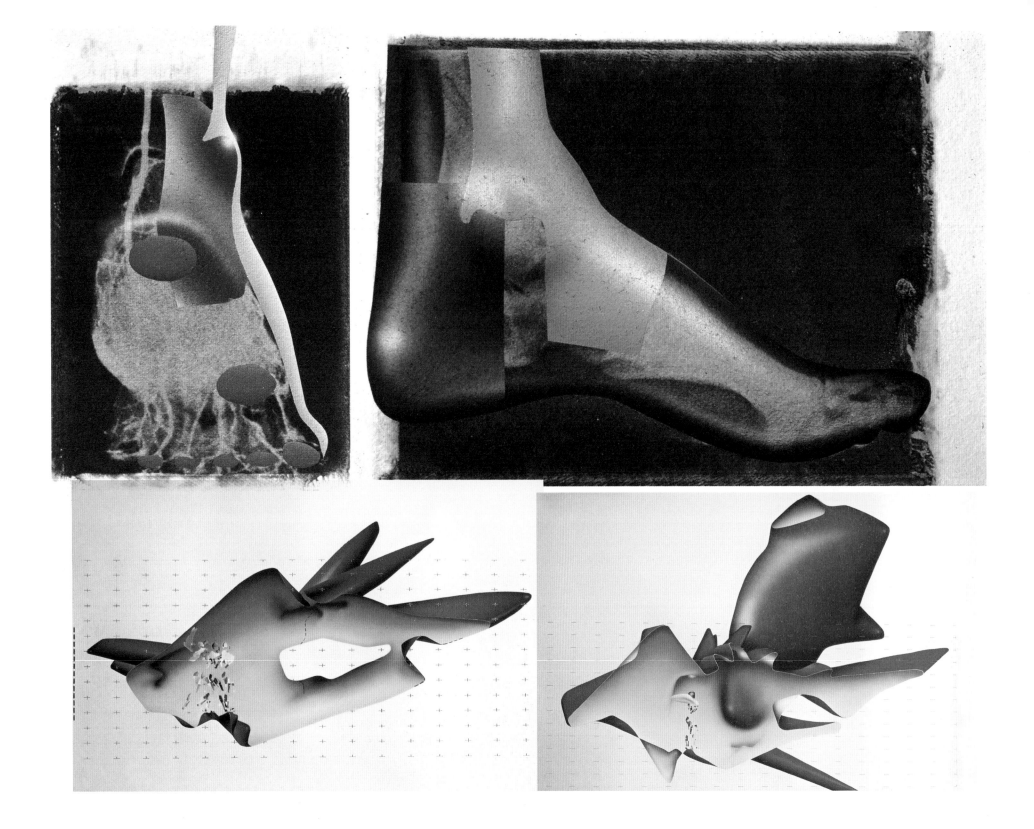

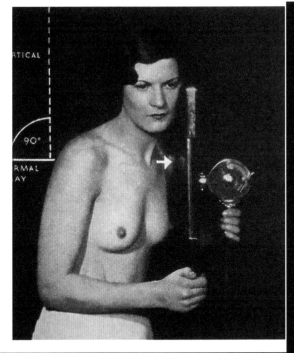

NAT CHARD

Head of the Department of Architecture at the University of Manitoba, Canada, Professor Nat Chard believes that when we draw, the tools we use bring their own constraints.

'When we draw with a pencil on a piece of paper everything is possible, a suffocating condition, but the limitations of a more restrictive process open up the possibility of what may be drawn within its specific capacity,' he says.

Chard creates his Architectural Body projects [80-83] as stereoscopic drawings—pairs of images that provide a 3D image when viewed through stereoscopic glasses, or if you look at them cross-eyed.

'There are many pleasures in finding a 3D resolution from a 2D drawing, not least the sense of what is drawn becoming the thing it depicts,' says Chard. 'But in this work the three dimensionality is also a spatial way to engage the observer with the drawing.'

The images are drawn with an airbrush, which, combined with the softening effect the hot press watercolour paper has on the Polaroid emulsion, provides a reasonable equivalence between what is drawn and what is photographed.

'As computer processes become more advanced I continue with this process, enjoying the lack of an "undo" button and the pleasure of having to commit to something, as well as the risk involved,' says Chard. 'The most disappointing outcome of any of my drawings is if they turn out as I imagined them before they were started.'

81

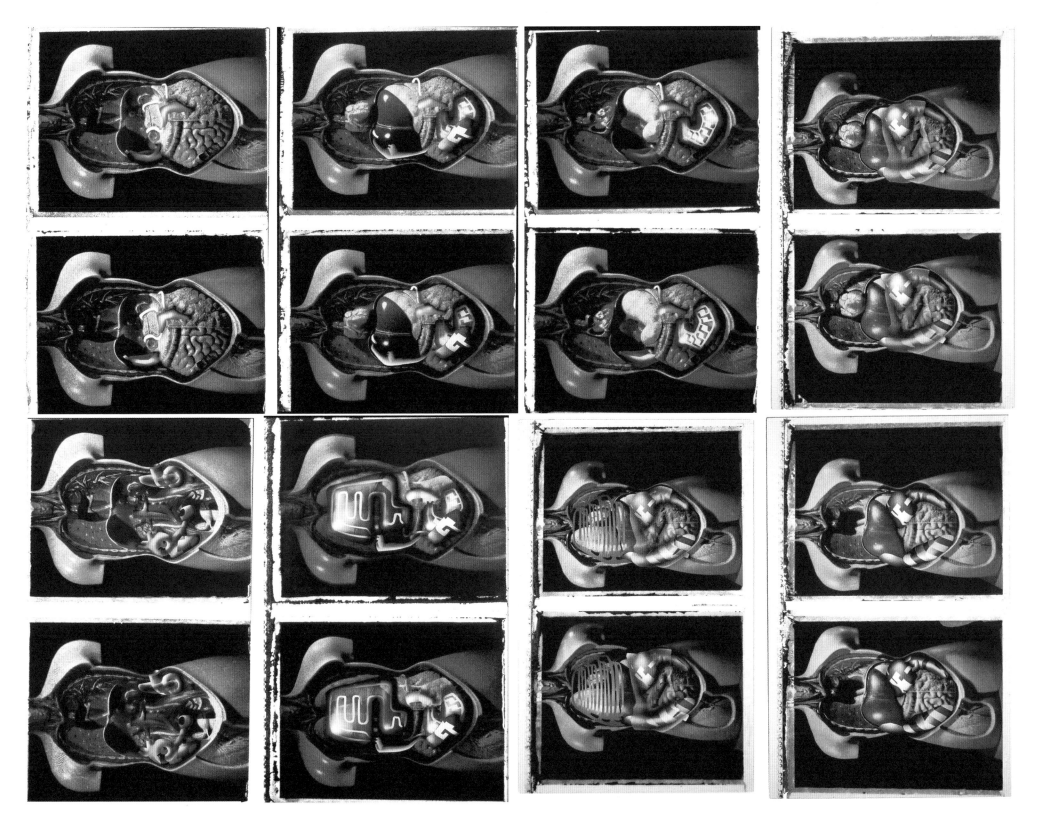

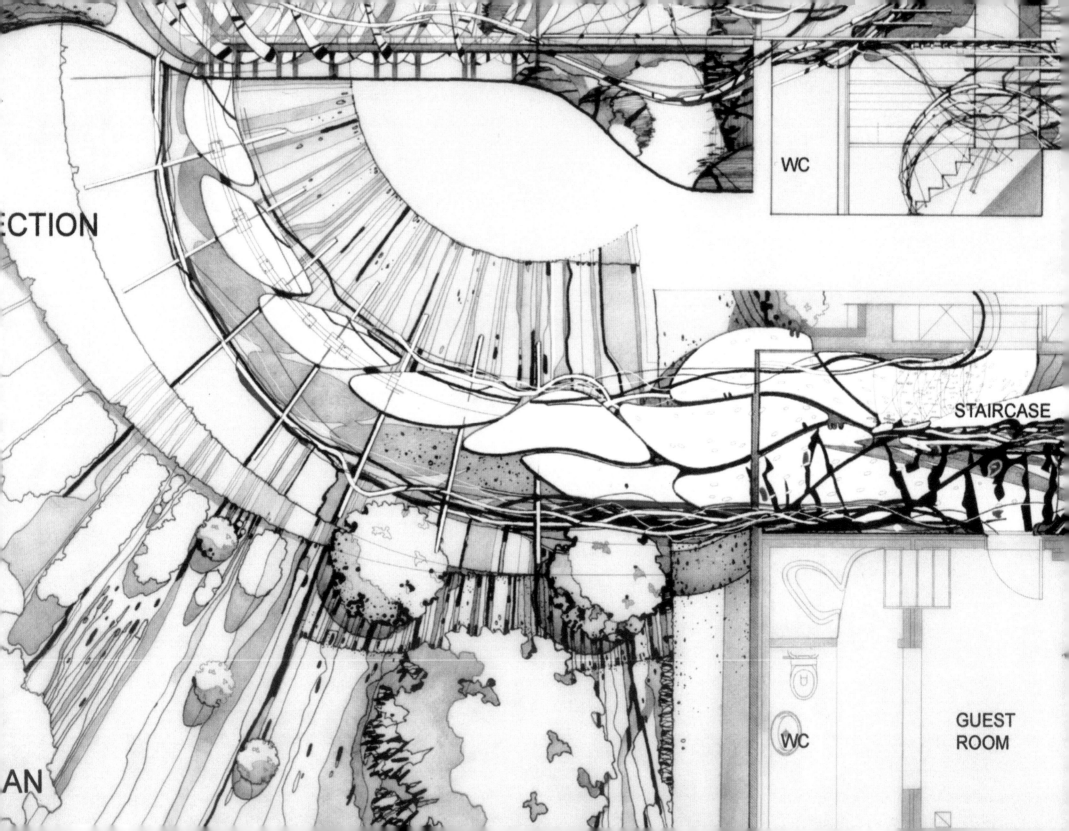

ECTION

WC

STAIRCASE

GUEST
ROOM

WC

AN

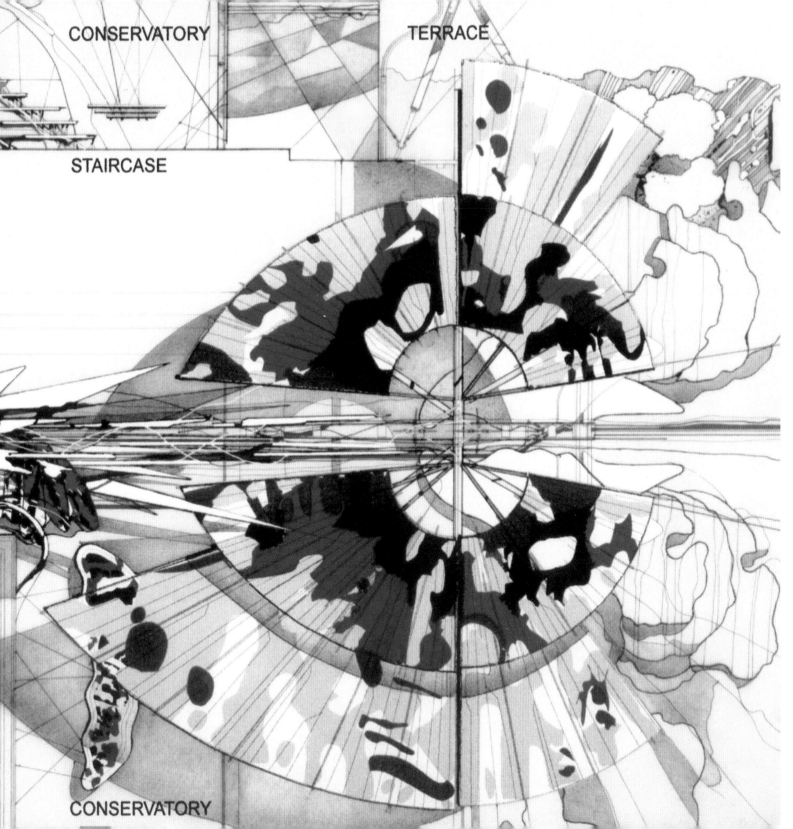

CONSERVATORY

TERRACE

STAIRCASE

CONSERVATORY

84–85

86–87

88–89

LAURIE CHETWOOD

Laurie Chetwood, of London-based practice Chetwoods Architects and Designers, has long railed against architectural students forgoing the sketch pad in favour of the computer. Yet he is no technophobe, instead feeling that a generation of AutoCAD designers lack the artistic inspiration to create buildings that appeal to users on multiple levels—functionally and emotionally.

Chetwood actually designs mostly using digital media. He uses a touch-sensitive tablet electronic notebook. 'It's like a digital sketchpad,' he says. 'I use it because it is just as portable as a traditional sketchbook but gives the designer extra freedom. Images can be manipulated in a multitude of ways. It is much more flexible and versatile than a paper pad, and can store information more effectively.'

Chetwood sees the sketch stage of the design process as an informal thinking phase, which allows the designer to relax and consider any possibility. Designs seen here include Chetwood's own home, the Butterfly House, in Surrey, UK [84–86], and over the page Paper City: Urban Utopias [87], a competition-winning concept. 'Sketching is the best time in a project's development, a time to really use your imagination—its also a brilliant device for unblocking designer block!' he says.

Chetwood's style of flowing, almost ethereal design is a world away from the Modernist ideals of many of his contemporaries. He believes that his artistic predilection has influenced this: 'The sketch is really important to me, and should be to all architects. It is particularly relevant to an organic style of architecture: the more informal and relaxed your style, the more beautiful, more inspirational your work.'

85

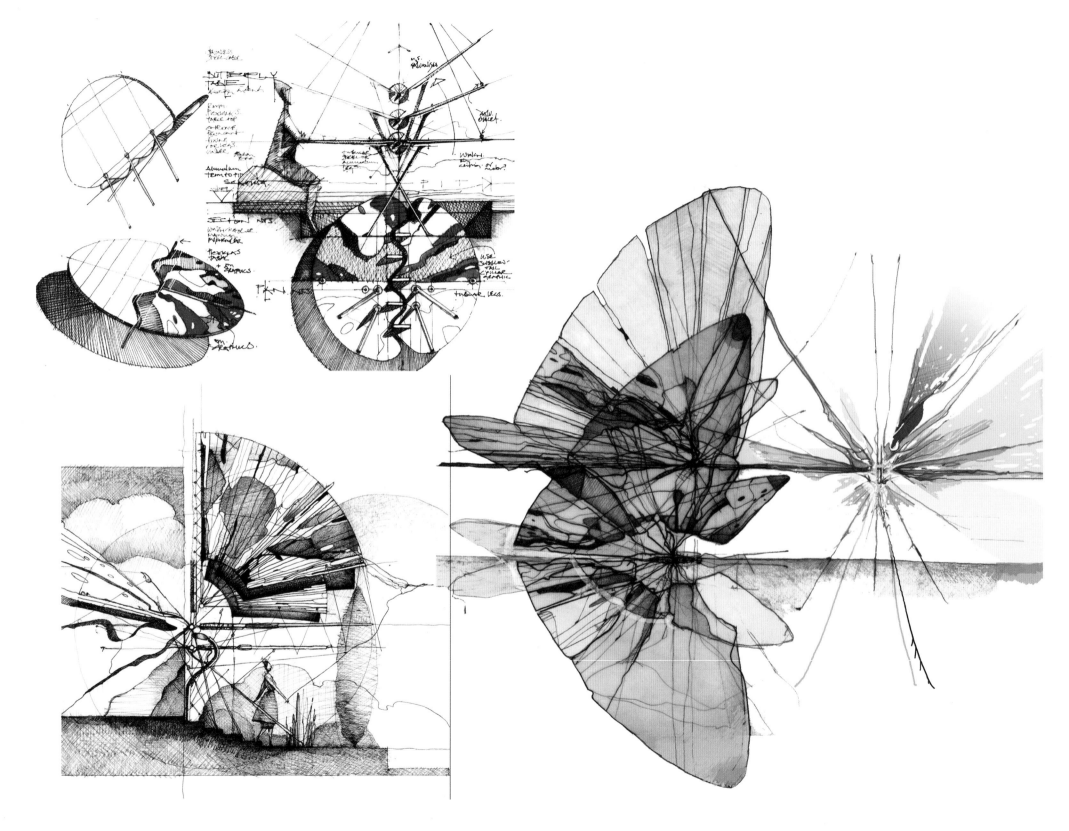

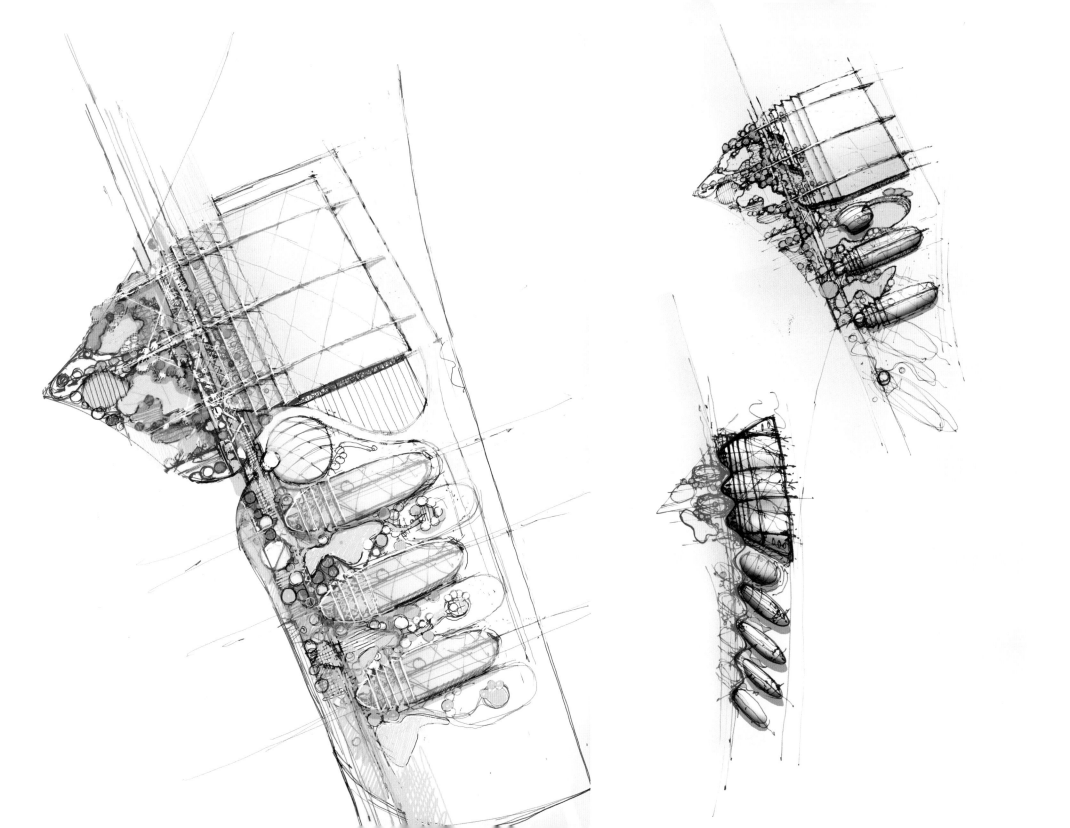

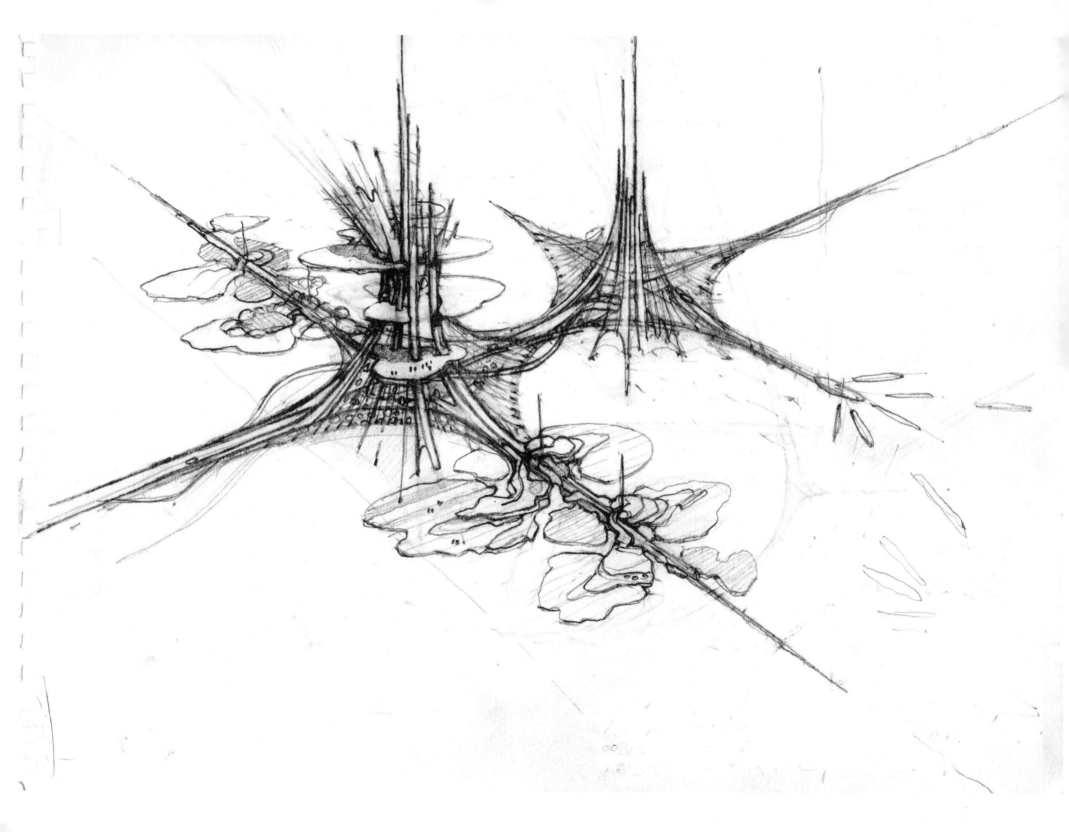

00.
BRIDGE
MARKET LEVEL 1

01
MARKET
LEVEL 2

02
HYDROPONIC 1.

FARM

CAFE +
RESTAURANT

CENTRAL CORE.

03
HYDROPONIC 2.

RESIDENTIAL

04.

05
FARM
LEVEL 5

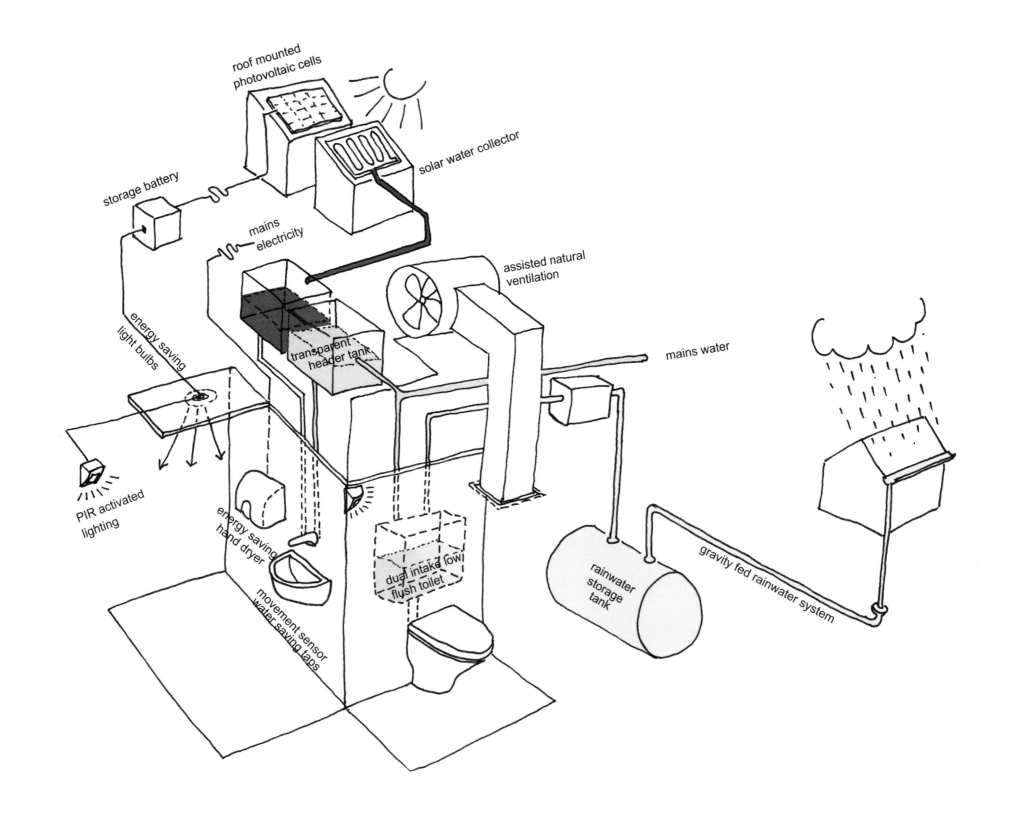

roof mounted
photovoltaic cells

solar water collector

storage battery

mains
electricity

assisted natural
ventilation

energy saving
light bulbs

transparent
header tank

mains water

PIR activated
lighting

energy saving
hand dryer

movement sensor
water saving taps

dual intake low
flush toilet

rainwater
storage
tank

gravity fed rainwater system

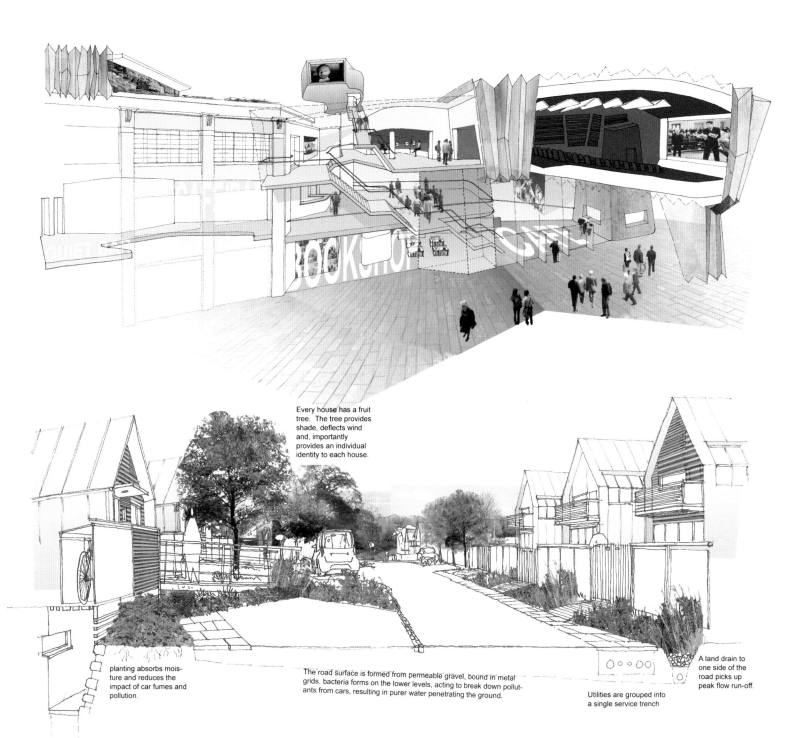

Every house has a fruit tree. The tree provides shade, deflects wind and, importantly provides an individual identity to each house.

planting absorbs moisture and reduces the impact of car fumes and pollution.

The road surface is formed from permeable gravel, bound in metal grids. bacteria forms on the lower levels, acting to break down pollutants from cars, resulting in purer water penetrating the ground.

Utilities are grouped into a single service trench

A land drain to one side of the road picks up peak flow run-off.

PRUE CHILES

'We use a combination of hand-drawn sketches and models to develop ideas,' says Prue Chiles, principal of Prue Chiles Architecture. 'We also often use a perspectival sketch that enables us to explore 3D relationships both within a building, and in its external environment. These are usually then rendered on computer, and annotated when discussed with a client. 2D and 3D explorations are made simultaneously.'

She uses this method because sketches allow a swift dialogue to develop both within the office and with the client, helping all concerned to focus on how the design evolves. 'This enables us to work through a number of thoughts and approaches very quickly without getting stuck on the details, even on small jobs,' she explains. 'Often as soon as a project is put onto a computer the thought process becomes more stilted, so it is important to keep sketching throughout the project.'

Although digital technologies have transformed architecture, Chiles believes that a quick photomontage accompanied by sketches can usually say more than elaborate computer-generated imagery. 'It is important to us that everyone can understand our drawings; they are not the private domain of the architect. Non-architects may be very sophisticated but they still struggle to visualize plans and sections, and so sketches are the drawings to show them.'

Chiles is not precious about her work and likes it when clients or builders draw on sketches and change things. 'Contractors might draw to understand a detail, or change dimensions. Clients can often be tentative but sometimes we can get them to make a mark, too.'

91

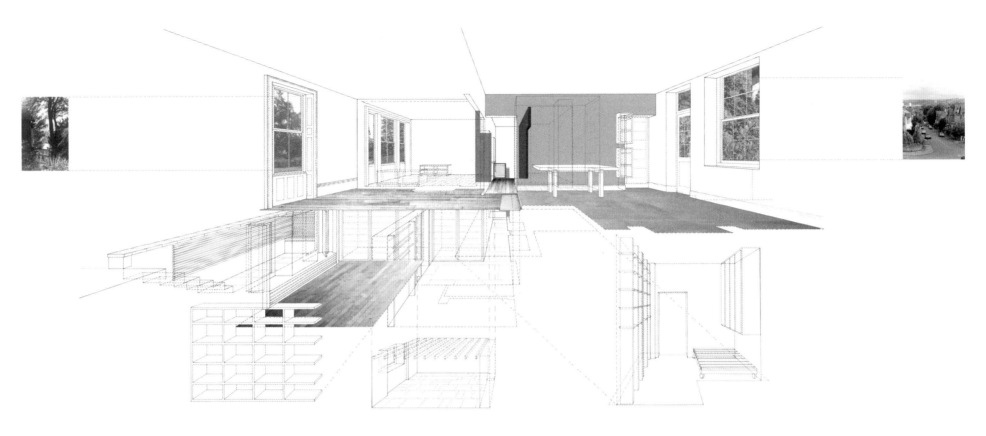

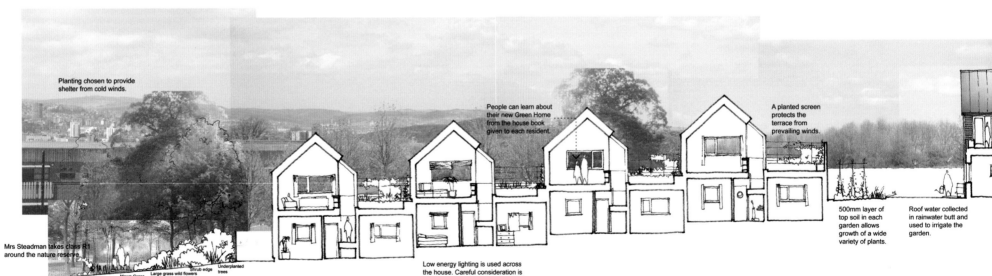

Planting chosen to provide shelter from cold winds.

People can learn about their new Green Home from the house book given to each resident.

A planted screen protects the terrace from prevailing winds.

Mrs Steadman takes class R1 around the nature reserve.

Mown Grass

Large grass wild flowers

Shrub edge

Underplanted trees

Ecotone

Low energy lighting is used across the house. Careful consideration is given to the position and provision of the lamps with a warmer colour rendering, in order to enhance the atmosphere.

500mm layer of top soil in each garden allows growth of a wide variety of plants.

Roof water collected in rainwater butt and used to irrigate the garden.

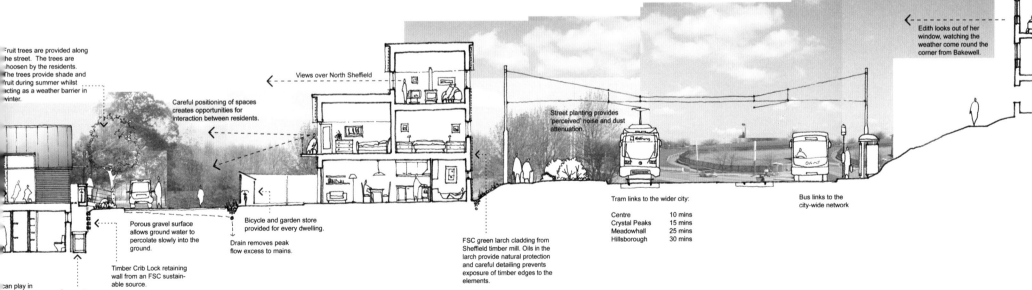

Fruit trees are provided along the street. The trees are choosen by the residents. The trees provide shade and fruit during summer whilst acting as a weather barrier in winter.

Careful positioning of spaces creates opportunities for interaction between residents.

Views over North Sheffield

Edith looks out of her window, watching the weather come round the corner from Bakewell.

Street planting provides 'perceived' noise and dust attenuation.

...can play in ... spaces.

Grey water collected and reused in WC's.

Porous gravel surface allows ground water to percolate slowly into the ground.

Timber Crib Lock retaining wall from an FSC sustainable source.

Drain removes peak flow excess to mains.

Bicycle and garden store provided for every dwelling.

FSC green larch cladding from Sheffield timber mill. Oils in the larch provide natural protection and careful detailing prevents exposure of timber edges to the elements.

Tram links to the wider city:

Centre   10 mins
Crystal Peaks   15 mins
Meadowhall   25 mins
Hillsborough   30 mins

Bus links to the city-wide network

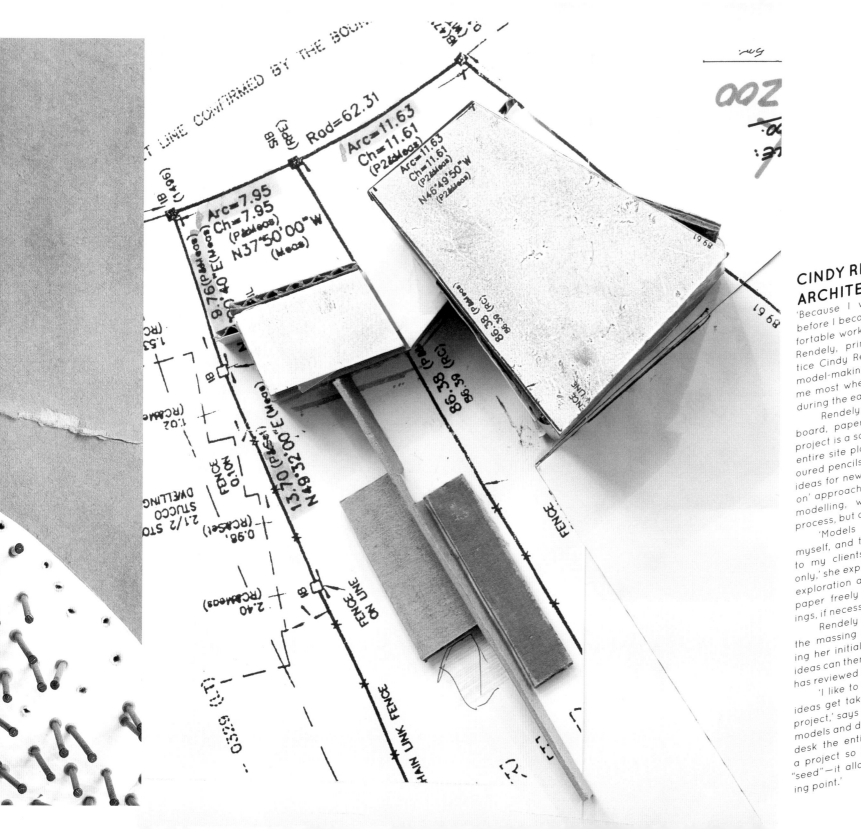

CINDY RENDELY
ARCHITEXTURE

'Because I was a goldsmith and jeweller before I became an architect I am very comfortable working with my hands,' says Cindy Rendely, principal of Toronto-based practice Cindy Rendely Architexture. 'Therefore, model-making and sketch models interest me most when I am exploring an idea in 3D during the early stages of a project.'

Rendely makes small models from cardboard, paper and Styrofoam, whether the project is a scale model of a new house or an entire site plan. She also sketches using coloured pencils and graphite when conceiving ideas for new works. She prefers this 'hands-on' approach of exploration to 3D computer modelling, which does enter the design process, but at a later stage.

'Models allow me to see quickly for myself, and to illustrate rapidly and clearly to my clients ideas in 3D rather than 2D only,' she explains. 'They allow for interesting exploration and I can manipulate card and paper freely to show options during meetings, if necessary.'

Rendely expects to have a clear idea of the massing and siting of buildings following her initial model-making process. These ideas can then be developed further once she has reviewed them with the client.

'I like to think that 100% of my concept ideas get taken through into the completed project,' says Rendely. 'I keep original sketch models and drawings close at hand, near my desk the entire time that I am developing a project so that I do not lose the original "seed"—it allows me to remember my starting point.'

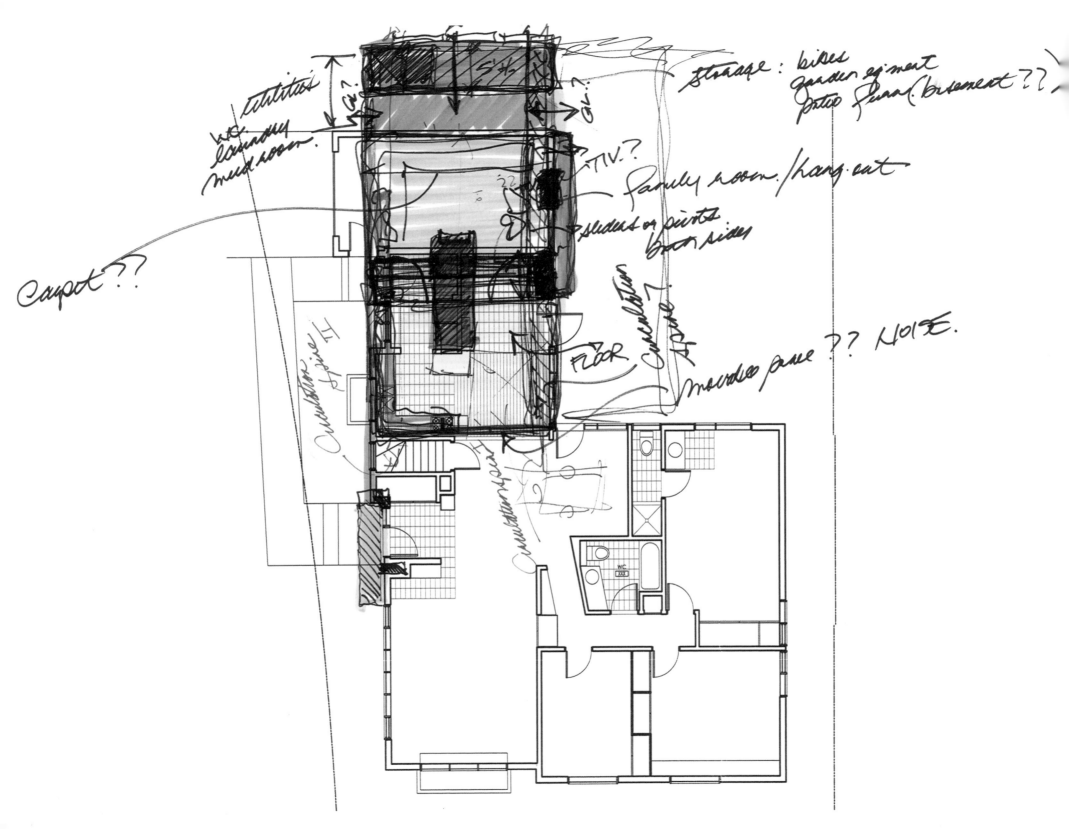

storage: bikes
garden equipment
patio furn. (basement ??)

w.c. utilities
laundry
mud room.

Family room. / hang. out

sliders or points
both sides

T.V. ?

G. ?

S.H.

Carpet ??

FLOOR

movable pane ?? NOISE.

WC

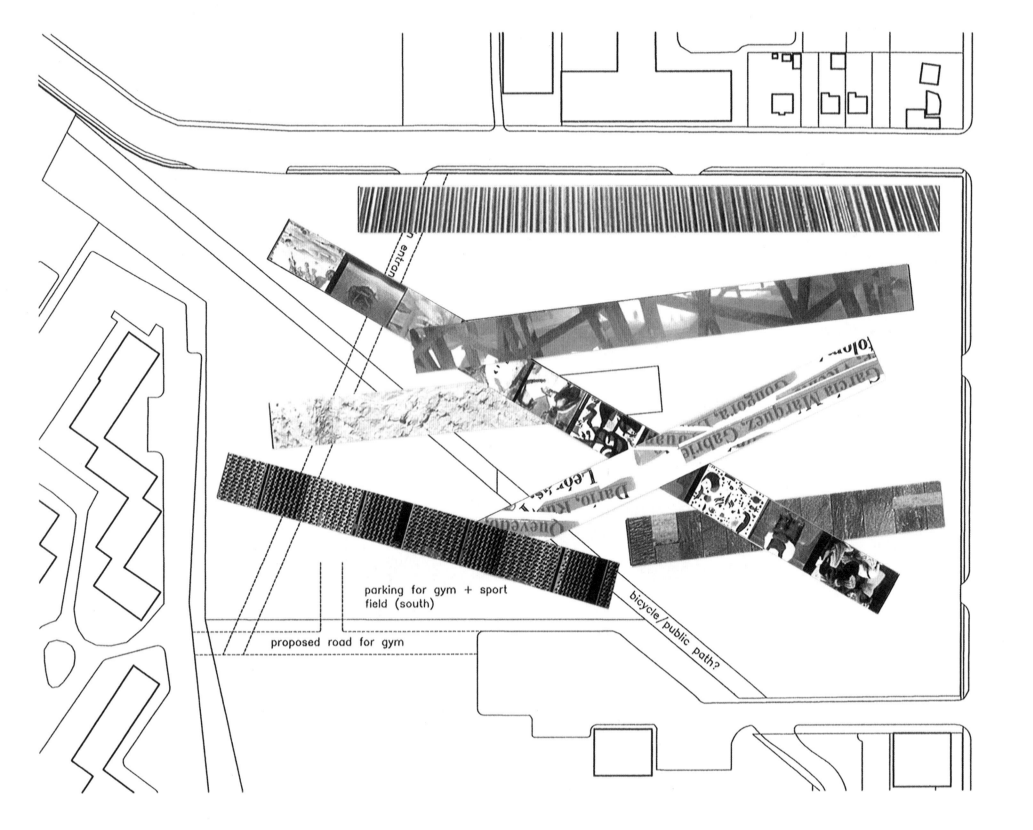

entran

parking for gym + sport
field (south)

proposed road for gym

bicycle/public path?

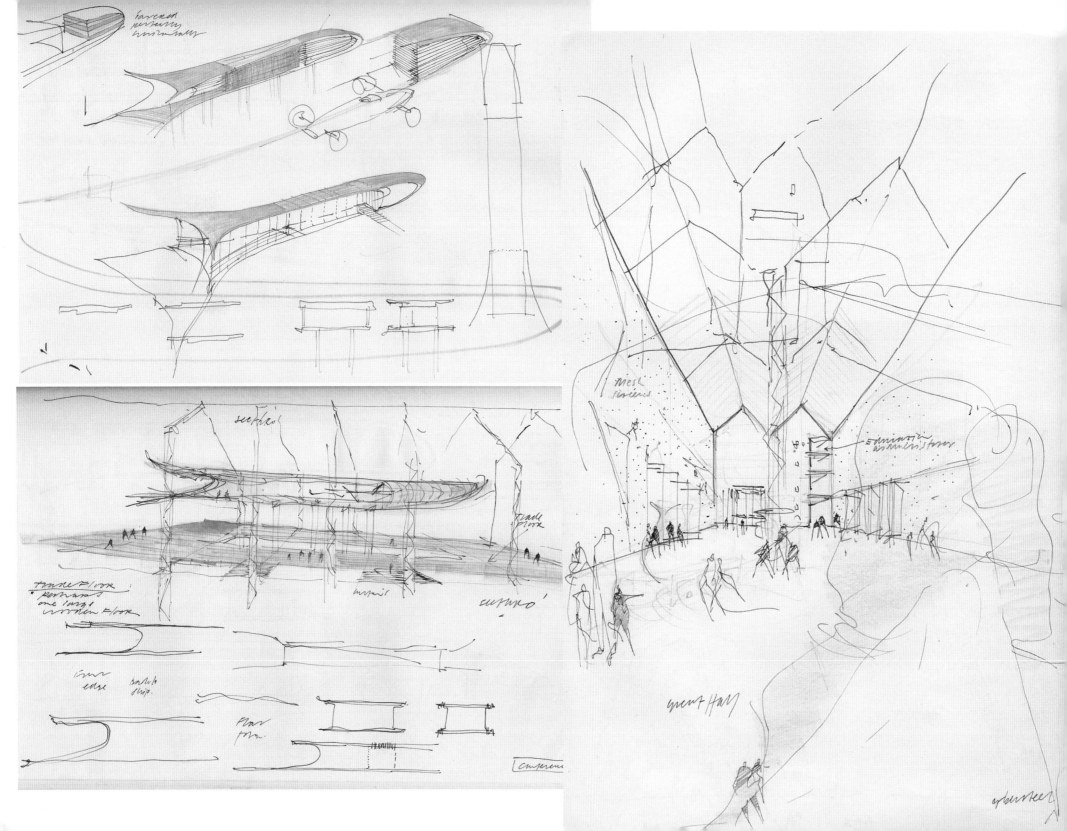

MAGNA

MAGNA

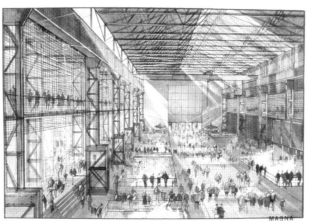

MAGNA

PETER CLASH

'I like to think of my initial sketch work as a sort of meditation through drawing,' says Peter Clash, principal of Clash Architects. 'Some architects seem to be able to conjure up a completed design in a single sketch, ...for me sketching is a gradual process; a way of exploring the potential of a project and slowly formulating the best ideas and solutions.'

Clash's sketches, here of Magna [98–99], an unrealized design for a derelict industrial building in Sheffield, UK, are predominantly in pencil, although pastels and watercolours are sometimes used to highlight certain elements, such as a type of material or spatial mood. Even when he has sketched numerous iterations of the same design and found a solution he likes, Clash says it is often beneficial to turn the page and carry on: 'then when you have taken time out, you can reconsider your options'.

Clash fills A4 sketchbooks with his designs, interspersed with pages of notes from meetings or 'to do' lists. 'The books aren't precious or project specific,' he says. 'They are filled with what I am thinking about at any given time.'

Page after page is covered with slightly different renderings of a single detail, other pages display ideas for how a building might appear from alternative perspectives. 'It takes time to develop the best scheme for any site,' says Clash. 'Architects need to take time to develop their position. Sketching is like dreaming. It is your own imagination, your own ideas. Spend time doing it and your work will be fresher, your ideas stronger, your architecture valid and vibrant.'

HOME GROWN

the Incredible Edible House

vertical axis wind turbine

rooftop evaporative reservoir

hydroponic panel and win-door storage

studio and garden deck level **3**

cross-ventilation adjustable win-door

sleeping level **2**

eating living level **1**

photovoltaic awning

desk level studio

garden deck

the nutty professor

tomatoes

arugula

chick peas

carob

jakub

green tea

storage

pre-fabricated

stair bay

wet bay

vent bay

living quarters

hydroponic skin

E

north

W

RIOS CLEMENTI HALE STUDIOS

FRANK CLEMENTI

'I wish I could draw better. I wish I knew what to draw. Trees shouldn't look like boulders on scaffolding—that's how mine turn out if I'm not careful,' says American Architect Frank Clementi. Although this is hard to believe, looking at images from his sketchbook [100].

'Initially my impulse is to draw diagrams of intangible ideas...unintelligible free-form drawings, a kind of note-taking of isolated perceptions and incongruous ideas without a known application or endpoint. None or all of these lead to "the" design. Hopefully all of them lead to something though. They aren't the answer but the process, a way to record thought.'

Clementi's curiosity and creativity extend beyond the borders of architecture into product design and graphic design. This cross-disciplinary approach is fuelled by time spent in Milan, working with iconic design group Memphis on aesthetic experiments involving products, graphics, packaging, ceramics, tableware and architecture. Even food is on the menu. Clementi is the designer of the Incredible Edible House [101]—a viable structure composed of edible materials.

'I got excited by architecture when I found out that it could be about ideas, and could be as culturally communicative as any art,' says Clementi. 'Drawing is a way of recording ideas in a proto-formal way. Ideas are intangible; buildings are fixed, formal and solid. Getting from intangible idea to built reality is the frustrating part.'

Sketches are the universal language of design, Clementi believes, and sketching in tandem—one drawing on top of the other's work—is something he enjoys. 'Co-sketching is a way of watching one another develop ideas, because the evolution of a drawing is narrative, like speech,' he says. 'The expediency of the hand drawing and the fact that it accretes subjectively makes it narrative. A wonderful design develops from a messy overlap of many of these narratives.'

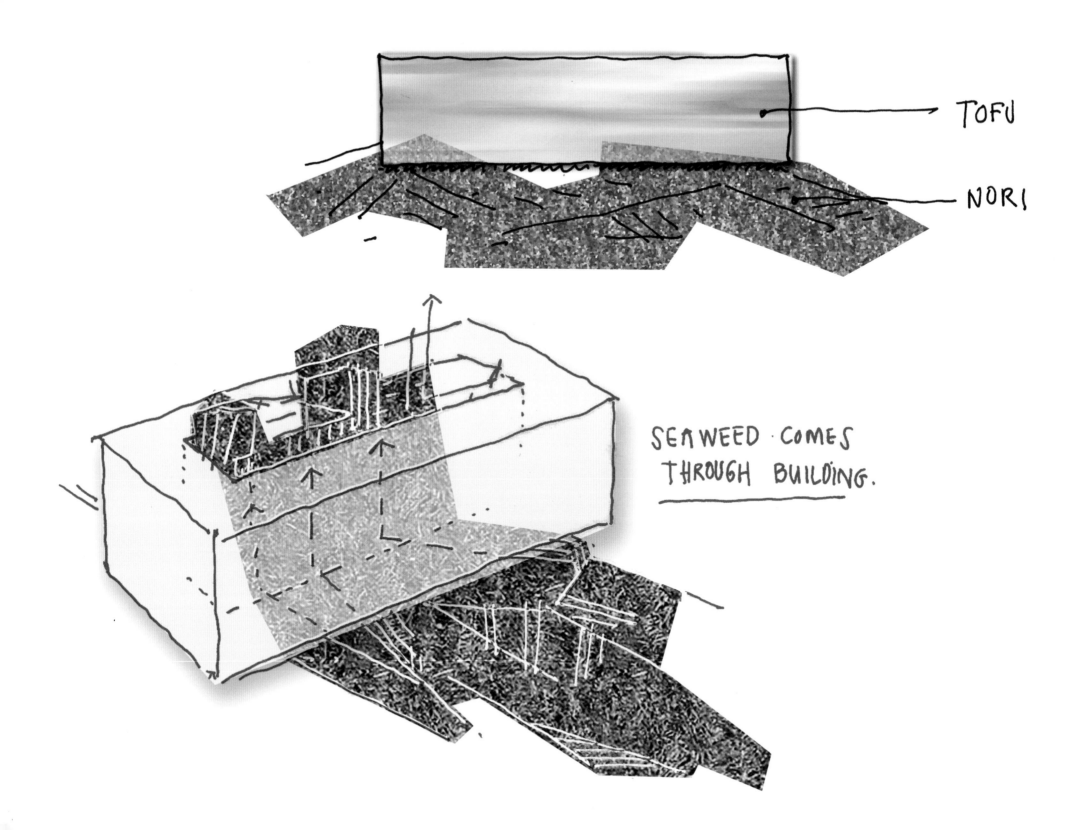

TOFU

NORI

SEAWEED COMES
THROUGH BUILDING.

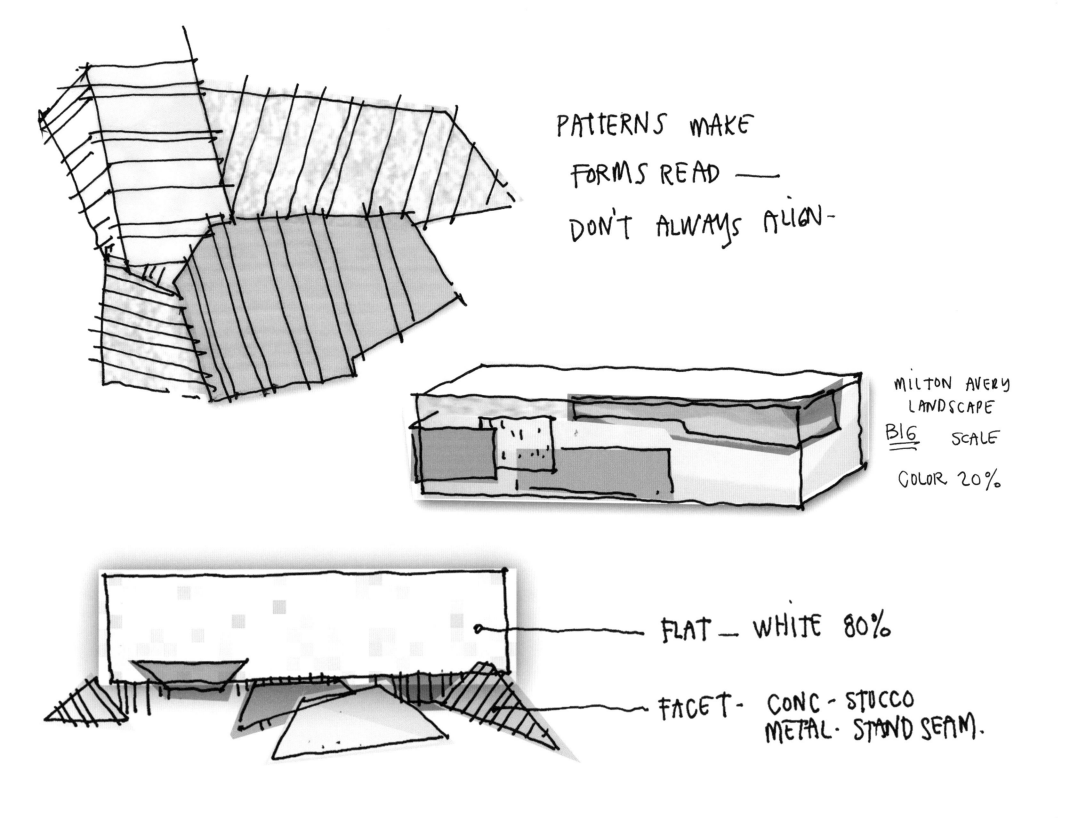

PATTERNS MAKE
FORMS READ —
DON'T ALWAYS ALIGN.

MILTON AVERY
LANDSCAPE
BIG SCALE
COLOR 20%

FLAT — WHITE 80%

FACET — CONC - STUCCO
METAL · STAND SEAM.

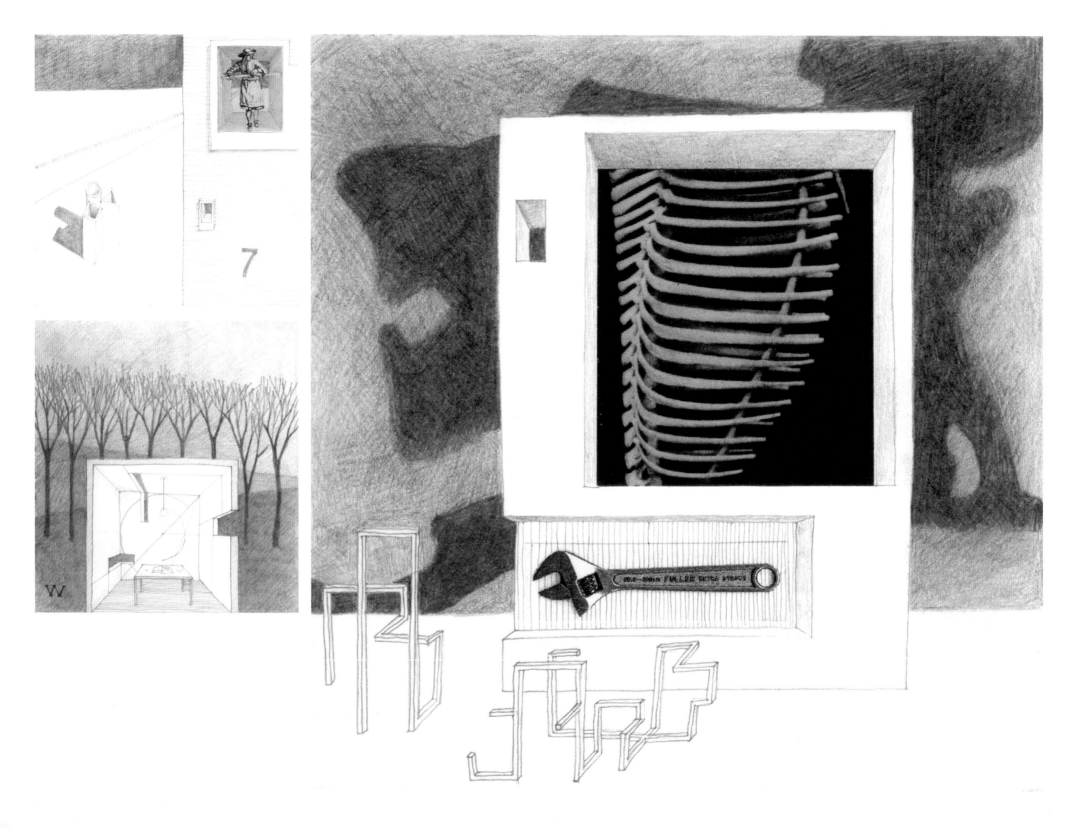

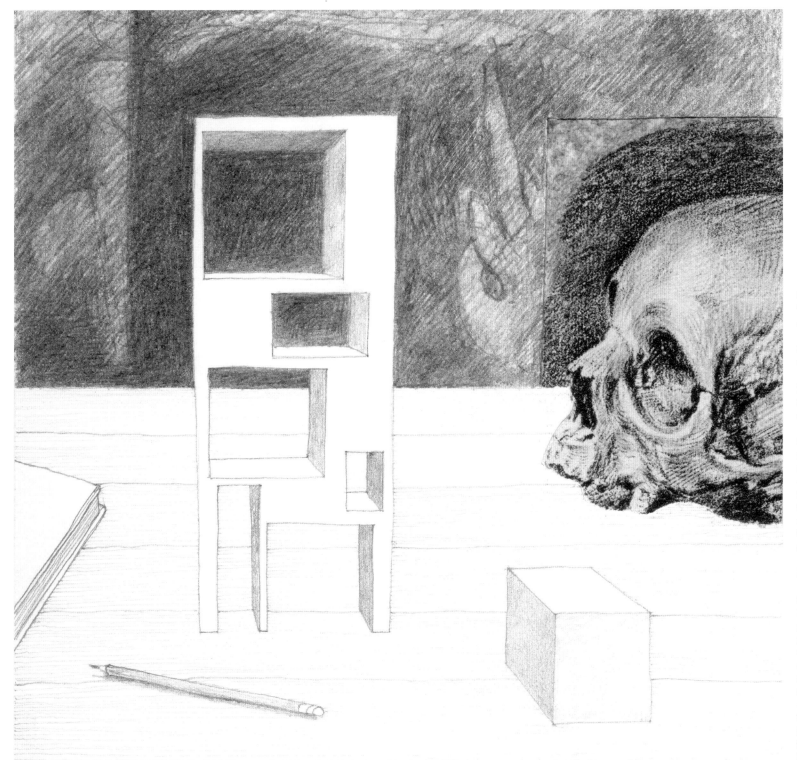

CALEB CRAWFORD

'The great gift of architecture is its ability to create worlds. We value architecture's utility but we prize its ability to astonish,' says Caleb Crawford. 'These drawings are a means of creating architecture, but they...have no immediate utility in the making of a building; they are autodidactic...a means of self-teaching; and they are poems in their desire to express...an ineffable quality.'

Crawford, the principal at Coggan + Crawford, exemplifies a surprisingly large number of architects who are influenced by Surrealist art and thinking. He might call his drawings 'useless', but they clearly rely upon—or modes of architectural representation—orthographic projection, axonometric drawing and perspective—at times mixing several techniques into a single sketch. They also draw upon the work of modern and contemporary artists such as Mondrian, Ernst, LeWitt, Miró, Klee and Duchamp.

Some drawings are intentionally narrative and pictorial, while in others Crawford blurs the line between an architectural representation and an abstract, geometric composition. 'I am constantly looking for ways of breaking habits and challenging my comfort level. Drawing involves becoming lost and discovering. Though logical rules for the making of form are employed, often there is no rational motivation for a form's presence. With these drawings, I really do not expect to be anywhere in a particular project but when the drawings are at their best, there is nothing left to say.'

105

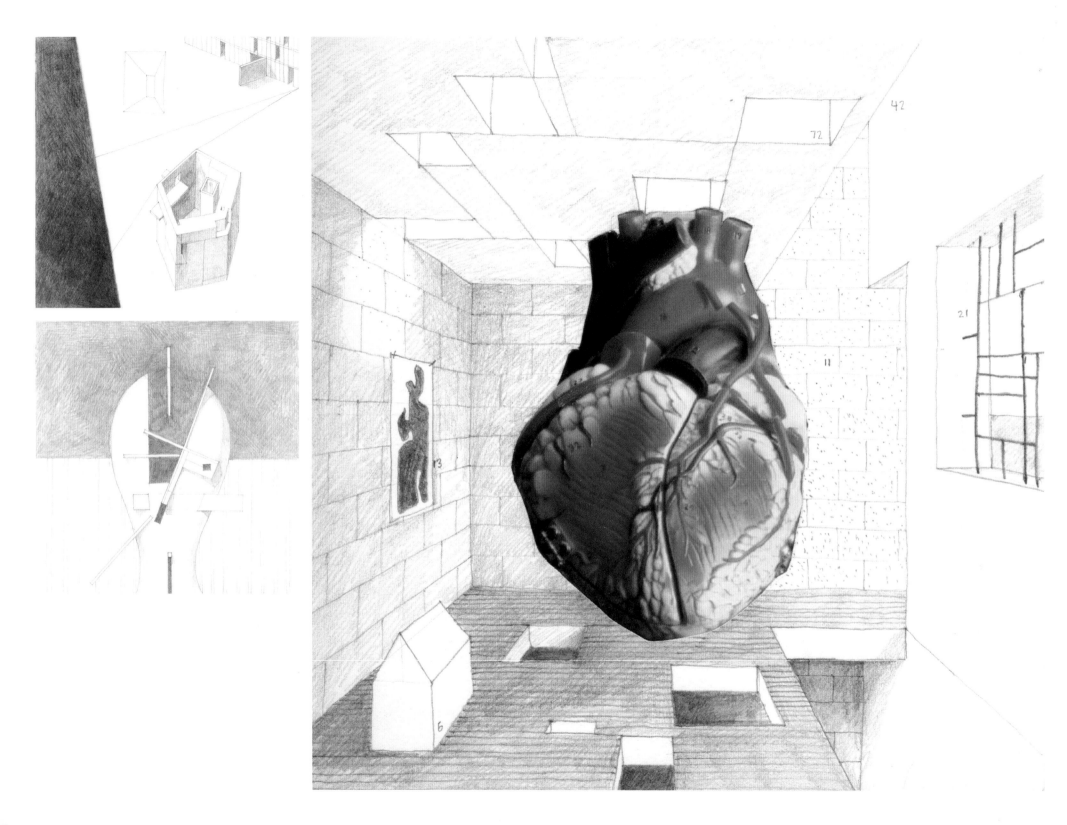

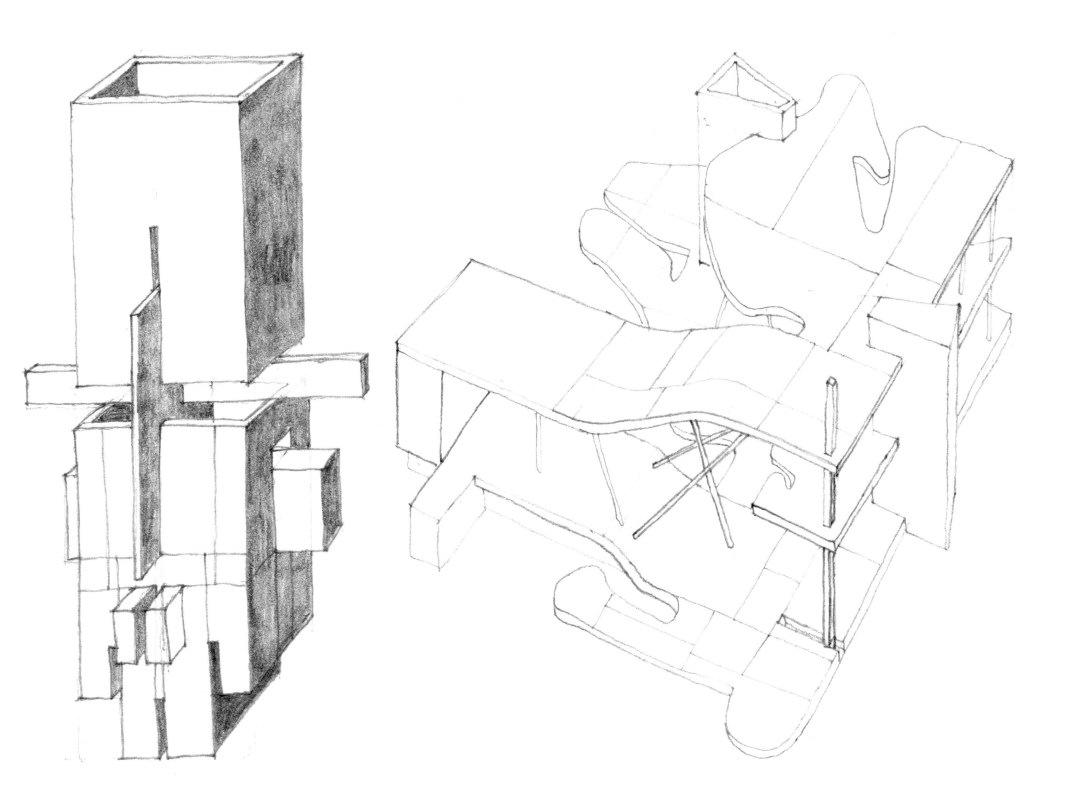

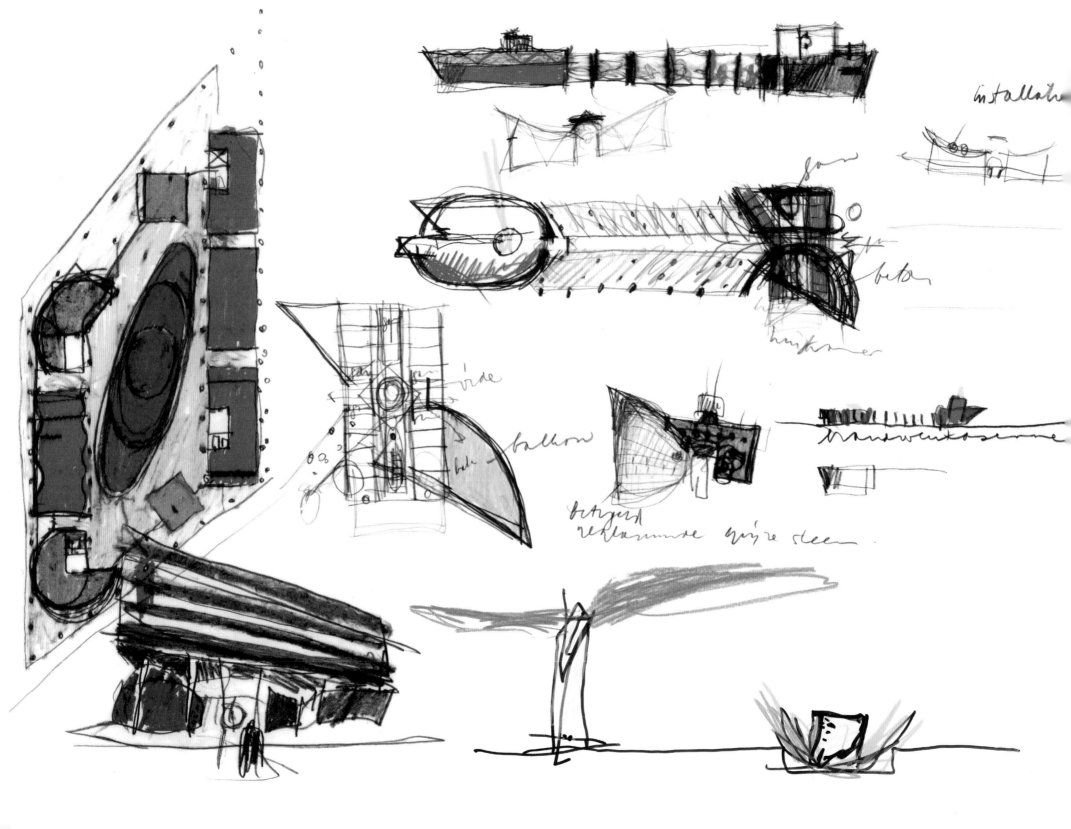

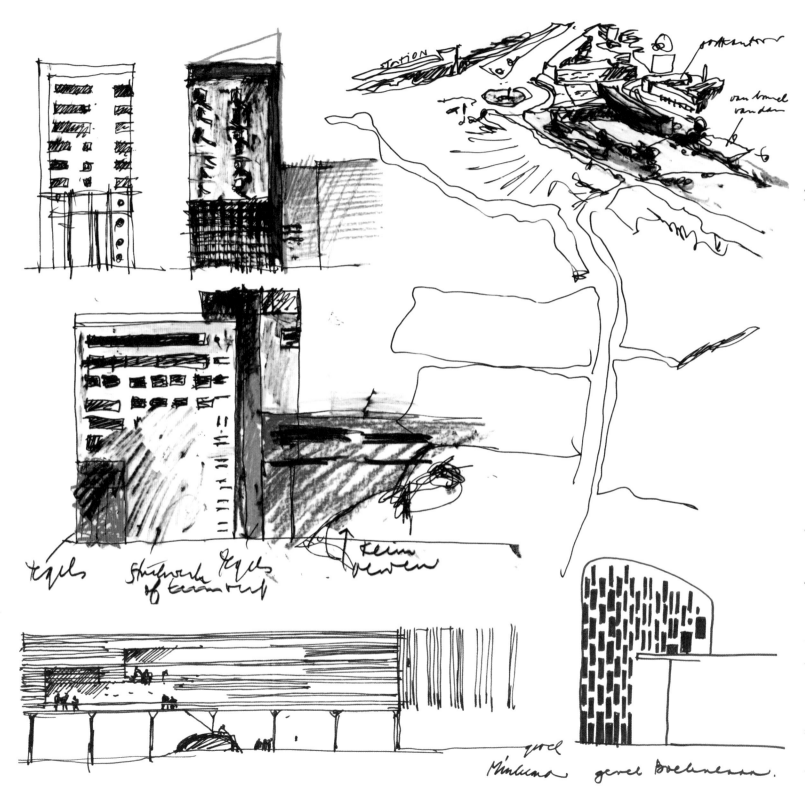

JEANNE DEKKERS

This Dutch architect has a rough-and-ready approach that comes across in her designs. Jeanne Dekkers's concept work is not about creating beautiful imagery, more about the distillation of what she calls 'the gift of the area' — the significance of a project's location, along with the desire and culture of the client and the user. However, whether a watercolour of a mosque or pen and ink sketch of an office design or site plan, the colourful nature of her work makes it a joy to look at.

Every design begins with the practice of getting thoroughly acquainted with the commission and studying four main aspects: the location; the brief; the purpose and background of the client and the user; and initially invisible factors. 'It is important for us to discover the essence behind the commonplace of the surroundings,' says Dekkers. 'In discovering the individuality of the area, the character of the client's desire and the uniqueness of the presently hidden significance, a new image is created that leads to a unique architectural interpretation.'

Dubbing her practice's working style 'poetic engineering', Dekkers advocates a multidisciplinary approach, in which several parties collaborate, each on the basis of their own particular know-how and expertise. 'Coordinating this process — poetry and engineering — is an extra challenge which results in excellence,' she says.

In each different case the concept sketch/painting is, while not minimal, sparse in detail. It is an indicator of the direction in which Dekkers wishes the project to proceed.

'Aside from materialization and detailing, key words that we do not lose track of are flexibility, durability and future-orientation,' says Dekkers. 'From these initial free-form sketches, the working method of the company makes our architectural ambition attainable and leads to a real, new building, a dream come true, as it were.'

111

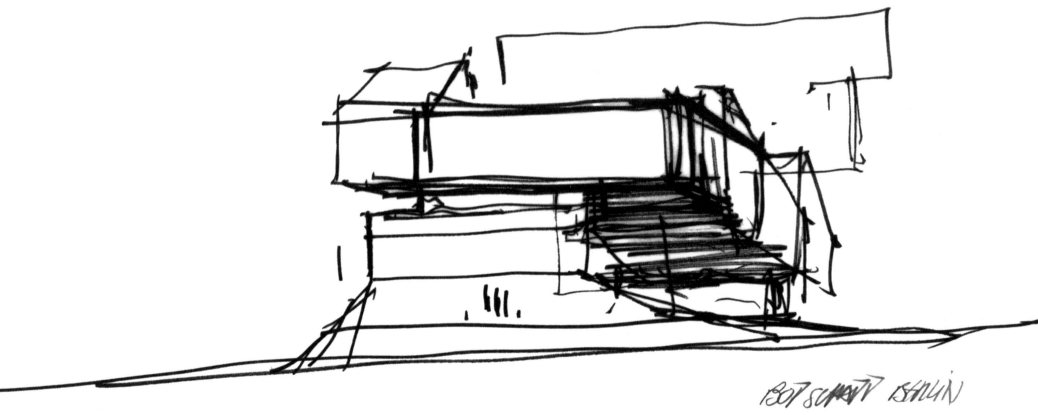

BOB SCHACHT ISHLIN

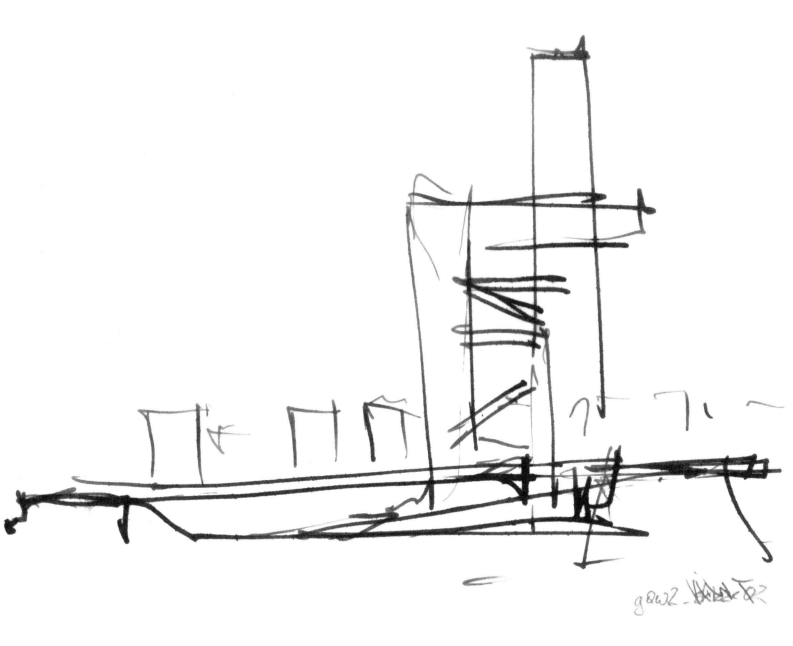

DMAA

'We see our office as a neutral cell, open within itself. Communication occupies the centre stage and discourse happens both inside and outside the office, echoing personal collected images and experience,' says DMAA. 'As such, the so-called star-architect represents a highly betrayed concept. Only the recognizability of his or her name is of significance. The contemporary office should act and work like a living structure, composed of varied independent systems; the result, a structural entirety that shares the common goal of generating architecture.'

This statement is indicative of the way in which DMAA approaches all projects, and the unique results of its architectural experimentation. Even a request for 'images that describe the way you work' for this book brought something different from that of any other architect [114–15]. The practice believes designing consists of letting accumulated knowledge 'rest in the mind' in order to unleash the senses from everyday influences, letting go of real images to generate creativity, and so opening up an alternate free space in the emotional world.

'Freedom of imagination is the cornerstone of every design. Experienced inner images are opened as mediators between the conscious and the unconscious. Comparable to dreams, they are windows into the latter. In order to generate this state of being the mind should be empty, the atmosphere should be like when one is in a doze: a neutral space, reduced to the essential. Emptiness signifies purity, which concentrates the mind on inner images. And so, the empty sheet of paper constitutes the beginning, the start of a visualization process powered by imagination. A series of lines overlap and finally show the growing organism.'

113

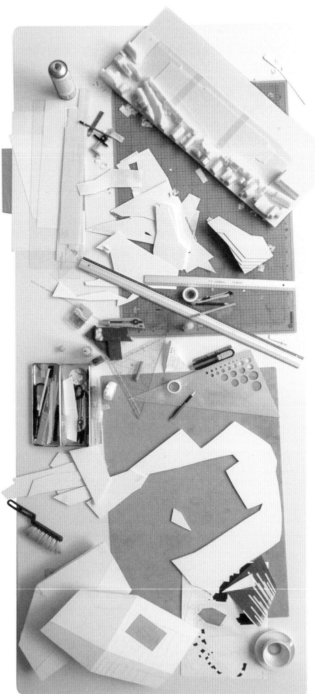

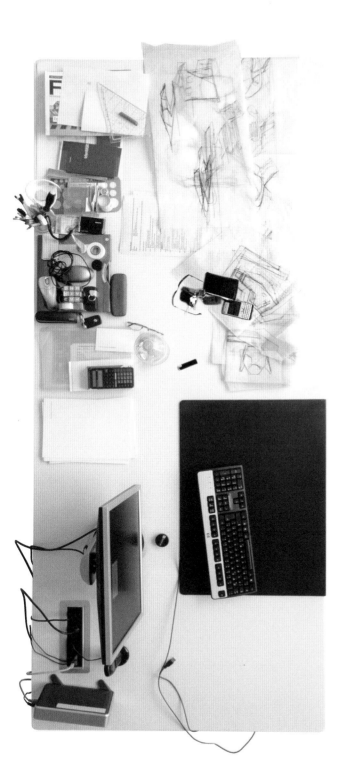

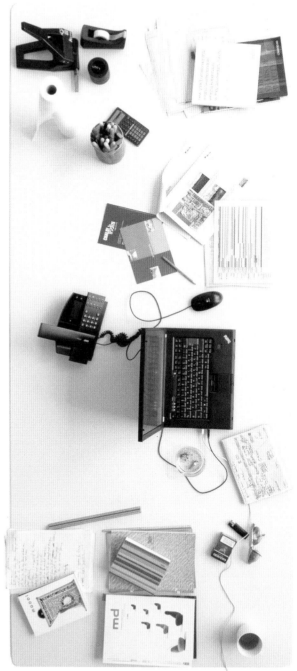

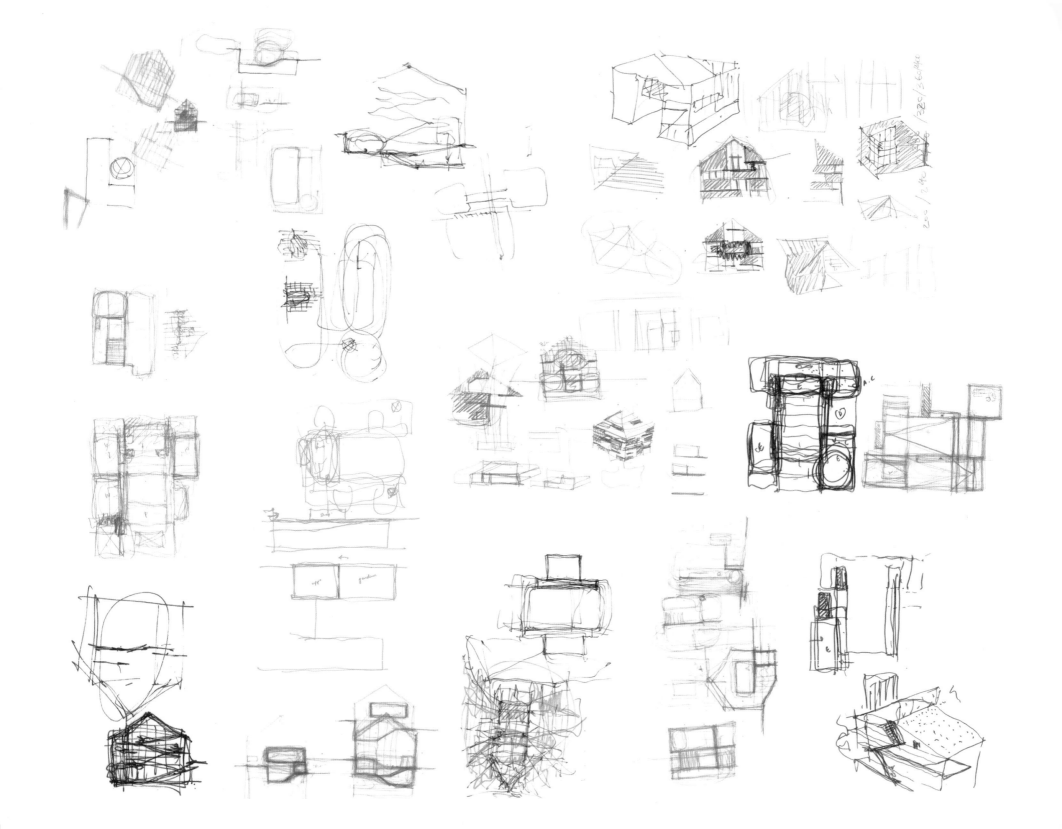

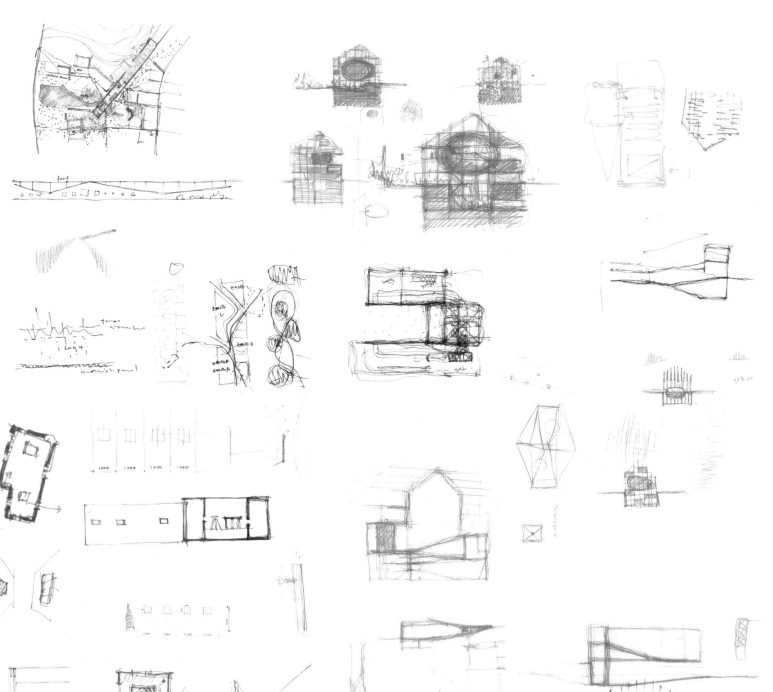

DORELL.GHOTMEH.TANE

'Initially, we illustrate ideas through words and sketching, as well as layering the sketches,' says Lina Ghotmeh. 'Models are also crucial in the process of design.'

Dorell.Ghotmeh.Tane is headed up by three architects: Dan Dorell, Lina Ghotmeh, Tsuyoshi Tane. This trio of different nationalities brings their diverse backgrounds, cultures and methodologies to bear on 'the production of space'.

Ghotmeh explains, 'As we are three partners leading the office, we have to use as many mediums as possible to communicate our ideas and develop them. Here, three different projects illustrate three different treatments—the first sketches [116–17], the second and third [118 and 119] photographs and the models, respectively. Words describe our intentions, thoughts, without physically defining them; they leave a large leeway for imagination in each one's mind. Sketches take shape and are initially a personal way of expression. The ideas are expressed through the specific hand of one person on paper or using 3D software. This sketch is often re-appropriated, re-layered by another partner architect. The idea for the space, the place, the architecture starts to take shape.'

Research plays a large part in the practice's work, as do different mediums, to communicate sketches and photography, to communicate the feeling or mood of a space. Finally models are used as the most complete medium for expressing ideas.

'Research, sketches, models, words are finally forced into crystallization because they reach a certain level of development,' says Ghotmeh. 'At this point what has been imagined has to be proven possible. Now, the design ideas are again contested and challenged, but we are pleased to see that the initial sketched inspirations often remain until the maturing of the project, to become the tie between the different aspects—function, materials and technical constraints.'

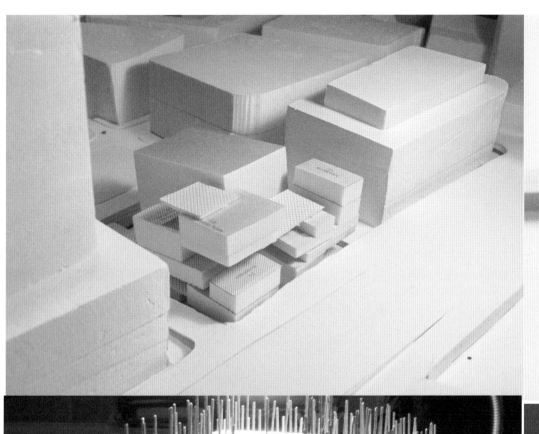

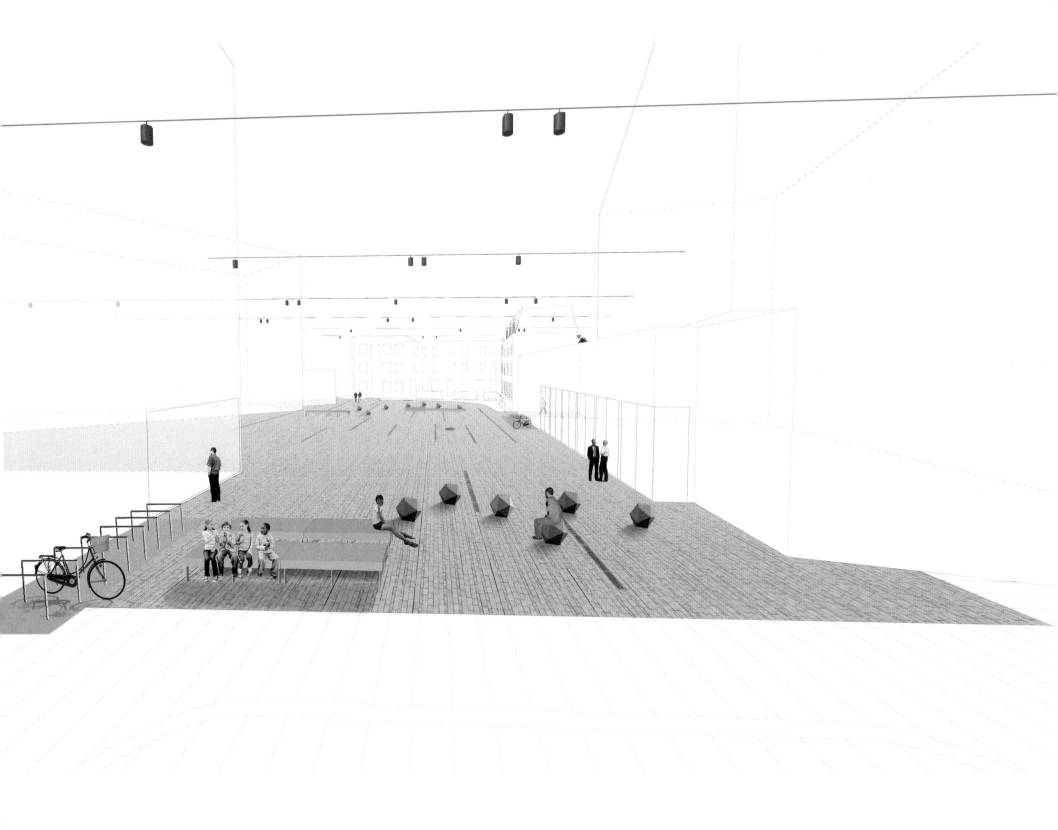

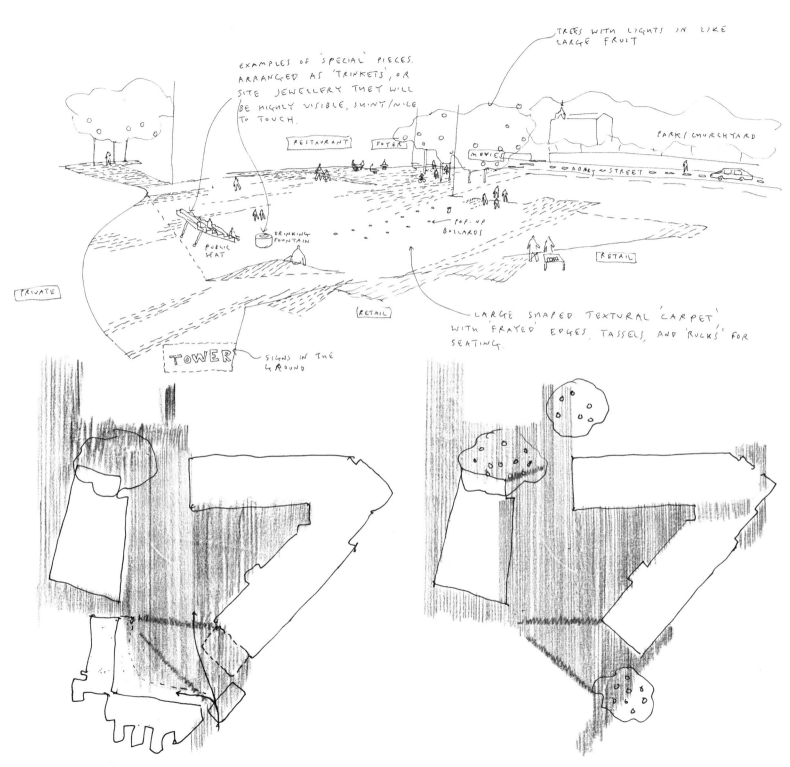

EXAMPLES OF 'SPECIAL' PIECES. ARRANGED AS 'TRINKETS', OR SITE JEWELLERY THEY WILL BE HIGHLY VISIBLE, SHINY/NICE TO TOUCH.

TREES WITH LIGHTS IN LIKE LARGE FRUIT

PARK / CHURCHYARD

RESTAURANT   FOYER

MOVIES

ABBEY STREET

RETAIL

PUBLIC SEAT

DRINKING FOUNTAIN

POP-UP BOLLARDS

RETAIL

PRIVATE

TOWER

SIGNS IN THE GROUND

LARGE SHAPED TEXTURAL 'CARPET' WITH 'FRAYED' EDGES, TASSELS, AND 'RUCKS' FOR SEATING.

EAST

'The drawings we do tend to be on large but flimsy and oddly-shaped pieces of paper. We stick more and more bits of paper to the first one to accommodate the growing design, which is drawn with four or even six hands,' say the architects of UK practice East. 'It feels like an occasion, with everyone sitting around the table, talking excitedly, adding more and more detail so that the thing on the table becomes complex and comprehensive.'

This collaborative working assists the practice to recall site visits and conversations and spell out clearly what is pictured in individuals' minds both verbally and on paper. 'It's one helping along the other. The more one draws, the more we all remember.'

On these pages sketches from an annotated site plan sketch and doodles [121] to a photomontage of the scheme [120]. The practice illustrates its quirky approach to design with a 'cut-out' diagram of an urban design study for Farringdon, London [122–23].

These initial sketches are, for East, about creating a shared understanding of the complexities of an urban situation, about trying to suspend judgment and design urges for a while, to get a sense of the places as they are. Drawing on ever-expanding sketching paper, using fine black pen, and writing what can't be drawn, the practice gradually builds this shared understanding: the design progresses through an iterative process, rather than lots of options.

The resulting models are often saved and cherished but the outsize, stuck-together sheets of paper that show East's design inspiration tend to get folded and accumulate in A3 folders tucked out of the way. 'Sometimes we come across them again with a small shock of delight, but more often they eventually get lost, mislaid, forgotten until a good idea surfaces again.'

121

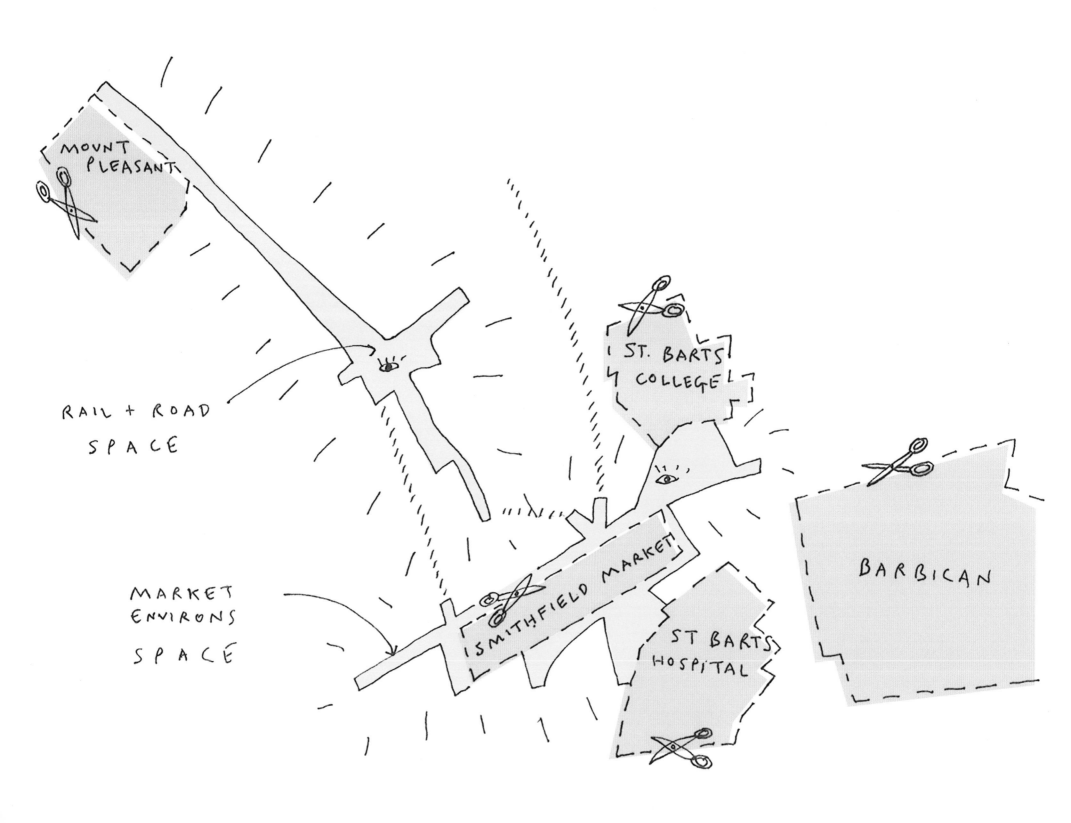

MOUNT
PLEASANT

RAIL + ROAD
SPACE

MARKET
ENVIRONS
SPACE

ST. BARTS
COLLEGE

SMITHFIELD MARKET

ST BARTS
HOSPITAL

BARBICAN

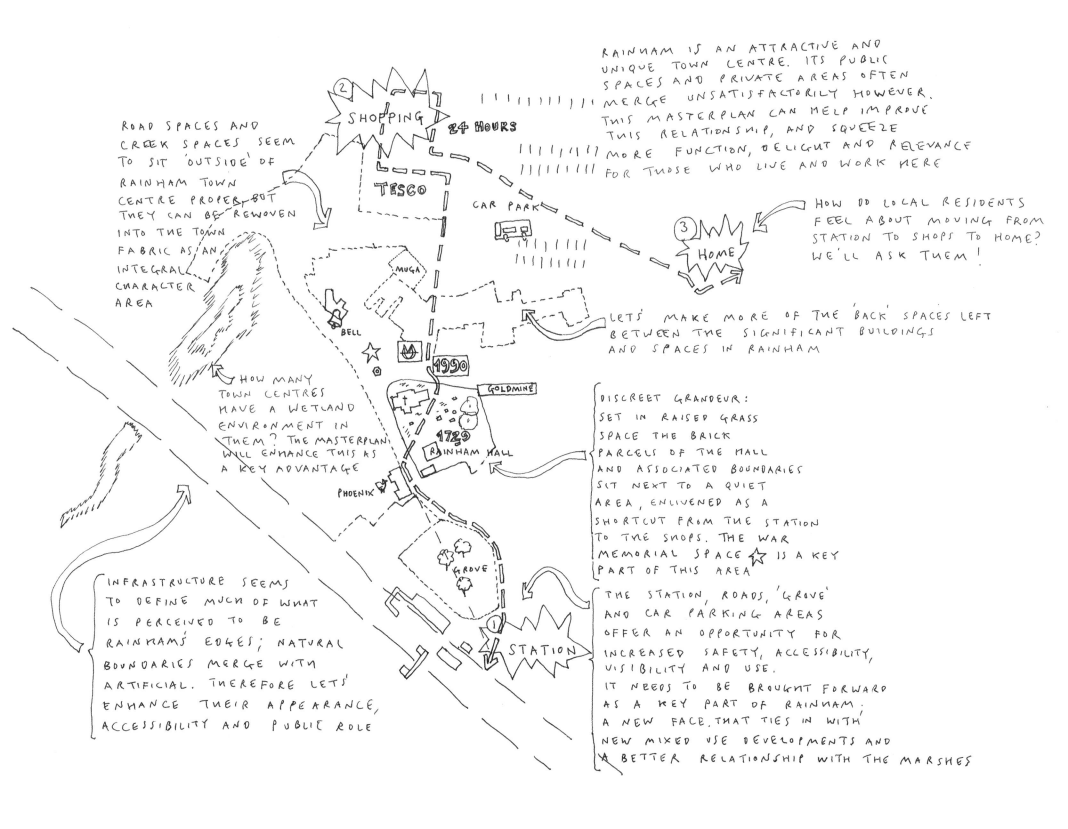

RAINHAM IS AN ATTRACTIVE AND UNIQUE TOWN CENTRE. ITS PUBLIC SPACES AND PRIVATE AREAS OFTEN MERGE UNSATISFACTORILY HOWEVER. THIS MASTERPLAN CAN HELP IMPROVE THIS RELATIONSHIP, AND SQUEEZE MORE FUNCTION, DELIGHT AND RELEVANCE FOR THOSE WHO LIVE AND WORK HERE

ROAD SPACES AND CREEK SPACES SEEM TO SIT 'OUTSIDE' OF RAINHAM TOWN CENTRE PROPER, BUT THEY CAN BE REWOVEN INTO THE TOWN FABRIC AS AN INTEGRAL CHARACTER AREA

② SHOPPING 24 HOURS

TESCO

CAR PARK

HOW DO LOCAL RESIDENTS FEEL ABOUT MOVING FROM STATION TO SHOPS TO HOME? WE'LL ASK THEM!

③ HOME

MUGA

BELL

LET'S MAKE MORE OF THE 'BACK' SPACES LEFT BETWEEN THE SIGNIFICANT BUILDINGS AND SPACES IN RAINHAM

1990

GOLDMINE

HOW MANY TOWN CENTRES HAVE A WETLAND ENVIRONMENT IN THEM? THE MASTERPLAN WILL ENHANCE THIS AS A KEY ADVANTAGE

1729 RAINHAM HALL

DISCREET GRANDEUR: SET IN RAISED GRASS SPACE THE BRICK PARCELS OF THE HALL AND ASSOCIATED BOUNDARIES SIT NEXT TO A QUIET AREA, ENLIVENED AS A SHORTCUT FROM THE STATION TO THE SHOPS. THE WAR MEMORIAL SPACE ☆ IS A KEY PART OF THIS AREA

PHOENIX

GROVE

INFRASTRUCTURE SEEMS TO DEFINE MUCH OF WHAT IS PERCEIVED TO BE RAINHAMS' EDGES; NATURAL BOUNDARIES MERGE WITH ARTIFICIAL. THEREFORE LETS' ENHANCE THEIR APPEARANCE, ACCESSIBILITY AND PUBLIC ROLE

① STATION

THE STATION, ROADS, 'GROVE' AND CAR PARKING AREAS OFFER AN OPPORTUNITY FOR INCREASED SAFETY, ACCESSIBILITY, VISIBILITY AND USE. IT NEEDS TO BE BROUGHT FORWARD AS A KEY PART OF RAINHAM; A NEW FACE THAT TIES IN WITH NEW MIXED USE DEVELOPMENTS AND A BETTER RELATIONSHIP WITH THE MARSHES

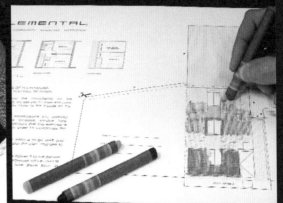

ELEMENTAL

Alejandro Aravena, architect and executive director of Elemental, looks to solve big problems using innovative, yet cost-effective solutions. 'If there is any agreement in the world today, it is that we need to correct the inequalities of our societies,' he says.

Looking to house poor families not on the outskirts of Santiago, Chile, but within the heart of the city, where the value of the properties built would be higher and so benefit new owners, Elemental devised a partly completed home that the owners will finish when they have the money.

The Construyendo Nuestro Futuro (Building our Own Future) project [124-25] consists of a 1.5-metre structural party wall element, two storeys high. This includes all the most complex parts of the house: bath, kitchen, stairs and ducts. It stands 3 metres from the next party wall so that within the void the families can expand in their own way, making their home personal to them and unique.

The architect explained his intentions to the prospective residents using a simple worksheet, plans of the building layouts and a cut-out-and-make paper model of the house. Residents were encouraged to decorate and assemble model houses—a fun exercise that encouraged them to engage with the project.

'In the end, when the given money is enough for just half of the house, the key question is, which half do we do?' says Aravena. 'We choose to make the half that a family individually would never be able to achieve on its own. We contribute using architectural tools, to answer non-architectural questions of how to overcome poverty. The rest of the house is up to the resident.

125

ELLIOTT + ASSOCIATES ARCHITECTS

The design philosophy of Elliott + Associates Architects is shaped from the theory that a space reflects the unique personality of the owner. 'We do not do cookie-cutter design,' says Rand Elliott. 'Each project, like each client, is unique.'

Based in Oklahoma, Elliott has a reputation for designing projects that not only 'fit' their respective sites but seem literally to 'grow' from the site, such as the McQueen Cabin [126–27]. He does this in a painstaking way that begins with 'word paintings'—single words, sentences, paragraphs or poems that describe the spirit of the project. Elliott explains, 'Words do not have form—they allow early ideas to grow with no stylistic preconception. It is easy to fall in love with a drawing and I try to avoid this trap.'

The design concept arrives after hundreds of words and sketches in an effort to find the breakthrough idea. Elliott uses notebooks initially; these doodlings and words are then scanned and printed on a large scroll that is unrolled at the feet of the client. 'I present the scroll with my client as we walk review each sketch with my client as we walk along the edge of the paper.' The longest scroll to date is over 32 metres.

'I do not focus on beautiful sketches, rather on words, ideas and emotions that can tell a story. My design approach is single-concept driven. One of many ideas will emerge as the appropriate solution to this specific problem. The early sketches and word paintings are realized and visible in the final design,' Elliott says. 'These sketches are very important to me. I am currently working in my twenty-eighth sketchbook, and once filled, they are kept in a bank vault.'

127

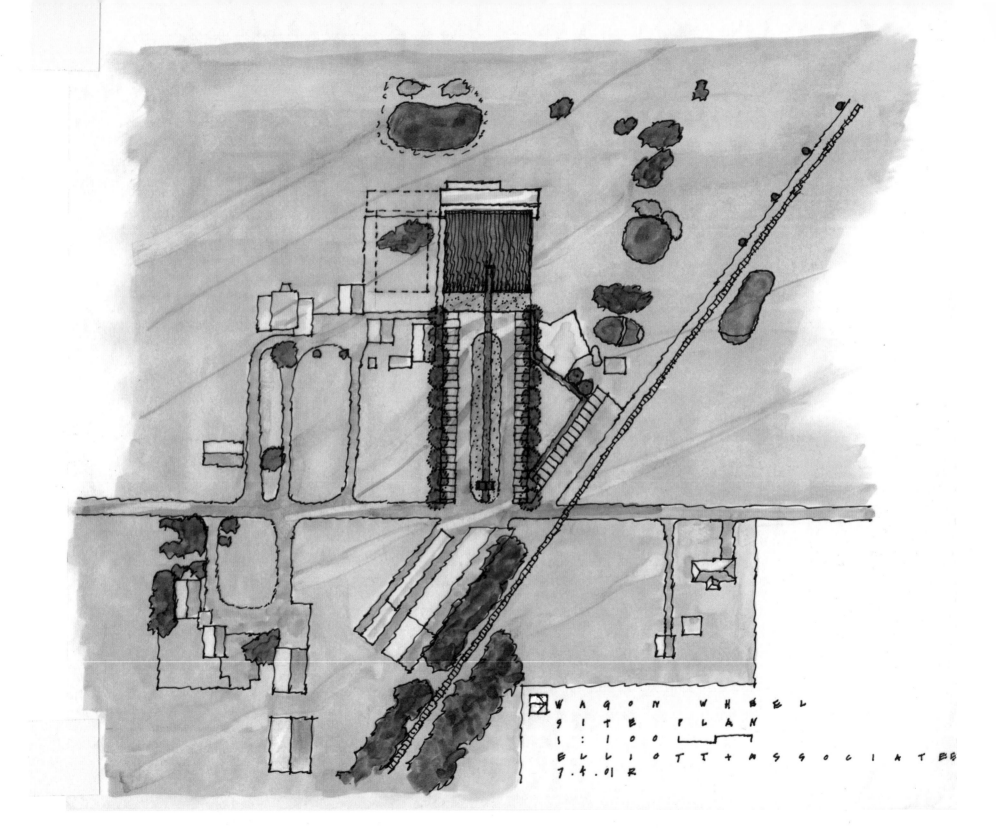

WAGON WHEEL
SITE PLAN
1:100
ELLIOTT+ASSOCIATES
7.4.01 R

connecting the earth and the sky

WW
5.22.01
1:20

East

5.22.01 Wagon Wheel

· Brick wall

· closer sides - no 180° view

· brick or stone wall
supports... views
· rusting steel panels?
· Brick form pushes thru
roof @ kitchen

· chimney is outboard of
roof edge... steel chimneys

G R O W
S P I R I T
L I G H T
S U N
S H A D E
V I E W
H O R I Z O N
R T 6 6
S U N S E T
R U S T
O P E N
F I R E
R E F L E C T I O N
W H E A T
R E D D I R T
F U R R O W S
too busy?
S U N R I S E

· make the entry "icon" fire...

· no panorama view... simplify

· Horizontal window
to North...
· move F chimney?

· earth form...
· protected N wall...
stone or brick

· put a fire pit on patio
not chimney...

· North elevation = Horizontal
window
· rusting steel chimney...
· Brick or stone

· is it friendly...

winter
south

winter
ESE

looking
West
· purple
color

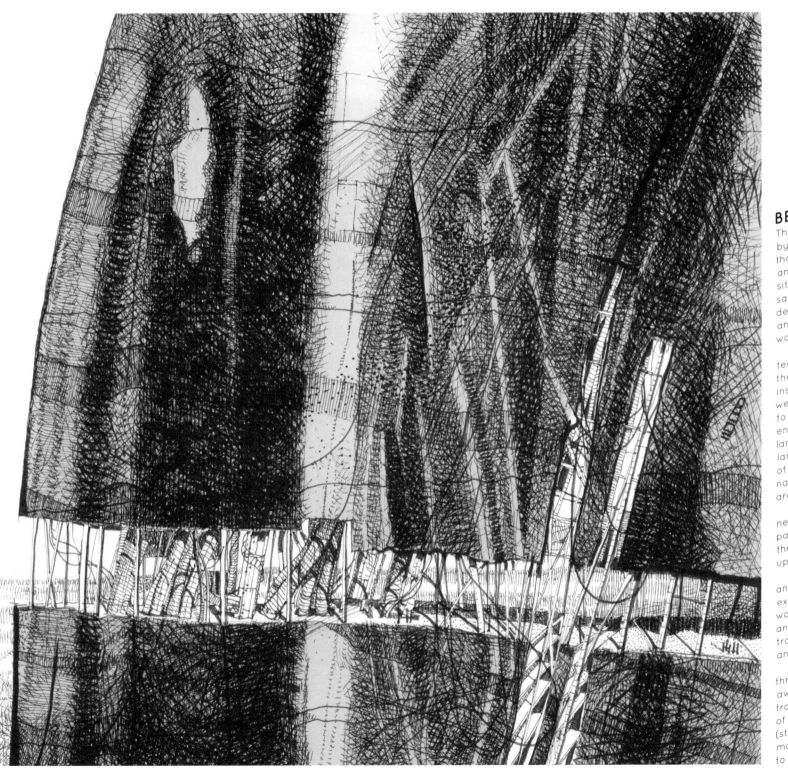

BEN EMMETT

The monumental scale of the drawings made by architect Ben Emmett is echoed in his thoughts about them. 'Large-format ink and graphite drawings articulate the intensity of light and dark in a wild landscape,' says Emmett. 'The energy of mark-making describes a latent atmosphere of mystery and rawness, gained only through time spent walking the land.'

Speaking as a poet as much as an architect, Emmett is passionate about his home in the west country of England. He takes much inspiration from walking and sketching in all weathers. 'It is important to draw from life to capture the spirit of the place. Camping enables me to immerse myself fully in the landscape. The drawings are inspired by landscape, myth and narrative. The process of sketching provides a link to a mythopoetic narrative where I can imagine structures that are an integral part of the landscape.'

In Emmett's drawings the structure is never wholly revealed, drawing the participant into the built form and landscape, while the use of scale—macro and micro—builds upon mythical structures and events.

Emmett works mainly with pen and ink, and graphite, to provide monochromatic expressions of fine detail and expansive tonal washes. He draws upon both contemporary and ancient architectural references to illustrate structures in a process of construction and/or decomposition.

Sometimes the inner workings burst through the façade, or the façade is peeled away to reveal the hidden. Emmett's formal training as an architect is clear from his use of contemporary construction components (steel, concrete, wiring, ductwork)—yet these materials are cunningly used in such a way as to simultaneously evoke a mythical feel.

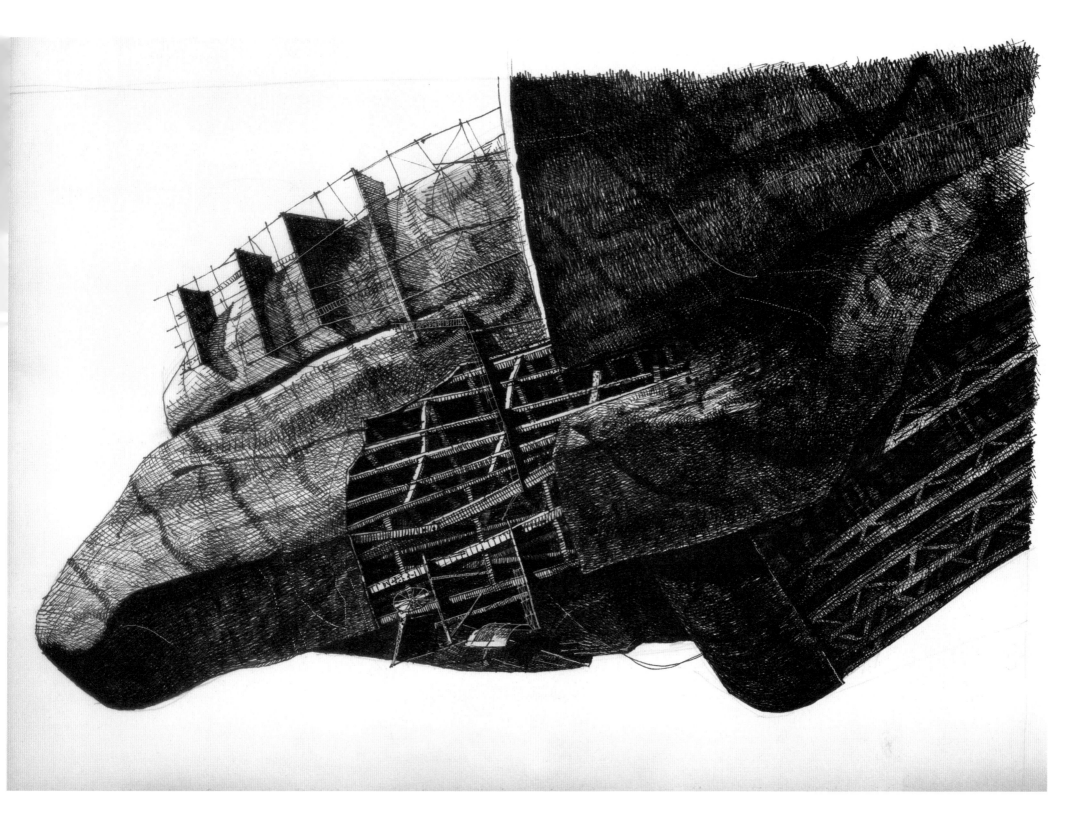

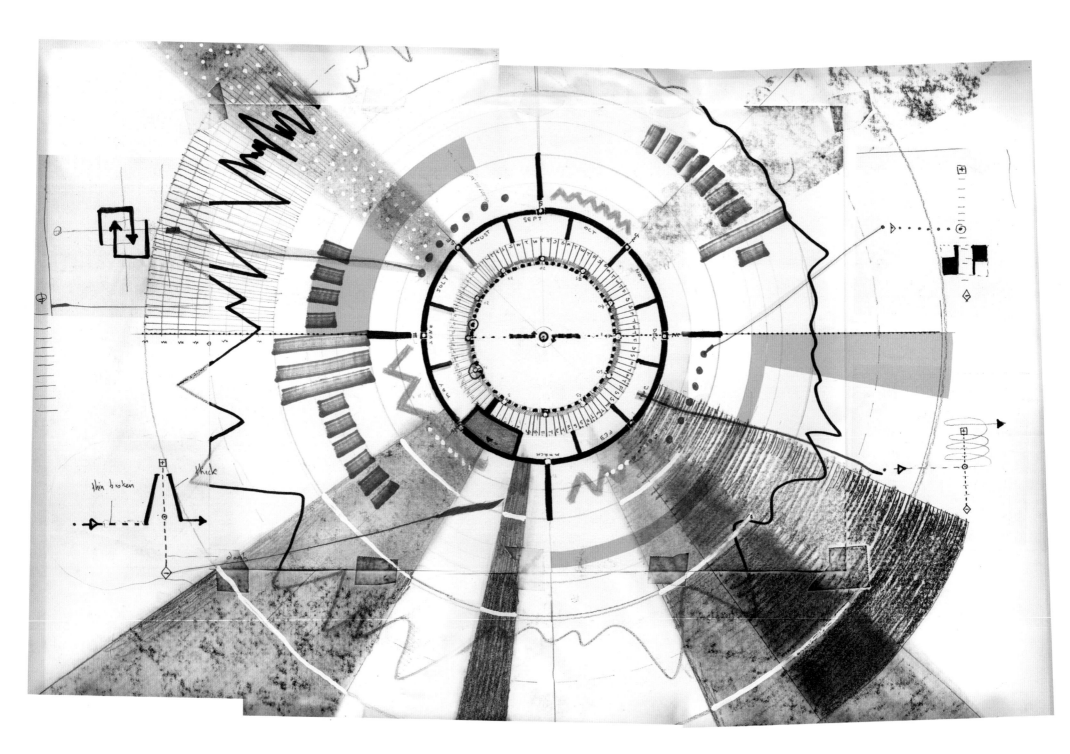

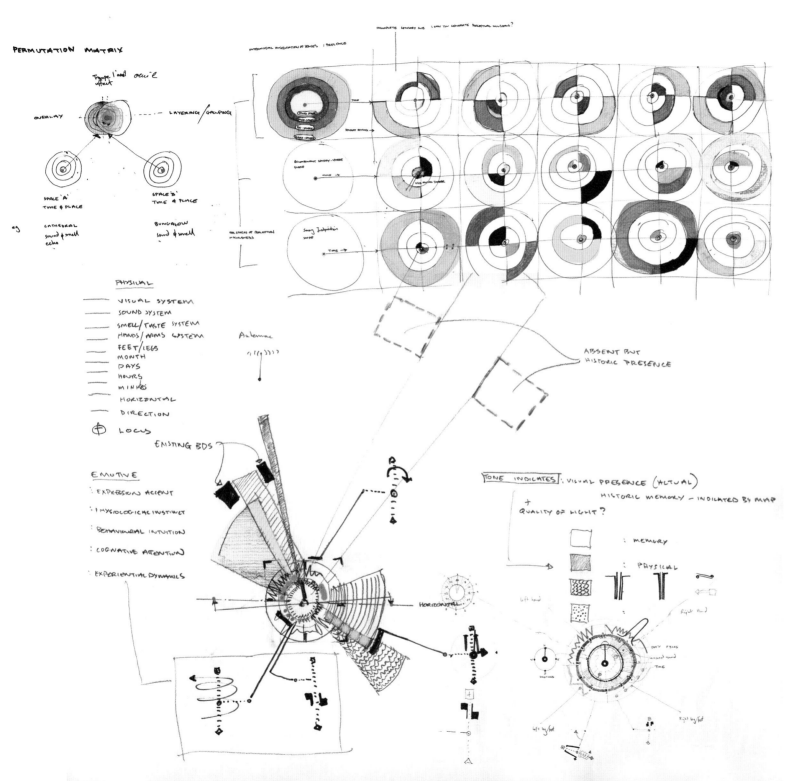

MATHEW EMMETT

'The work vivisects space and time, representing the praxis of mental, sensual and physical creation,' says British architect Mathew Emmett. 'Drawing amplifies the imagination, ramps up the theory and transmits the code—deployed to emit spores of polyspatial thought, mediating between perception, knowledge, manipulation and communication.'

Emmett's projects demonstrate what he terms the varying bandwidths of architectural thinking, ranging from conceptual prospecting and researching to testing and deciphering complex, idea-led scripting. All of these processes seek to transmit information at both technical and emotional levels. 'Exploration through drawing maps the mediation of cognition, affording more dexterity and criticality in the shifting dimensions of the imagination,' he says. 'Drawing is thinking, as modelling is multidimensional viewing, seeing the concept from different angles—looking behind the diagram.'

Emmett's sketches and models start off very loose; the initial explorations establishing lines of enquiry. Thinking-drawings investigating discovery by asking questions, investigating the mental, sensual and physical domains simultaneously. Diagrams explore the potential of an idea, where the methodology treats the drawing or model as a form of research, emphasizing the analytical, multi-perspective investigations of space.

The works shown here [134–37] were created as part of research projects aimed at developing an ordination tool for visualizing statistical analysis. The projects use process-orientated design methods to demonstrate a systematic exploration of space and investigate new developments in spatial constructs. Emmett says his theories 'generate polydimensional geometries, pushing at the limits of space-making and fostering new forms/systems of architectural design'.

THE END /
THE BEGINNING

FANTASTIC NORWAY

Founded by Håkon Matre Aasarød and Erlend Blakstad Haffner, this architectural practice uses a diverse and unusual range of media and methods to communicate its designs and aims. Believing that conventional architectural language is limiting, Fantastic Norway make use of alternative media such as cartoons, TV and exhibitions.

Bottled Message [138–39] is an animated film exploring Norwegian national identity and coastal culture. The cartoon expresses these notions through the narrative of a small, traditional house that sets off on an extraordinary journey. The story begins with images of abandoned cities and fragile settlements along the coast of Norway. Throughout history these settlements have depended on the unpredictable nature of the ocean—it could enrich the community bringing sailors and travellers (along with their unknown traditions and tools) or it could equally destroy that same community.

As the cartoon unfolds, a small worndown house on the windy island of Hysvær is revealed. 'Coastal houses should not be connected to the mainland. They should be lifted and free,' remarks Håkon Matre Aasarød. Fantastic Norway's architectural response is to cover the house with mirrors to reflect people and the cultures it encounters. The house's foundation of compressed salt is worn down over time by water slowly dissolving it, and so, when it touches the water the house floats away like a boat to encounter famous places, strange environments and new cultures. Finally, the small house reaches a place where it settles.

'Coastal identity is not something static or constant but rather an ephemeral and ever-changing notion. Architecture in these places must prepare for the unknown. One day, something will happen,' warns Aasarød.

139

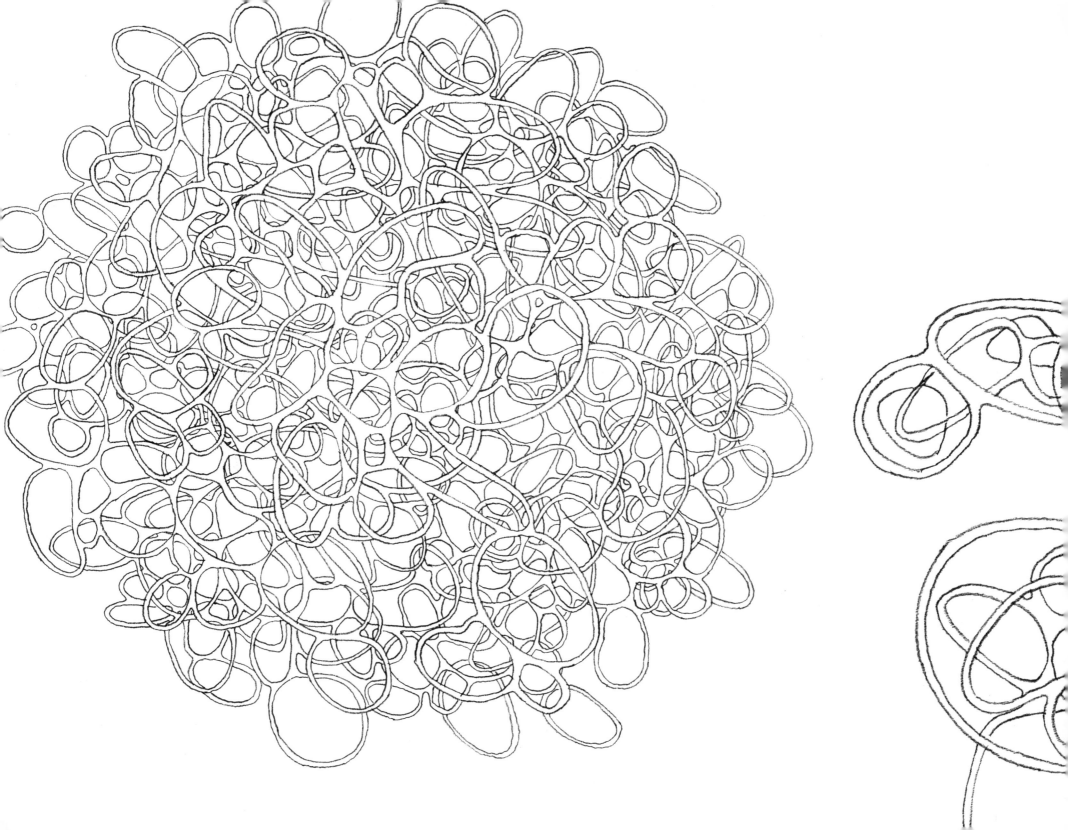

THOM FAULDERS

American architect and professor Thom Faulders (founder of Faulders Studio) explores the interfaces between space, perception and context. His work presented here—Particle Reflex [140–41] and Deform House [142–43]—places the practice of architecture within a broader context of 'performative research and material investigations that negotiate dynamic relationships between users and environments'.

This forward-thinking approach to architecture is often the realm of those enamoured with digital design. However, Faulders uses sketching in nearly all of his projects and understands the importance of this oldest form of architectural 'note-taking'.

'Prior to beginning digital design drawings, I'll sketch on a stack of white letter-size sheets of paper—nothing precious, just plain space upon which I can play around with ideas graphically,' he says. 'It is important that the process is non-precious and non-linear. I'll reshuffle the drawings, throw some out, post others on the walls. I'll also scan these small sketches into the computer, enlarge them and print out them as very large images. The initial sketch takes on a new dimension, one that can be further worked and developed at the larger scale.'

Faulders's architecture is pursued not as static form or pre-programmed space, but as an arena for adaptive and responsive behaviours. His work is an active and opportunistic architecture, articulated through and defined by spontaneous, constantly changing relationships between a building and its surroundings.

'These simple drawings are graphical concepts, used in tandem with written conceptual texts,' he says. 'Often sketches begun in one project will be pulled and used on another. Ideas are fluid and adaptable.'

141

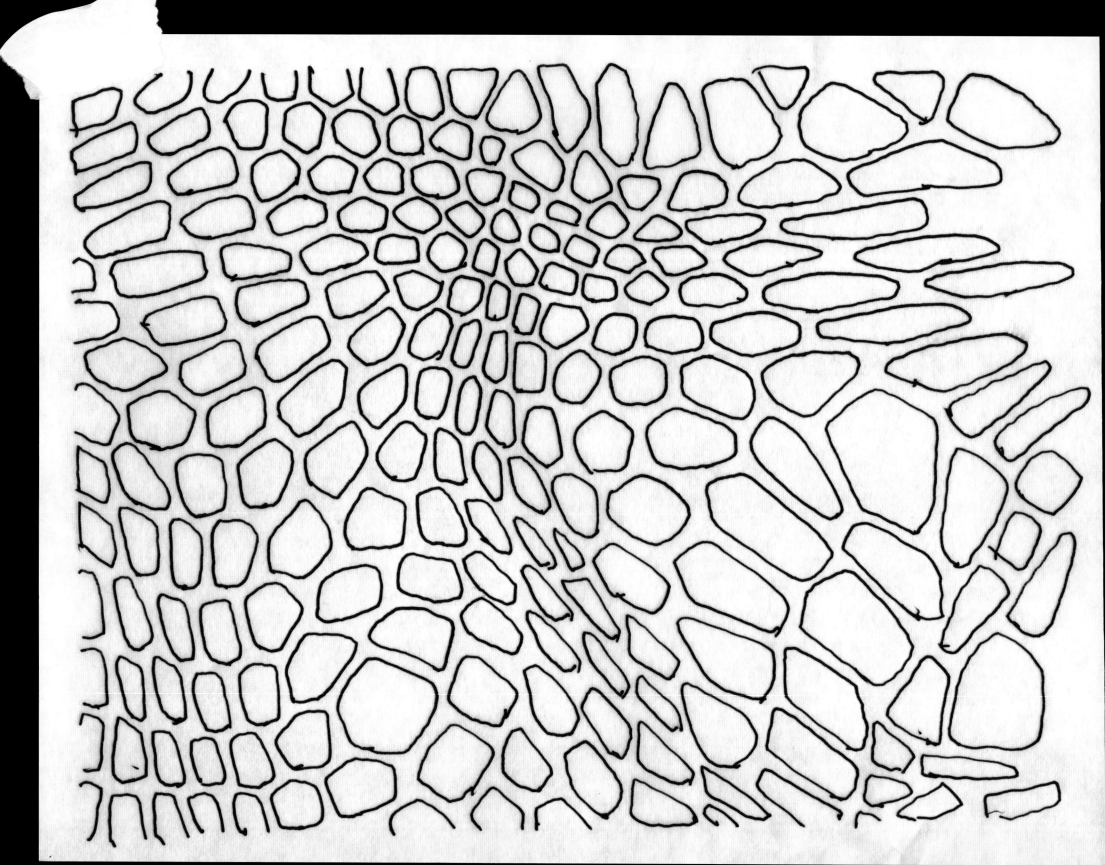

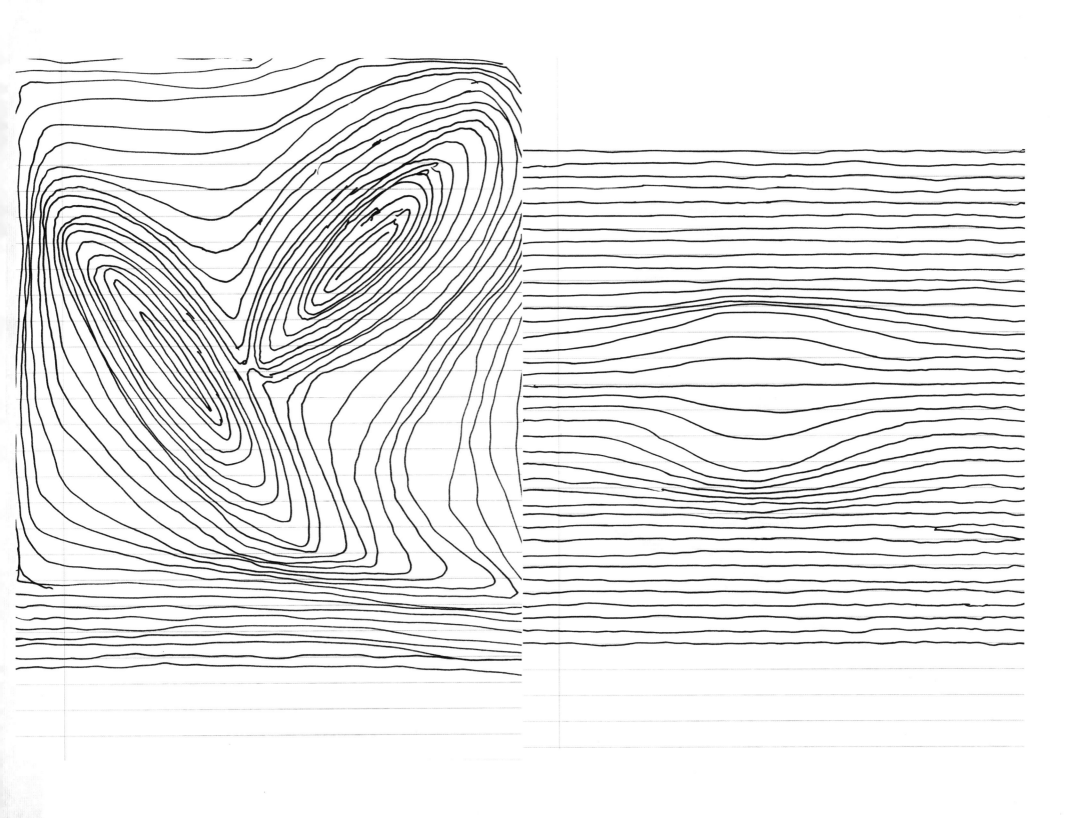

① consider
a hierarchy
w grids

grids
within
grids

more atmosphere!

+ ceiling plane

it has the
potential to be
more
richer
with
shadows
& transition patterns
ABU DHABI

NF Feb '06

← tower

tower

NORMAN FOSTER

'I sketch all the time,' says Norman Foster, founder and chairman of Foster + Partners. 'Although the computer has revolutionized the way we work, we still draw by hand, and model-making plays a central role in our studio.' This revered architect bemoans the idea, common among students, that the power of sophisticated computer equipment has somehow rendered the humble pencil if not obsolete, then certainly second rate. He states: 'The pencil and computer are very similar in that they are only as good as the person driving them.'

Foster sees sketching as a means of communication. In a meeting or a design review, he uses drawing to communicate a point. 'I find that I'm furiously scribbling away while I talk, so it is part of a dialogue in that sense as well.' See the comparison with classical architecture in Foster's sketch of the Carré d'Art and Médiathèque, Nîmes [148–49]; and sketches of an entire project in Sierra Leone [146], or details of Chesa Futura [147], a scale-clad office block. These pages feature sketches of the Central Markets, Astana, Kazakhstan [144] and the Commerzbank Headquarters, Germany [145].

'Architecture is as much about the fine print as the headlines—the tactile details, which are literally close enough to touch. Sketching, for me, is a vital way of exploring these concerns,' he says.

Foster's many sketches have been exhibited around the world alongside models of his buildings, but he is still reticent about showing them. 'I have never thought of the sketches as precious and, in the past, I was rather reluctant to exhibit them. I have certainly never thought of the sketches as "works of art".' Instead, he sees them as stepping stones in the design process. 'I'm always excited by the potential that lies within a sketch. I sometimes get so locked into the design process that it becomes compulsive and the sketches become dimensioned cartoons—a basis for more formal drawings, the absolute first step towards a new building.'

A school
for Sierra Leone

NF
04/09

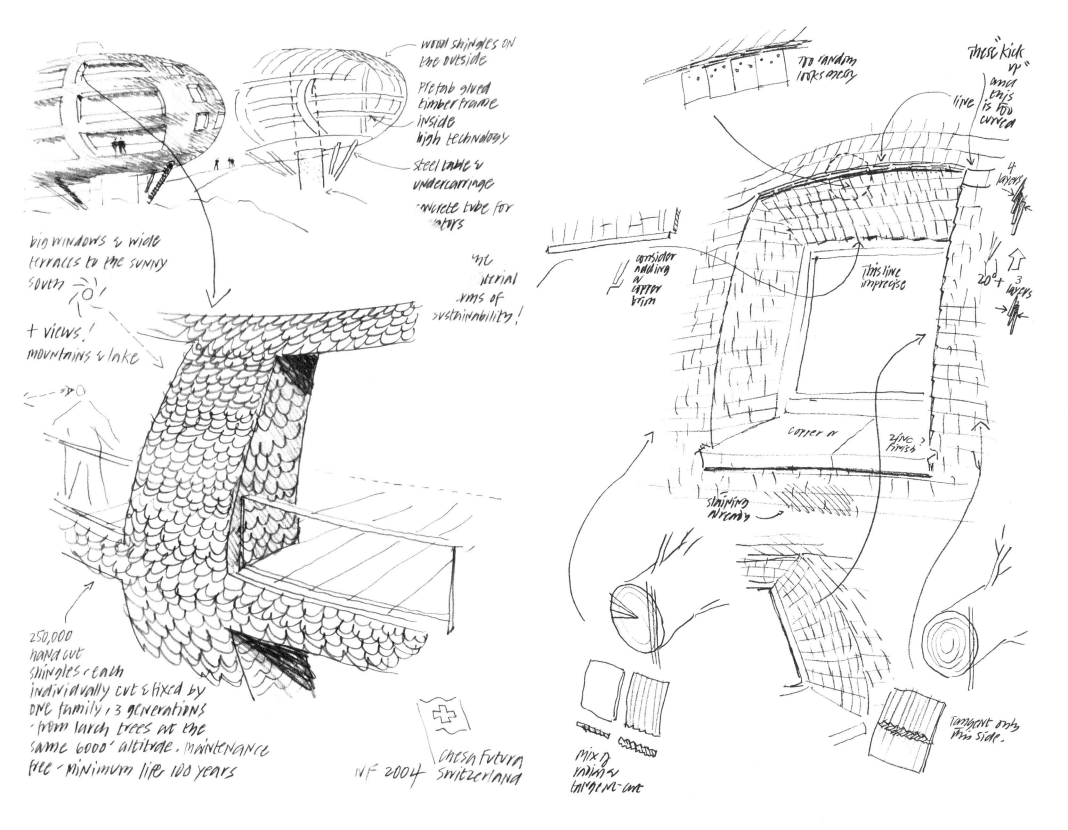

wood shingles on the outside

Prefab glued timber frame inside high technology

steel table & undercarriage

concrete tube for ~ators

big windows & wide terraces to the sunny south!

+ views! mountains & lake

the ~erial ~rms of sustainability!

250,000 hand cut shingles · each individually cut & fixed by one family, 3 generations · from larch trees at the same 6000' altitude. Maintenance free · minimum life 100 years

NF 2004   Chesa Futura Switzerland

too random looks messy

these "kick up" and this is too curved

live

4 layers

consider adding a copper trim

this line imprecise

20° + 3 layers

copper ~

zinc? finish

staining already

mix of ~~~ tangent-cut

tangent only this side

The new building fills the same site as the original 19c Opera House - since destroyed by fire.
The "Place de la Maison carrée" - the setting of the Roman Temple - therefore remains unchanged
The height, mass & geometry of the new building defer to the surrounding "background" buildings

The main facade to the "Place" recreates the
"Portico" extending over the pavement · a simple
inviting public gesture as well as a climatic

The bulk of the new building above ground is rea
penetrating deep below pavement level · small
-backs & pavement lights bring light & views

LINKS WITH THE PAST · CENTRE FOR CONTEMPORARY ART & MEDIATEQUE · NIMES

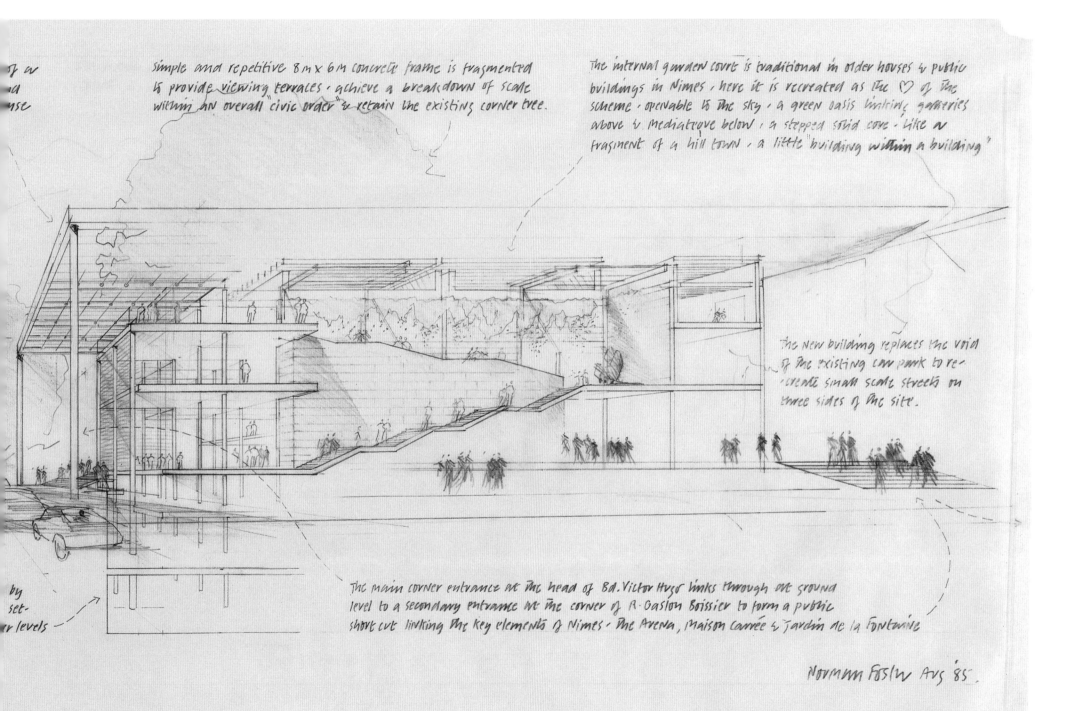

simple and repetitive 8m x 6m concrete frame is fragmented
to provide viewing terraces · achieve a breakdown of scale
within an overall "civic order" & retain the existing corner tree.

The internal garden court is traditional in older houses & public
buildings in Nimes · here it is recreated as the ♡ of the
scheme · openable to the sky · a green oasis linking galleries
above & mediatheque below · a stepped solid core · like a
fragment of a hill town · a little "building within a building"

The new building replaces the void
of the existing car park to re-
create small scale streets on
three sides of the site.

The main corner entrance at the head of Bd. Victor Hugo links through at ground
level to a secondary entrance at the corner of R. Gaston Boissier to form a public
short cut linking the key elements of Nimes · the Arena, Maison Carrée & Jardin de la Fontaine

Norman Foster Aug '85.

by
set-
levels

TONY FRETTON

Founded in 1982 and headed by partners Tony Fretton and James McKinney, Tony Fretton Architects has had a strong influence on regional arts in the UK. Their buildings include the Lisson Gallery in London; ArtSway, a centre for visual Arts in Sway, Hampshire; and the Quay Arts Centre for visual and performing arts in Newport, Isle of Wight.

Given this connection, the art of architecture is tremendously important to Fretton: 'Sketches maintain the potency of the ideas and form as they develop. My sketches provide imagery and conceptual direction for a project in its early stages, and ideas for how the pragmatics and social elements of a project can be given form.'

The two projects featured here illustrate the transition from sketch to model. An administrative centre in Belgium [150–51; 152, right; 153, right] and the Fuglsang Kunstmuseum in Denmark [152, left; 153, left], are represented by simple sketches and their subsequent model forms.

Fretton also believes that collective working makes for the best designs. He and his colleagues study and develop each project in small teams. Periodically the design is then critiqued by a larger group. 'Throughout this process I contribute sketches,' Fretton says. 'They not only address the issues specific to a project but also encapsulate aspects of other buildings I have seen, which I think are communicative.'

During design, sketches are removed page by page from Fretton's sketchbook and stored in a project file for members of the design team to consult. Later they are scanned for publication and potentially exhibition.

151

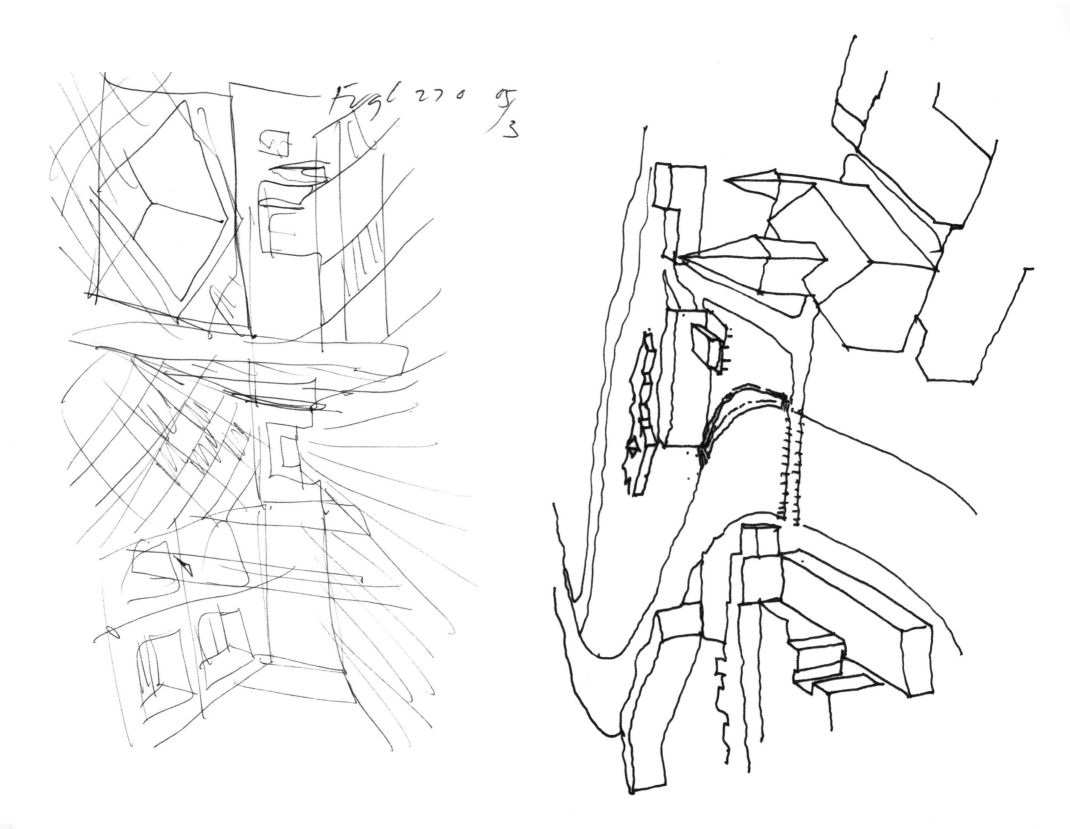

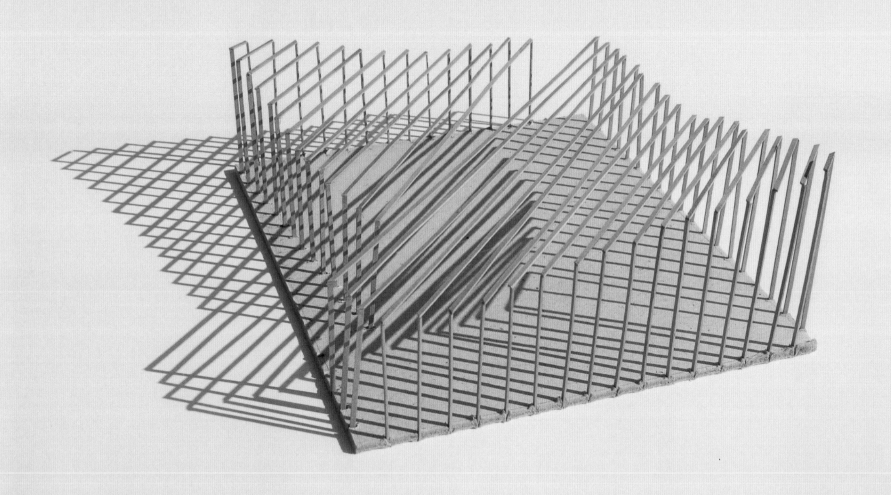

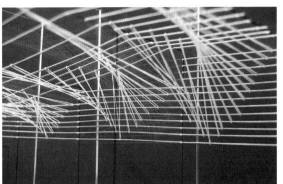

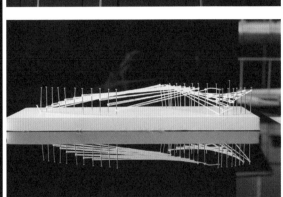

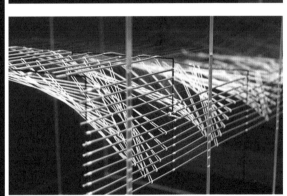

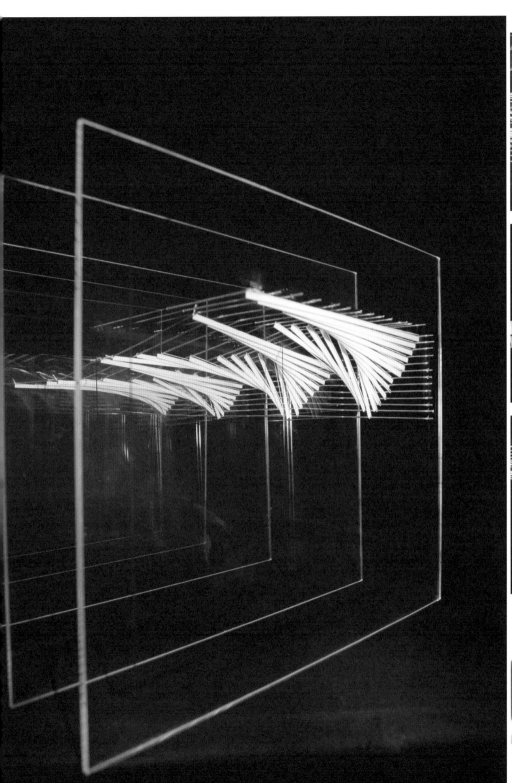

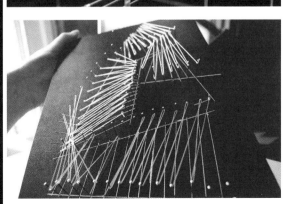

GLOWACKA RENNIE

'Models, models, models! We make models like other architects sketch,' says Agnieszka Glowacka. This does not necessarily mean models of the whole proposal, but often fragments of an idea. The practice might initially concentrate on a particular experience it wants to create within a project and test it through conceptual physical models. 'We are experimental,' says Glowacka. 'One series of models for a competition scheme we did ended up in the office freezer!'

On these pages are models for the Victoria & Albert Museum womens' amenities, London [155] and Rogerstown visitors' centre in Ireland [154]. Over the page are the Bridge of Reeds, near Cambridge [156] and an installation for the Hong Kong Shenzen Biennale [157].

The practice also photographs fragments of models to create atmospheric images showing what it might be like to experience the spaces in reality. These 'experience' models inform larger, more 'overall' models, which in turn help to develop CAD models, too.

But why be model-makers when CAD can do it for you? Glowacka believes that 'The hands have an instinctive link to the brain and eye. The often intuitive process of making is very creative. Seeing something physically manifested in a model, so that it can be picked up and peered through, makes it much more real and engaging. You can get excited about an effect, a view being created, and this concept seed then germinates into a proposal based on that initial excitement.'

Glowacka believes that the thrill and insight inspired by these models is retained in almost all of the practice's completed assignments. 'The project obviously transforms in response to new information but almost always the essence, the spirit and character, of those first models remains. Having concept models helps us to remember what we found exciting about the project in the first place and helps us to not lose that quality.'

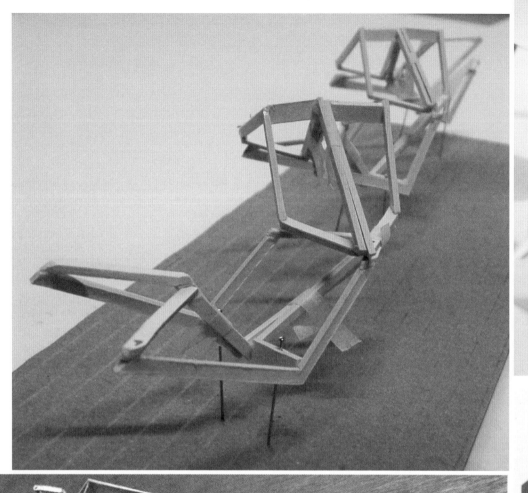

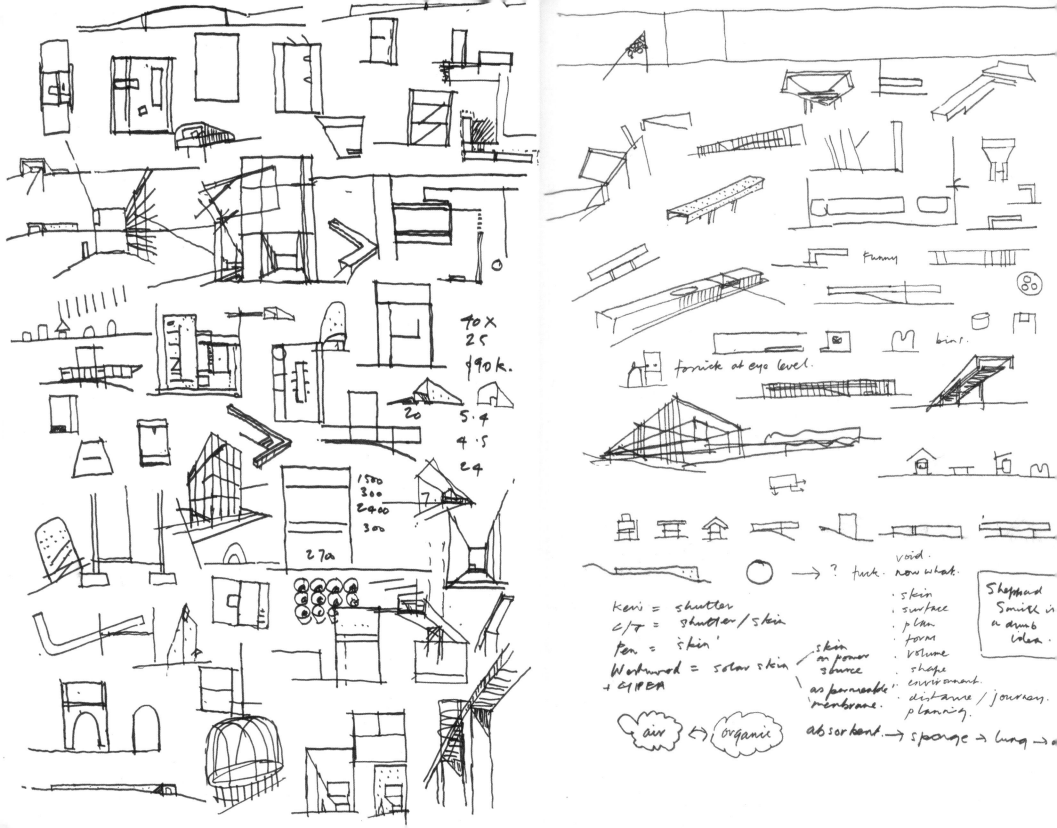

40 X
25
$90k.

20   5·4

4·5

1500   24
300
2400   7.
300

27a

Funny

bins.

Forrick at eye level.

void.
→ ? fuck. now what.

· skin
· surface
· plan
· form
· volume
· shape
· environment
· distance / journey.
· planning.

Kevi = shutter
c/τ = shutter/skin
Pen = skin'
Westwood = solar skin
+ GIPEA

skin
as power
source

as permeable
membrane.

air ↔ organic

absorbent. → sponge → lung →

Sheppard
Smith is
a dumb
idea.

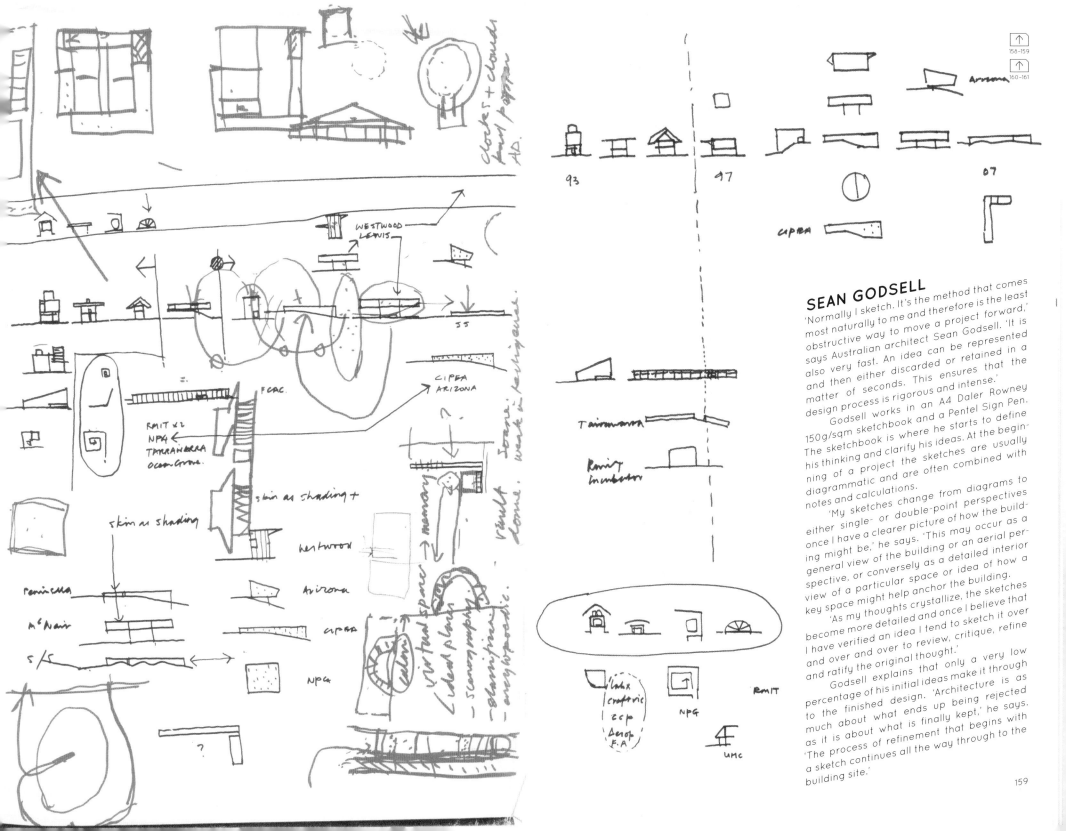

SEAN GODSELL

'Normally I sketch. It's the method that comes most naturally to me and therefore is the least obstructive way to move a project forward,' says Australian architect Sean Godsell. 'It is also very fast. An idea can be represented in a matter of seconds. This ensures that the design process is rigorous and intense.'

Godsell works in an A4 Daler Rowney 150g/sqm sketchbook and a Pentel Sign Pen. The sketchbook is where he starts to define his thinking and clarify his ideas. At the beginning of a project the sketches are usually diagrammatic and are often combined with notes and calculations.

'My sketches change from diagrams to either single- or double-point perspectives once I have a clearer picture of how the building might be,' he says. 'This may occur as a general view of the building or an aerial perspective, or conversely as a detailed interior view of a particular space or idea of how a key space might help anchor the building.

'As my thoughts crystallize, the sketches become more detailed and once I believe that I have verified an idea I tend to sketch it over and over and over to review, critique, refine and ratify the original thought.'

Godsell explains that only a very low percentage of his initial ideas make it through to the finished design. 'Architecture is as much about what ends up being rejected as it is about what is finally kept,' he says. 'The process of refinement that begins with a sketch continues all the way through to the building site.'

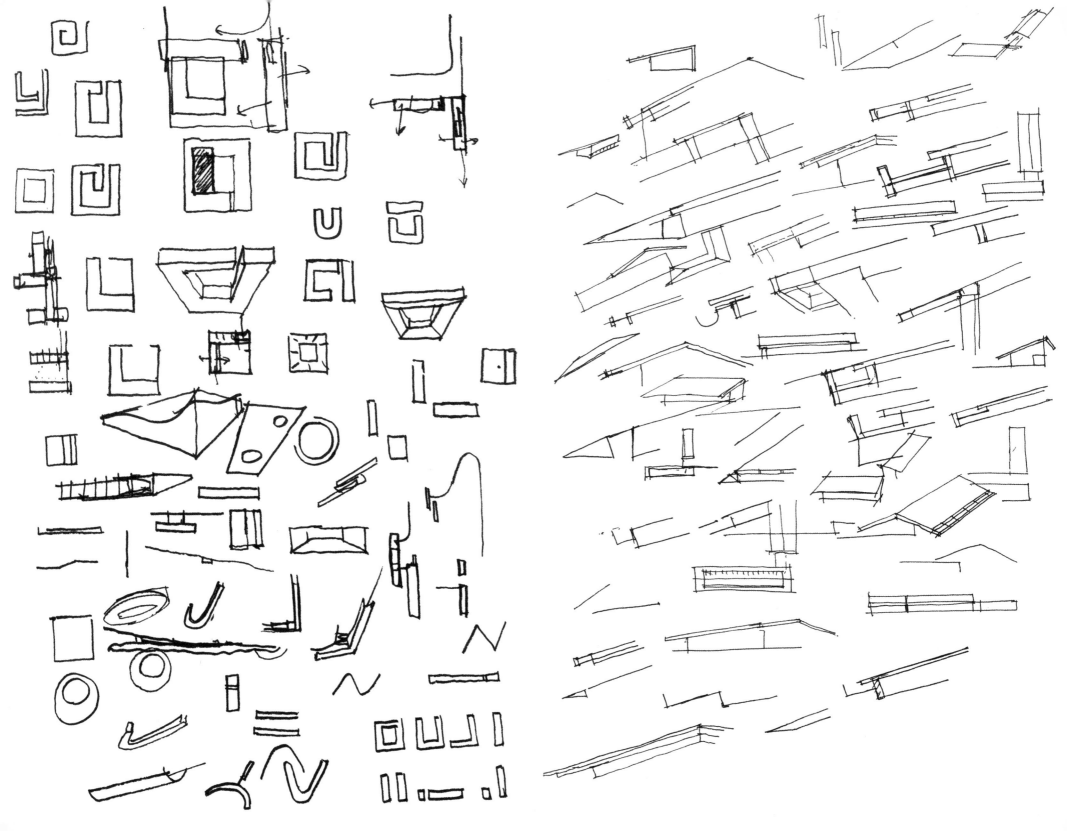

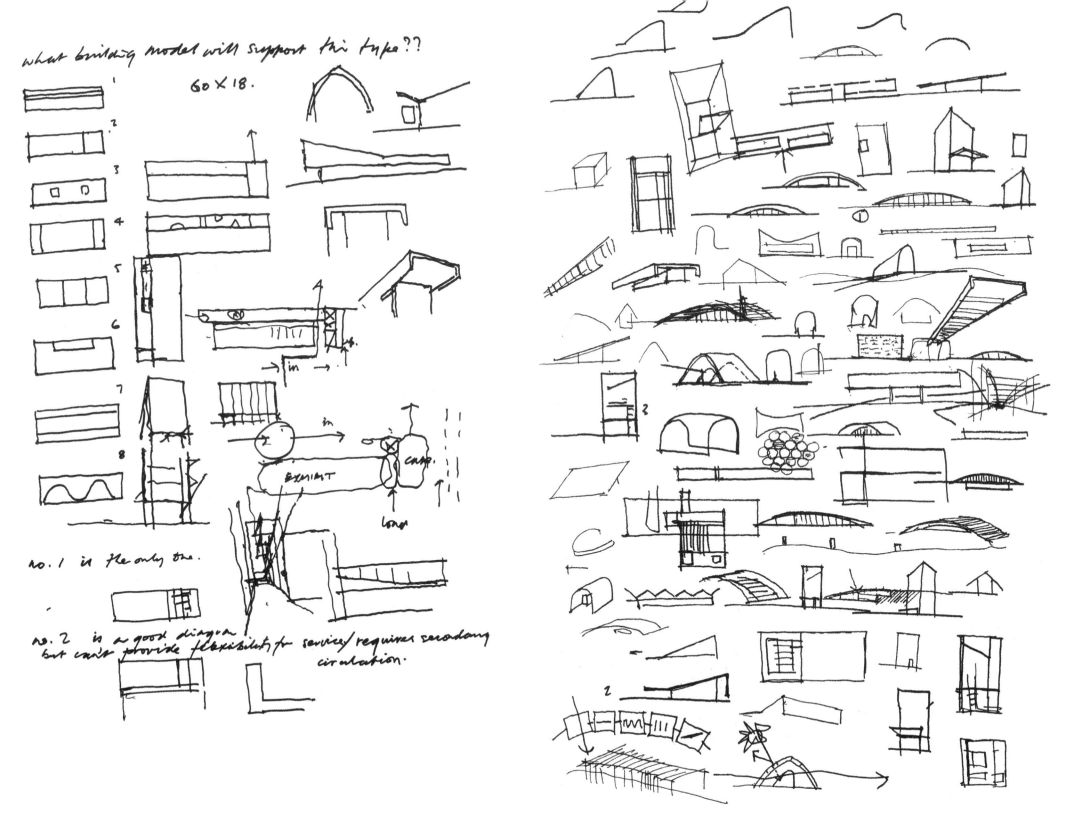

what building model will support this type??

60 × 18.

no. 1 is the only one.

no. 2 is a good diagram but can't provide flexibility for services/requires secondary circulation.

PENELOPE HARALAMBIDOU

Architect and lecturer at the Bartlett School of Architecture in London, Penelope Haralambidou uses sketches, collages and drawings to visualize her work.

'These can be simple line sketches in pencil or more elaborate compositions,' she says. 'I also make sketch models and digital animations to explore the narrative or performative nature of projects. However, I see the sketchbook as a first site for ideas. The physicality of the book or a single page plays an important role in the generation of the ideas.'

What is important for Haralambidou about sketching is that it is not just the representation of ideas but also a process whereby ideas are generated. Model-making is also crucial and she is a strong believer that drawing and model-making techniques influence design ideas. 'For instance,' says Haralambidou, 'if you develop your design out of a model made of wood, you will have a different result from the one you would get if you were making the model out of cardboard.'

Haralambidou's unusual graphic style has given rise to intriguing imagery. Some of her sketches and drawings acquire the status of 'pictures' for the architect because they have an aesthetic value or capture in an eloquent manner the unfolding of the thought process. 'I am fascinated by drawings as traces of thought, not only in architecture but also in other fields such as medicine, engineering and of course art.'

This fascination remains from Haralambidou's days as a student. 'I was always impressed by the fact that although the design process was very long it was the essence of the very first sketches that drove the design.'

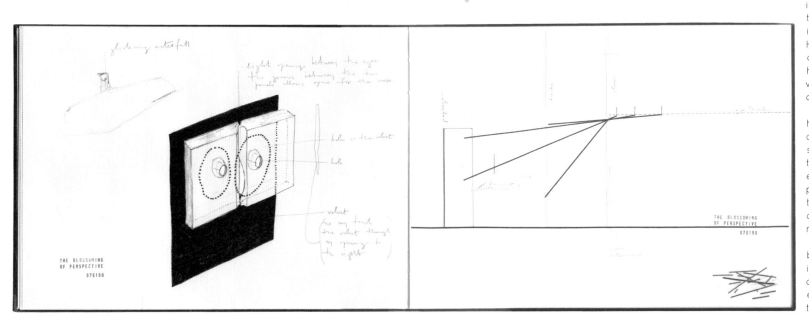

THE BLOSSOMING
OF PERSPECTIVE
070100

THE BLOSSOMING
OF PERSPECTIVE
070100

163

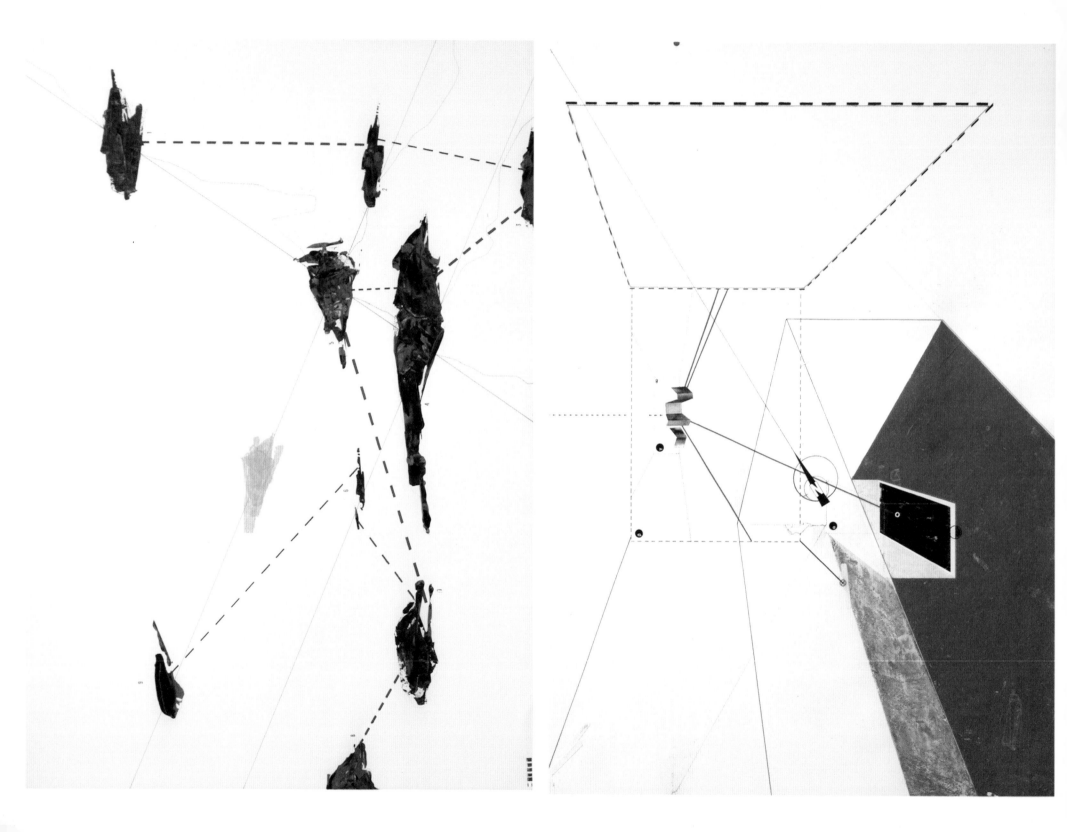

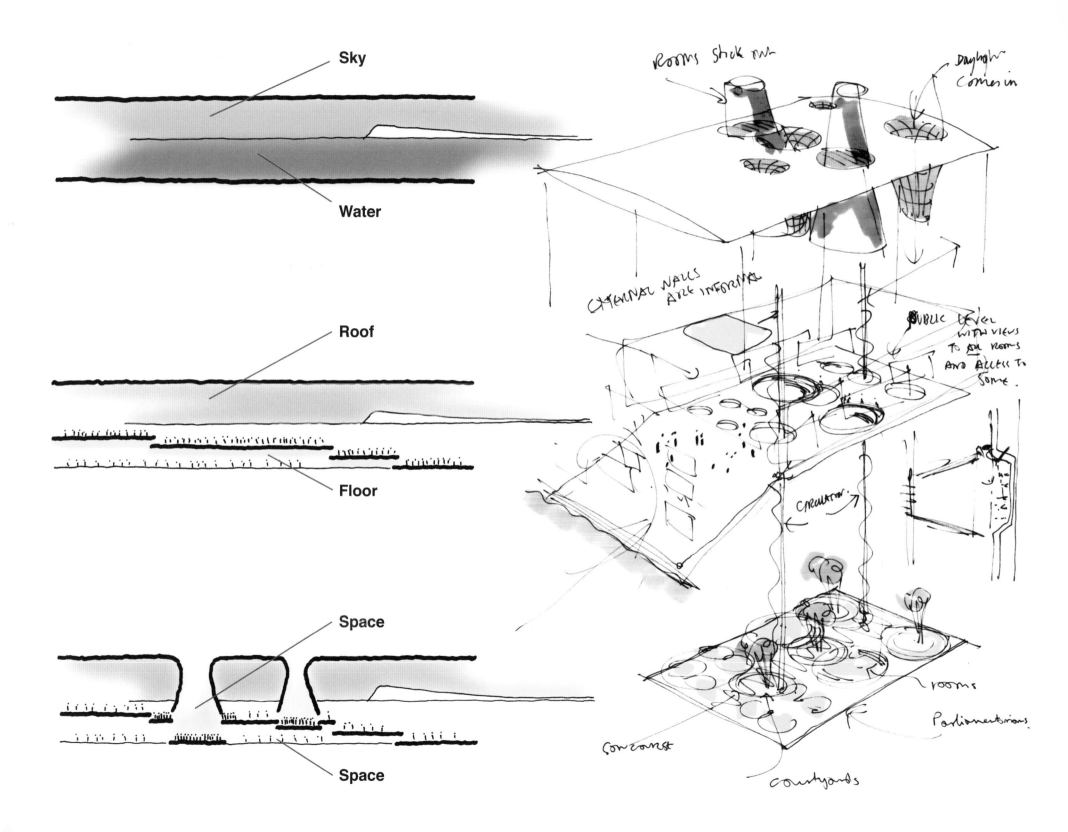

Sky

Water

Roof

Floor

Space

Space

rooms stick out

Daylight comes in

EXTERNAL WALLS ARE INFORMAL

PUBLIC LEVEL WITH VIEWS TO ALL ROOMS AND ACCESS TO SOME.

CIRCULATION

rooms

Parliament rooms

concourse

courtyards

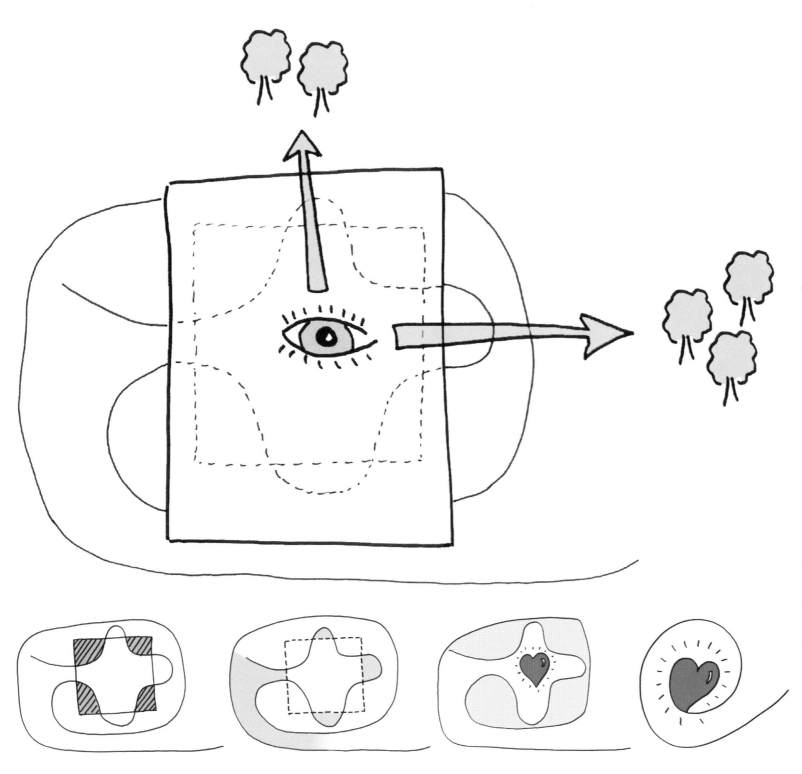

IVAN HARBOUR

Design director at Rogers Stirk Harbour + Partners, Ivan Harbour joined Richard Rogers in his London studio in 1985. He cut his teeth on the Lloyd's building in London and subsequently led the design of award-winning buildings, including the National Assembly for Wales, Cardiff; Terminal Four, Barajas Airport, Madrid; and the European Court of Human Rights, Strasbourg.

When asked how he initially illustrates his ideas, Harbour states that he uses anything to hand, apart from a mouse: 'an image of something else, pen, pencil, whiteboard, paper, tablecloth...whatever is to hand that will communicate my thoughts. It just has to be fast, to enable me to demonstrate the essence of the idea without getting too complex.'

Sketches are part of a bigger picture and not something to be viewed as precious in their own right, Harbour says. 'Sketches are the beginnings of a project, the initial seed. They are works in progress and never complete. None of my sketches ever show the finished design because a sketch illustrates an idea. They aren't easily explicable in any logical way; they are snapshots of moments within the project. If the idea is robust then it goes on to become the design.'

Here, the idea for how a building will 'work' grows from the building's heart and progresses to show circulation and views/exits out of the space in the simplest of draft forms [167]. Opposite, a landscape inspires built form, step by step [166].

Harbour sees each design as a unique response born out of a pursuit of the optimal solution, combined with a thorough questioning of design proposals. His sketches are fine workings within this quest and as such most of them are set aside over the course of the project. 'Some are saved though—the ones that sum up important elements of a design.'

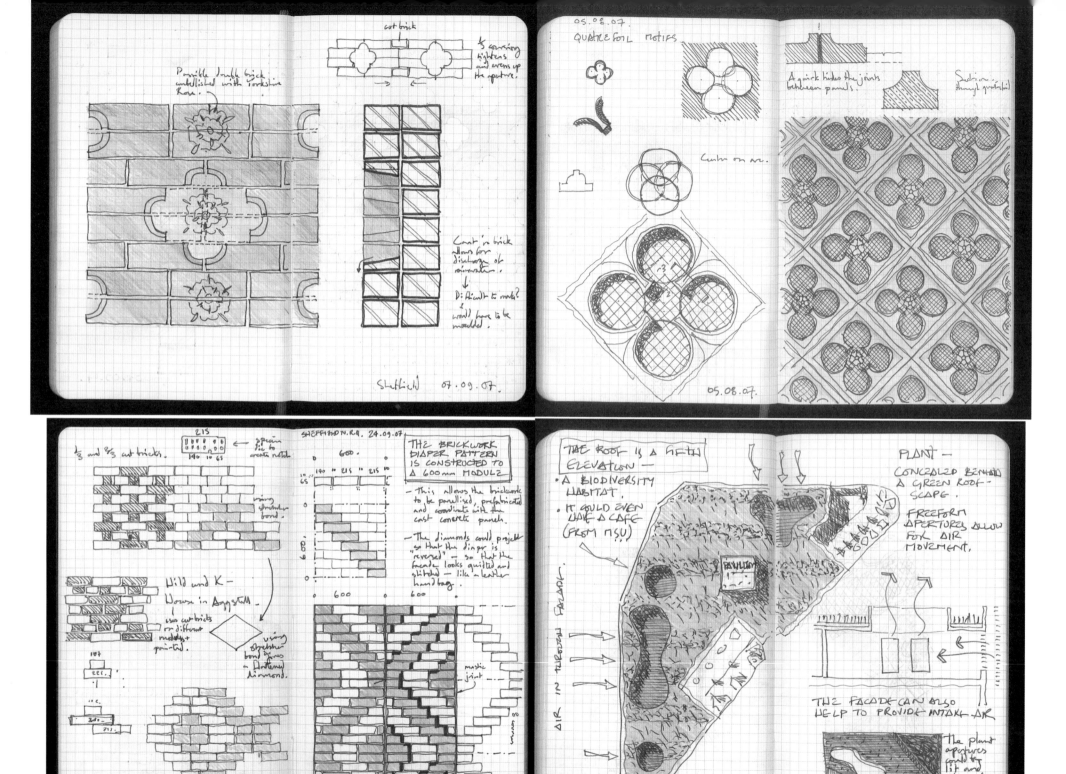

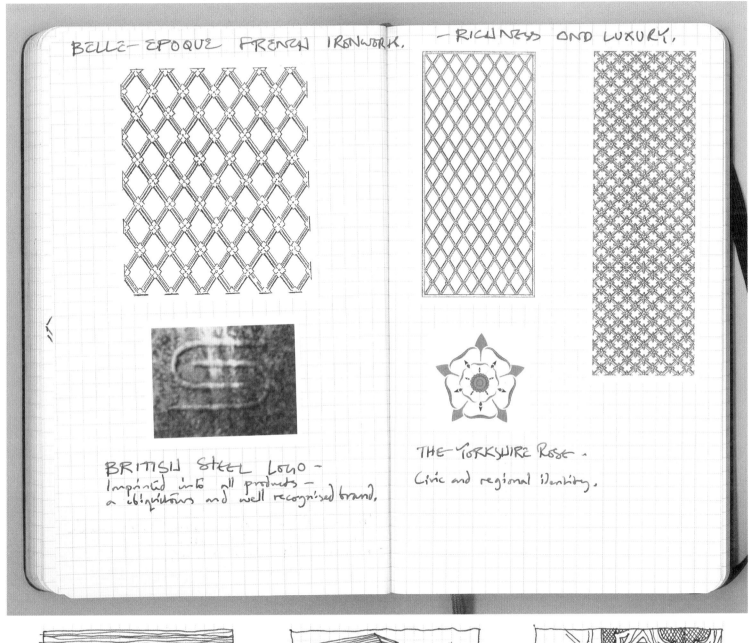

BELLE-EPOQUE FRENCH IRONWORK.

- RICHNESS AND LUXURY.

BRITISH STEEL LOGO -
Imprinted into all products -
a ubiquitous and well recognised brand.

THE YORKSHIRE ROSE.
Civic and regional identity.

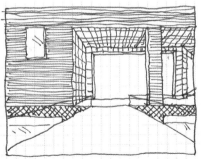

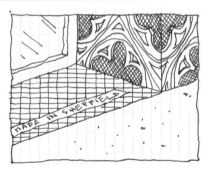

HAWKINS\BROWN

A quote from the practice's website reads: 'Architecture is a pragmatic, negotiated, commercial, mediated and compromised art.... Design at Hawkins\Brown is generated by 'infection' rather than dictation. Ideas are gathered from everyone, using all our experiences and seeking cross-fertilization from current projects. Then they are tested. The best ideas win.'

This approach is something that associate Seth Rutt is keen to emphasize. 'Architecture needs to be collaborative. We will often segue from a sketch to a foam model to a computer model in SketchUp, subsequently rendered in Cinema 4D, and back again.'

But, synergistic as the firm's methods may be, the art of sketching and its individual nuances still come to the fore. 'A lot of us prefer to capture our thoughts in our sketchbooks. I carry mine at all times, as invariably a train journey or a quiet moment offers the opportunity to draw without distraction,' says Rutt. 'In such moments, sketching is the most immediate method of capturing an idea. Also, at moments of creative impasse, the discipline of forcing oneself to draw can be cathartic and yield at least a little forward movement.'

Rutt's attention to detail in his sketches can be easily seen in the designs for retail project Sevenstone in Sheffield [168–71], where sketch details and patterns have been directly transferred to CAD visualizations and models. Regarding digital tools, however, Rutt has a word of warning: 'I believe that over-reliance on computers has resulted in a loss of confidence in hand drawing. Consequently, we encourage our staff to use sketchbooks and develop drawing skills in parallel with other methods of expression.'

169

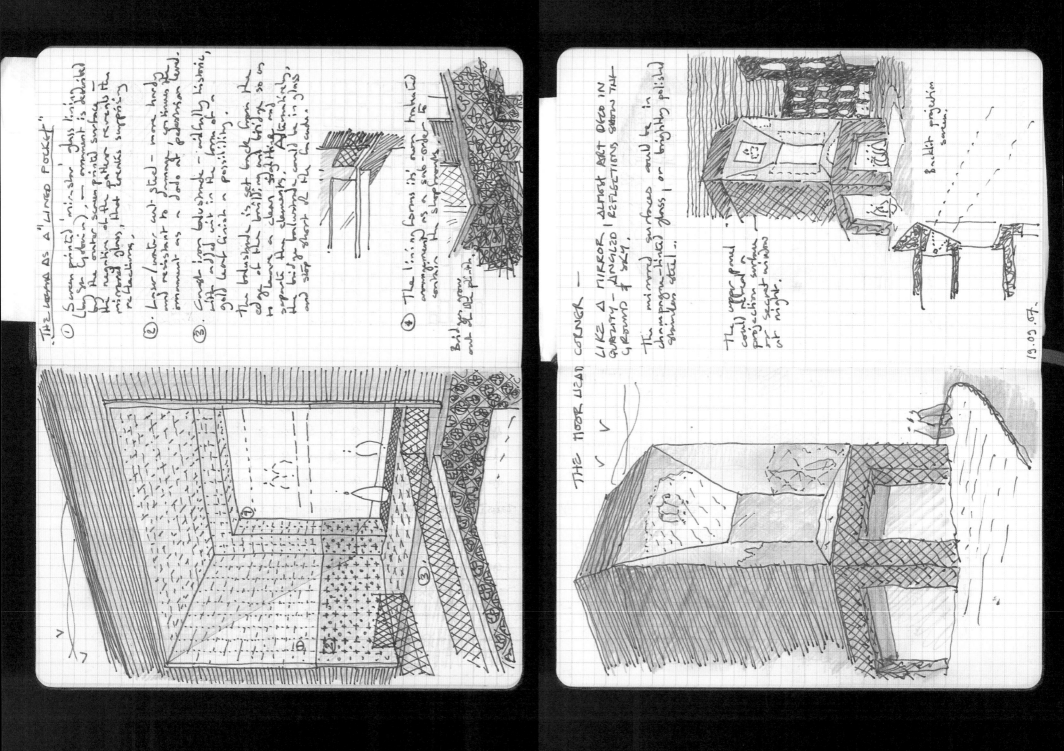

. THE LINING AS A "LINED POCKET"

① (Screen printed) 'micron' glass lining (by Sir Epstein) — an internal surface is printed, the outer screen printed surface the magnitude of the milan mirrored glass, that breaks surprising reflections.

② Laser/water cut steel — more hardy and resistant to damage, cast more economic as a slot if...

③ Cast iron balustrade — wildly historic, soft wood in the form of a gilt and a possibility.

④ The lining forms its own frame/as arranged as a sub-order to the staircase within.

Bed, grey in and grey plan.

THE FLOOR HEAD CORNER —

LIKE A MIRROR, ALMOST ART DECO IN QUALITY — ANGLED REFLECTIONS SHOWN THAT GROUND & SKY.

The mirrored surfaces could be in champagne-tinted glass, or brightly polished stainless steel..

They could be a projection surface for backlit window at night.

Backlit projection screen.

19.03.07

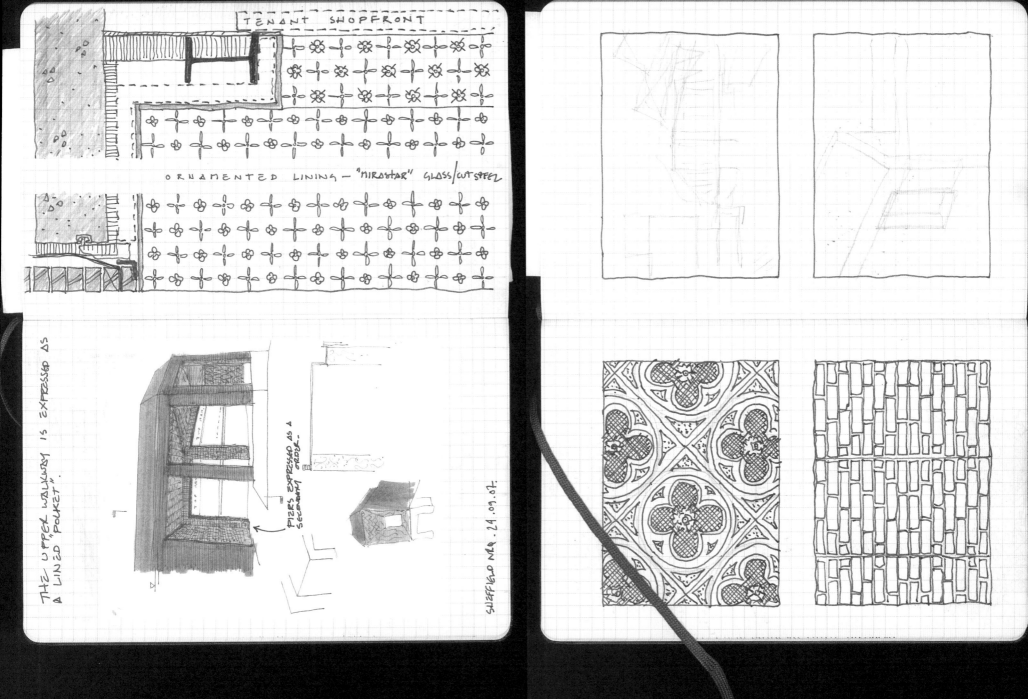

TENANT SHOPFRONT

ORNAMENTED LINING — "MIRASTAR" GLASS/CUT STEEL

THE UPPER WALKWAY IS EXPRESSED AS A LINED "POCKET".

PIERS EXPRESSED AS A SECONDARY ORDER.

SHEFFIELD MKT . 24.09.07.

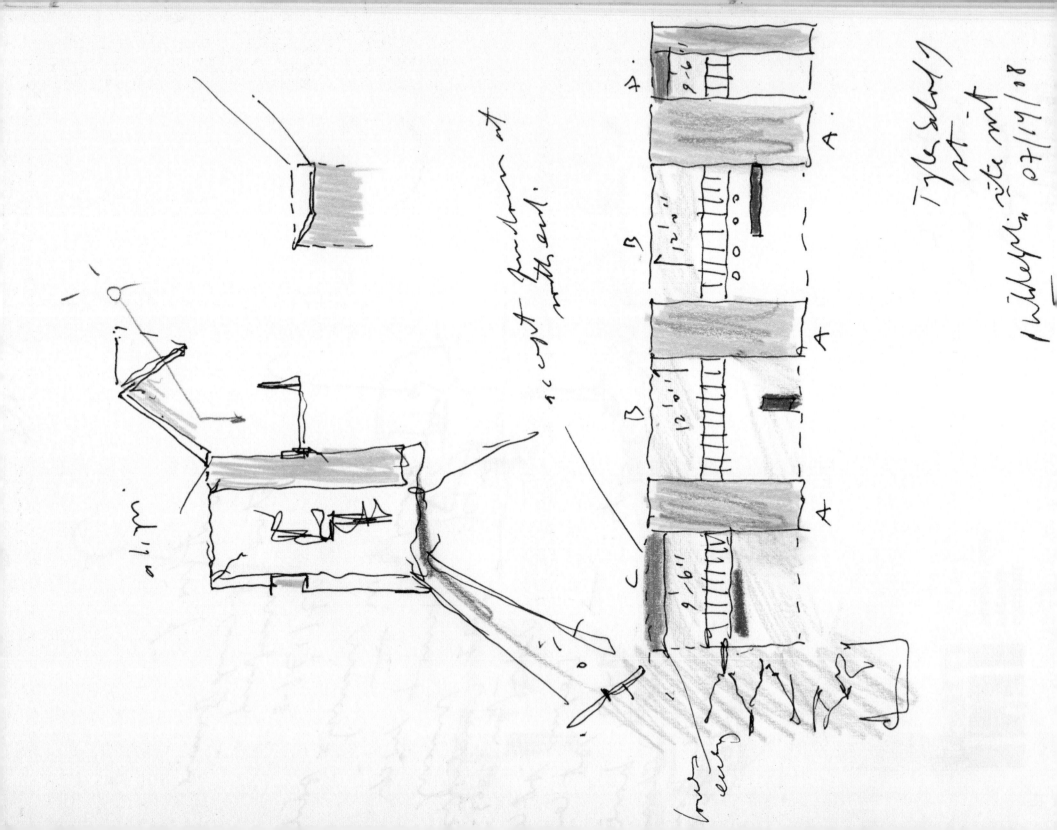

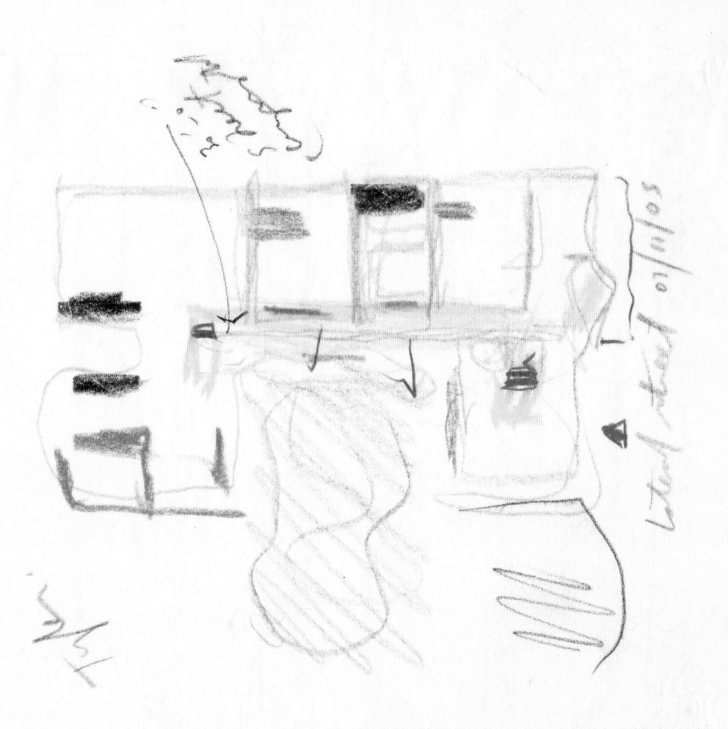

CARLOS JIMÉNEZ

'For me sketching is an intuitive action, one that records precise or fleeting thoughts; it is that might capture an immediate response that might capture a sudden idea, a possible concept, or an interesting possibility,' says Carlos Jiménez, architect and professor at the Rice University School of Architecture, Houston. 'There is always an urgency to these initial drawings. I might be driving (in Houston one drives a lot) and suddenly I see something on the road that elicits a connection to an idea that I am developing: I have to stop and draw it.'

Jiménez sees sketching as pictorial shorthand that allows him to quickly record a thought. He describes it as a 'free, necessary and intuitive search' and a means of remembering or recording an ephemeral instant in time. This approach of capturing fleeting impressions can be seen in his sketched designs for the Tyler School of Art at Temple University, Philadelphia [172–75]. Displayed together, they have a feeling of progression and evolution.

'A sketch has a germinal purity and an enigmatic "what if" quality to it,' he says. 'It is a critical part of my design process. I rely on the agility and memory that a sketch conveys more than I do computer drawings. The latter are mechanical, traceable, and automatic; I have great respect for them but they don't interest me very much.'

Jiménez insists his colleagues have pens, pencils and paper by their stations so that they can draw, and so 'break the hypnotic tempo of the computer screen'. 'Drawing, building models and the construction site are the domains where I feel the closest to making architecture,' says Jiménez.

'I sketch primarily on large (8.5 × 11 in., 21.75 × 27.5 cm) canvas-covered sketchbooks. I like the loyal presence of each white page, not knowing what is going to come out next or what is going to happen next month.'

173

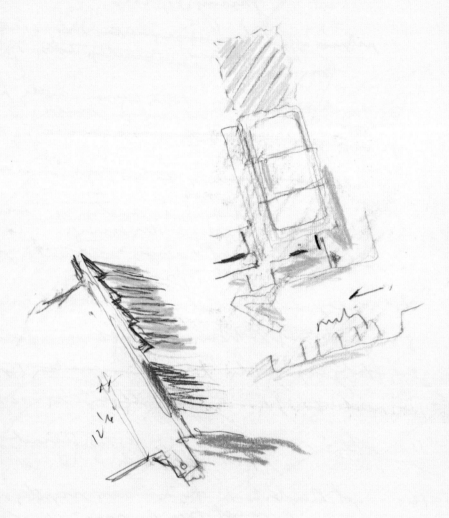

primary elevation

natural grade

Ocean Vista Center
01/30/06

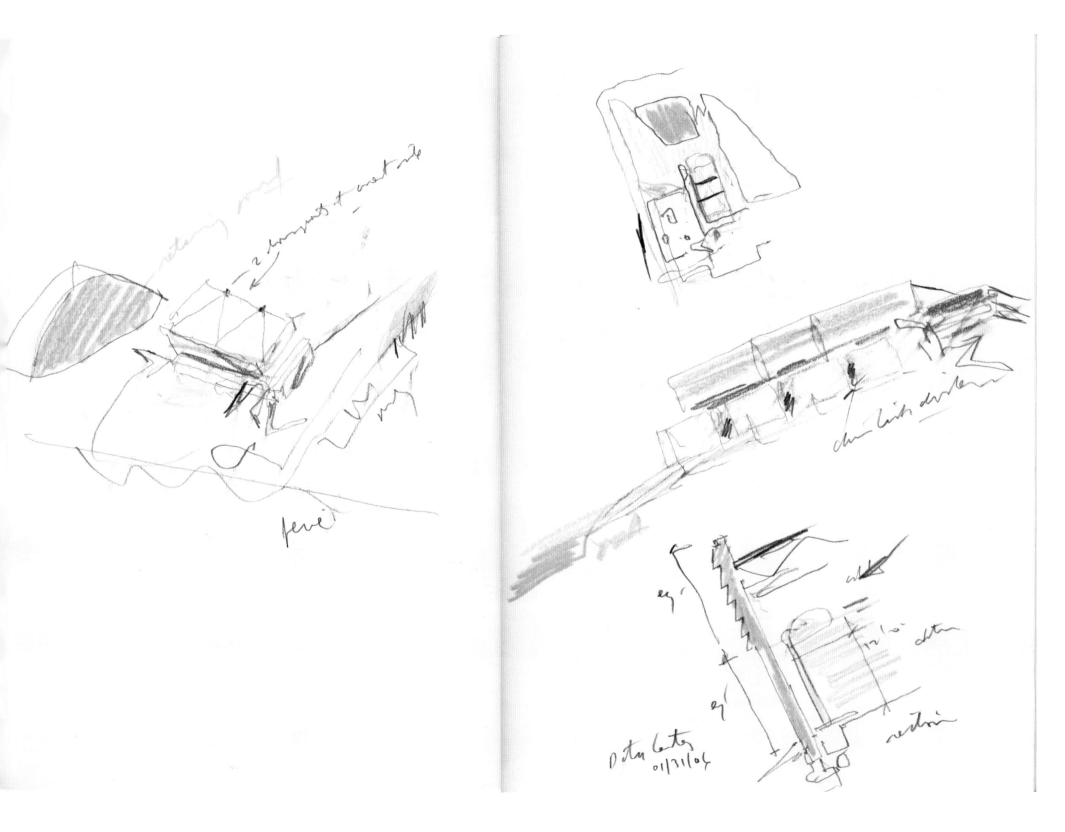

SERVICES

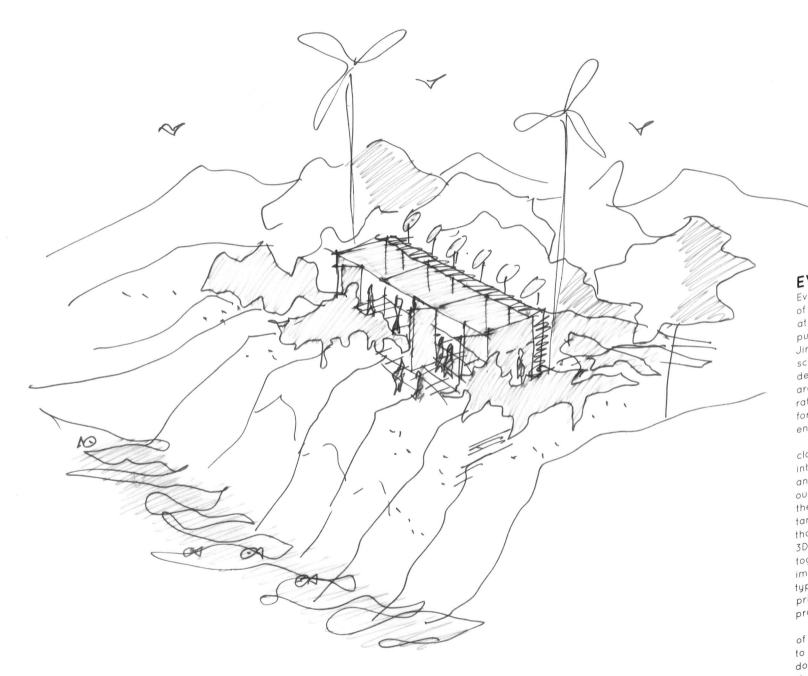

EVA JIRICNA

Eva Jiricna has an easy, almost languid style of sketching that looks as if it takes no effort at all. 'I can't say that I work on this style purposefully,' says Jiricna, principal at Eva Jiricna Architects. 'I just start sketching and scribbling until I reach the point where I can describe in words what I am doing. I know architects who start writing a story or a narrative, some make models, some start looking for an associated image…. We all have different ways of expressing ourselves.'

Jiricna sees her sketches as tools to clarify in her mind what she is doing. A visual interpretation that is easy to understand and which has a clarity that the ambiguous written word cannot offer. Sometimes the sketches themselves suggest an important idea; sometimes they include embryonic thoughts about the problem; alternatively, 3D sketches suggest how things might come together, creating a more comprehensive image out of previous thoughts. 'I suppose the type of sketch somewhat reflects the order of priorities as seen at different stages of the project,' she says.

'I can't put a percentage on the number of original sketches that get carried through to the completed design. I will say that it does happen but it is very rare that the first sketch would be the final solution. But, it does happen occasionally and it is great when you can refer to the sketch at the end of a project and see that it was the right solution, which survived all the subsequent tests.'

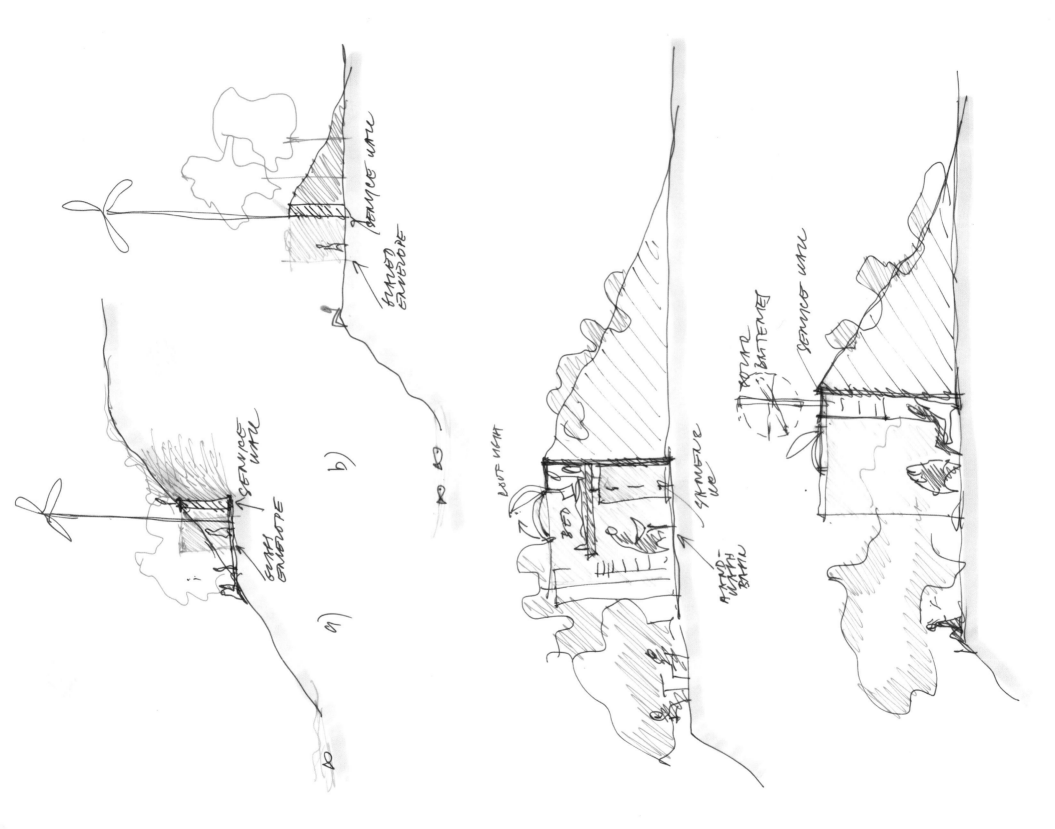

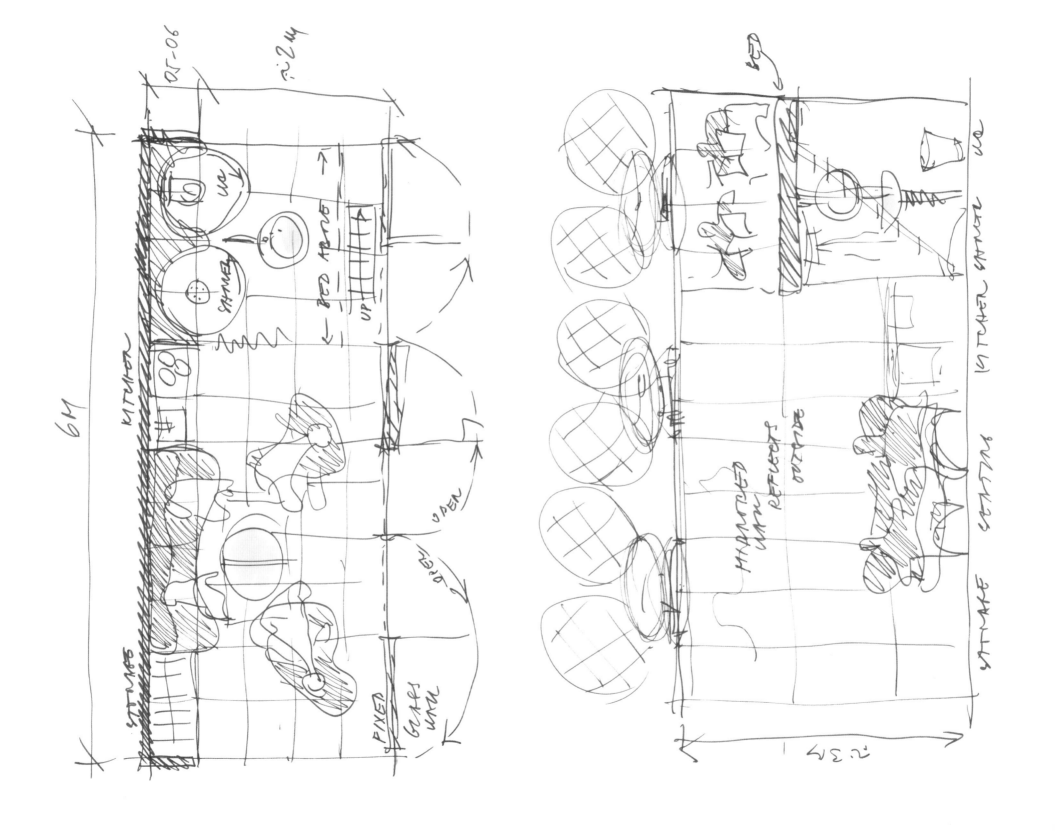

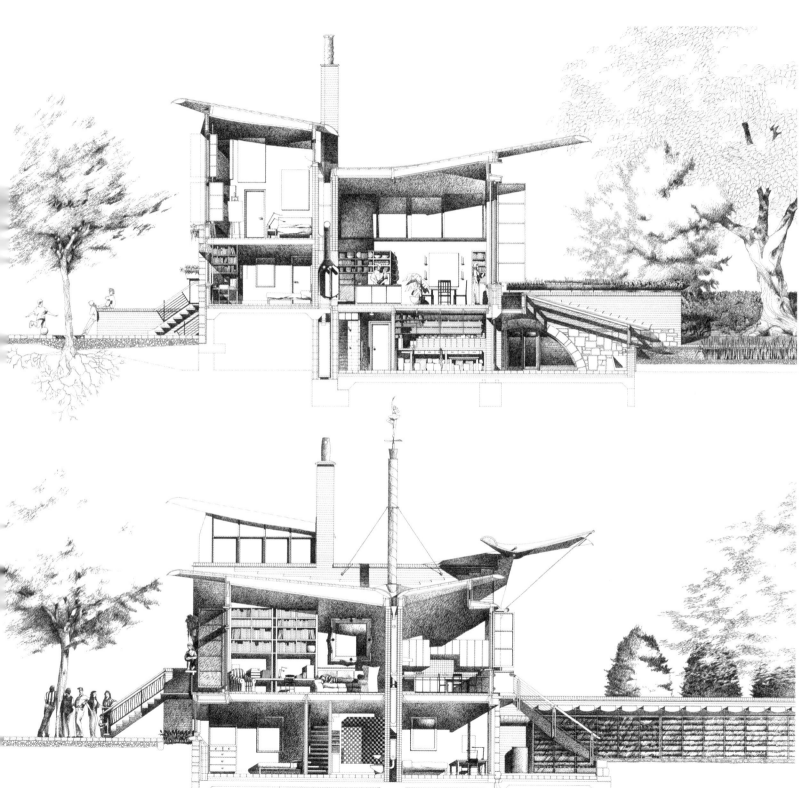

STEVEN JOHNSON

'I begin sketching in a hardbound sketchbook to pull comments and reactions from the client, if they are present. If not, I sketch in the same notebook and scan images for emailing to receive feedback,' says Steven Johnson, principal of The Architecture Ensemble.

The immediate involvement of the client gives them confidence in Johnson's capacity to understand what they are asking for, and to put ideas onto paper in a convincing way. 'I feel that clients get far more out of hand drawings than computer images,' says Johnson.

If 'in the right mood', his sketches will be 3D images, showing form, light and structure. If it doesn't flow on the day, Johnson plays it safe with plans and sections, saving the 3D work for later. His sketches and models are fairly specific about the building's physical traits and underlying form, and almost all of Johnson's final designs directly reflect the initial sketching process.

In addition to sketching and modelling, Johnson also experiments with words. 'I've begun writing narrative descriptions of projects taken from the viewpoint of a fictional character walking through a site or building. It's like producing a verbal sketchbook.'

Through this process, Johnson is forced to think about the project with all his senses. 'It forces me to describe in words how light enters a space, sound and smells filter through open windows, colours clash or complement.' He finds that writing has a surprisingly large impact upon the way he thinks about a project and, almost more than drawings, he believes words have a captivating effect on clients who absorb stories better than pictures.

181

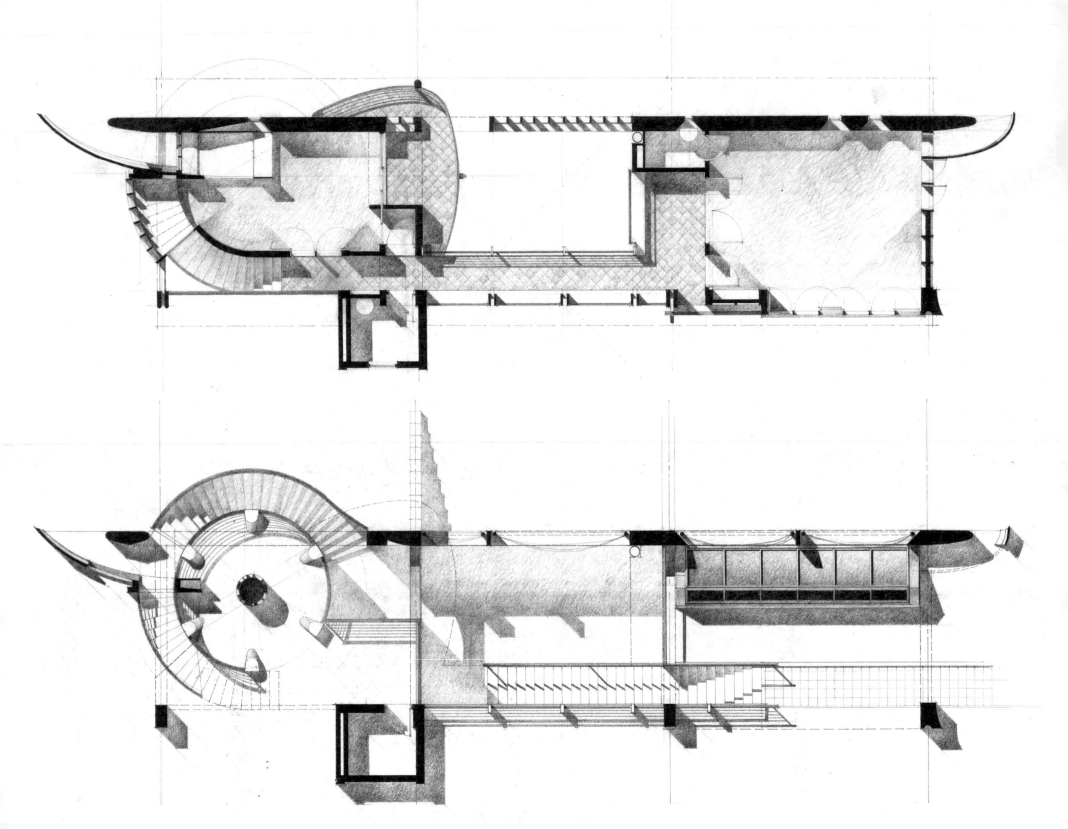

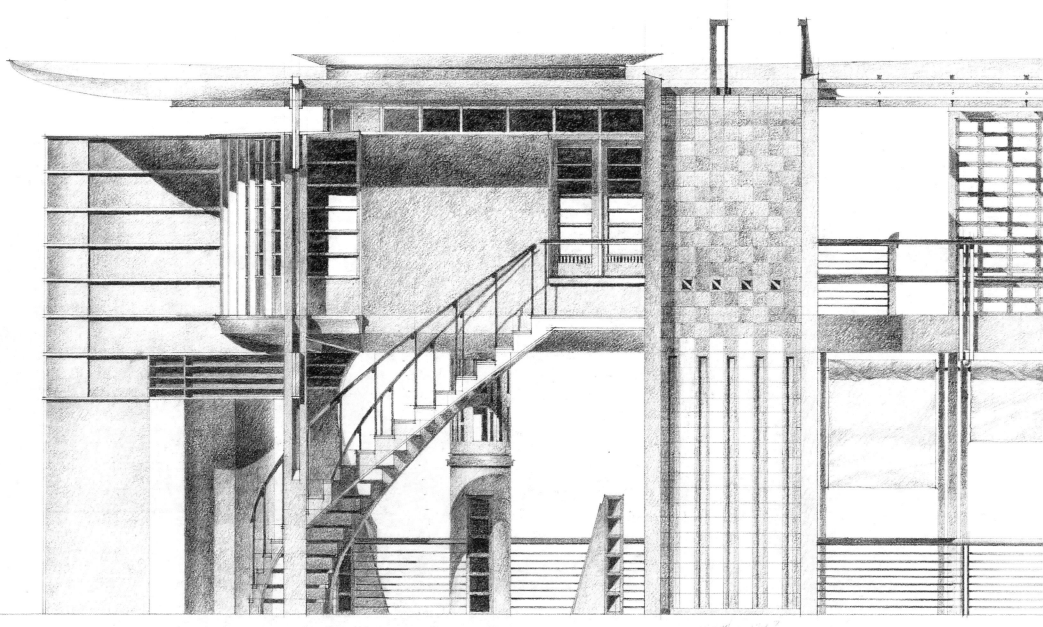

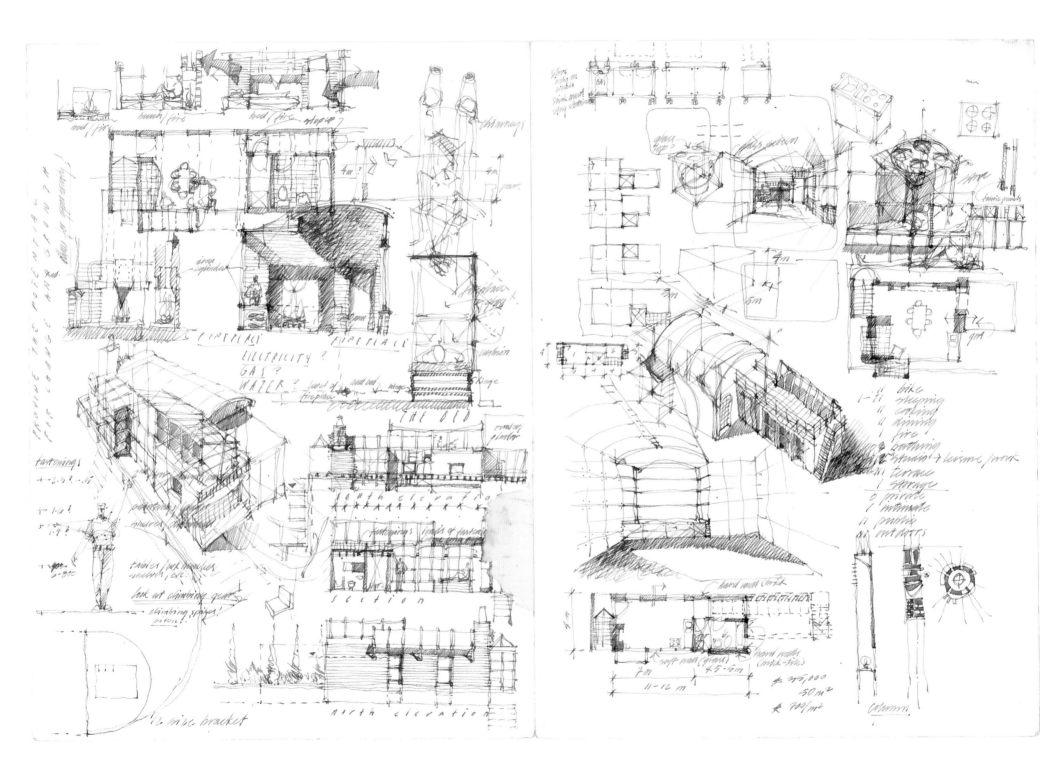

FIREPLACE   FIREPLACE

ELECTRICITY ?
GAS ?
WATER ?

THE BED

south elevation

section

north elevation

1–11 bike
11 sleeping
11 cooking
11 dining
11 fire
11 bathing
11 studio → leisure/work
11 terrace
11 storage
9 private
11 intimate
11 public
11 outdoors

hard wall (brick)

soft wall (glass)   hard walls (mud-brick)

7 m   4.5–5 m

11–12 m

$ 315,000
50 m²
$ 700/m²

column

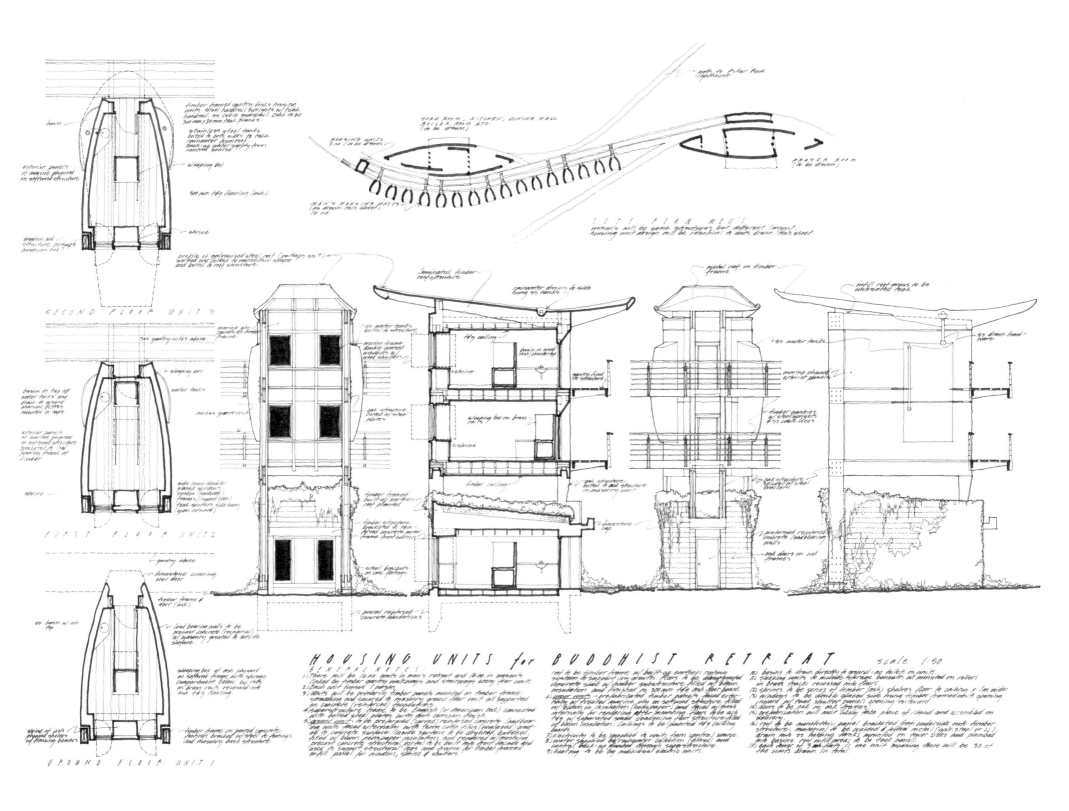

HOUSING UNITS for BUDDHIST RETREAT   scale 1:50

JUNYA ISHIGAMI & ASSOCIATES

Still in his thirties, Junya Ishigami is already making waves in the architectural world with his surrealist take on Japanese architectural minimalism. His first completed building, the facility at Kanagawa Institute of Technology, is a shared workshop where students engage in creative projects in conjunction with the local community.

Reminiscent of a bamboo forest, the facility is a single space, 154 × 151 ft (47 × 46 m), littered with slender steel columns distributed apparently at random across the interior. A steel roof crowns the building and a frameless glass perimeter seals it. There are no walls or partitions, people and furniture are left free to inhabit the space as they wish. The architecture is lost within a scene that appears both natural and somehow fantastic.

'I would like the things I create to have something of that combination of reality and surprise,' says Ishigami, consequently his designs—sketches and models—appear almost ethereal. Figures float through buildings and worlds, shrouded in a fine mist. Buildings are light, weightless apparitions in dreamlike landscapes.

'I want to create a new kind of space with very ambiguous borderlines,' he says. 'I try to avoid the abstraction that is characteristic of diagrams; a diagram compresses and abbreviates information. Rather than distilling the information, I try to keep it all present. What I would like to do is to grasp the ambiguity of this variety, and develop abstractions from that.'

Ishigami's sketches and models are beautiful and other-worldly, but his greatest talent is the ability to translate these phantoms into built form.

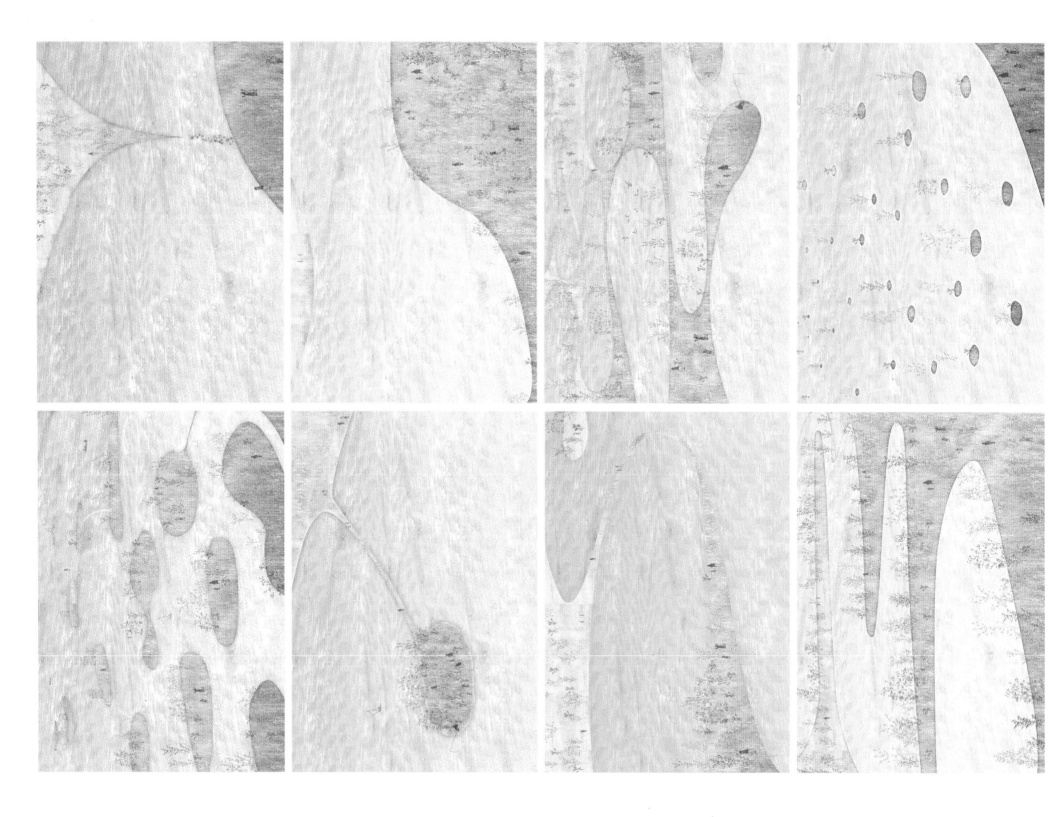

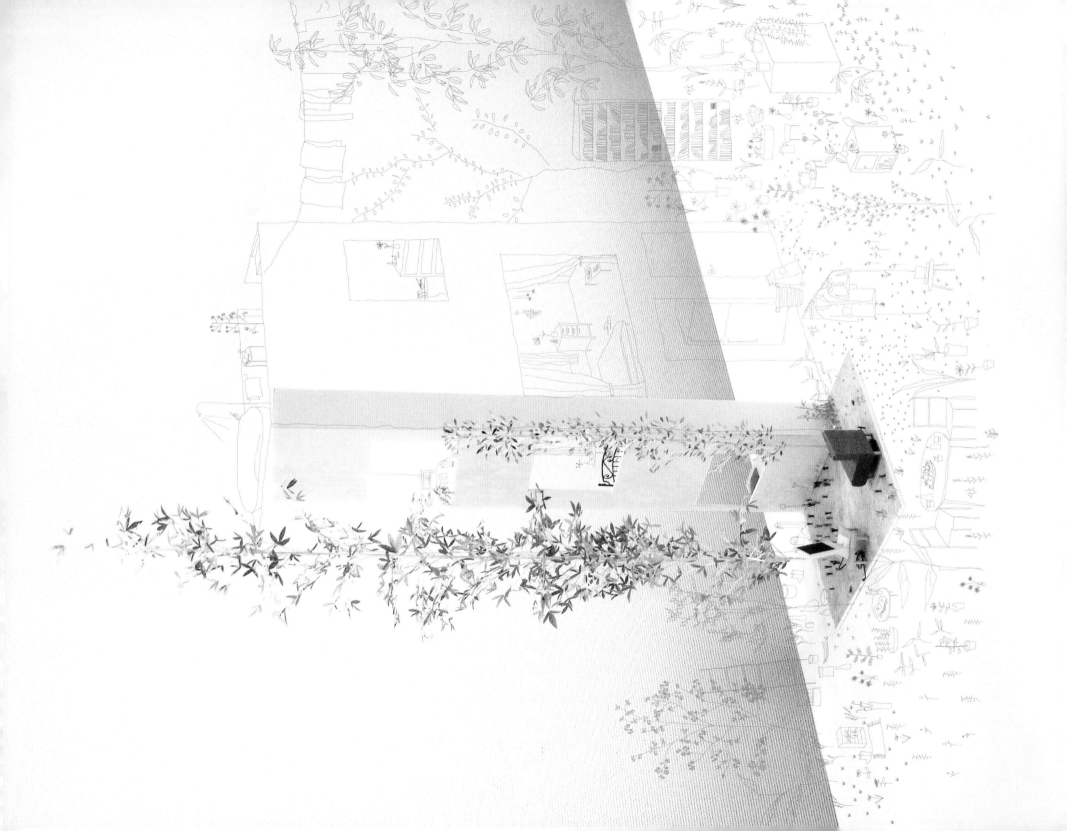

KRISTOFER KELLY

'I draw to understand the world. Some people speak eloquently, others write, I draw,' says Kristofer Kelly. 'A sketchbook is to me a free plane on which to gesturally explore ideas.'

Kelly, a newly graduated architect from Calgary, Canada, has already been lauded for the quality of his sketching in major publications including the USA's Architectural Record magazine. He works with a variety of media, including ink, graphite and charcoal. The sketches happen quickly, usually on site and catch the atmosphere, spatial relationships, body rhythms (the way in which people interact with space) and other qualitative characteristics of a place.

'These sketches capture my gut reactions to the site—reactions that have the potential to become design interventions,' he says. 'Only rarely do I come back to these drawings to annotate or colour them. The idea of the "thinking hand" is a good way of describing this process.'

His drawings become what Kelly describes as 'living artifacts' to be referenced later in the design process. 'While I continue to sketch through the life of an assignment, the first sketches remain critical because they capture my initial reactions to the context,' says Kelly. They are a touchstone that he sees as vital for maintaining the conceptual lineage of a project; 'Designs should evolve and change through their development but those early sketches can serve as guideposts to remind the designer of that initial spark.'

Kelly, in fact, values this part of the process so much that not only does he keep his own sketchbooks, he also acquires those of other designers who are willing to part with them: 'Drawing is a powerful tool in interdisciplinary collaboration and critical analysis is always necessary.'

193

GREY NUN

ROBEN stein
1981
Rose

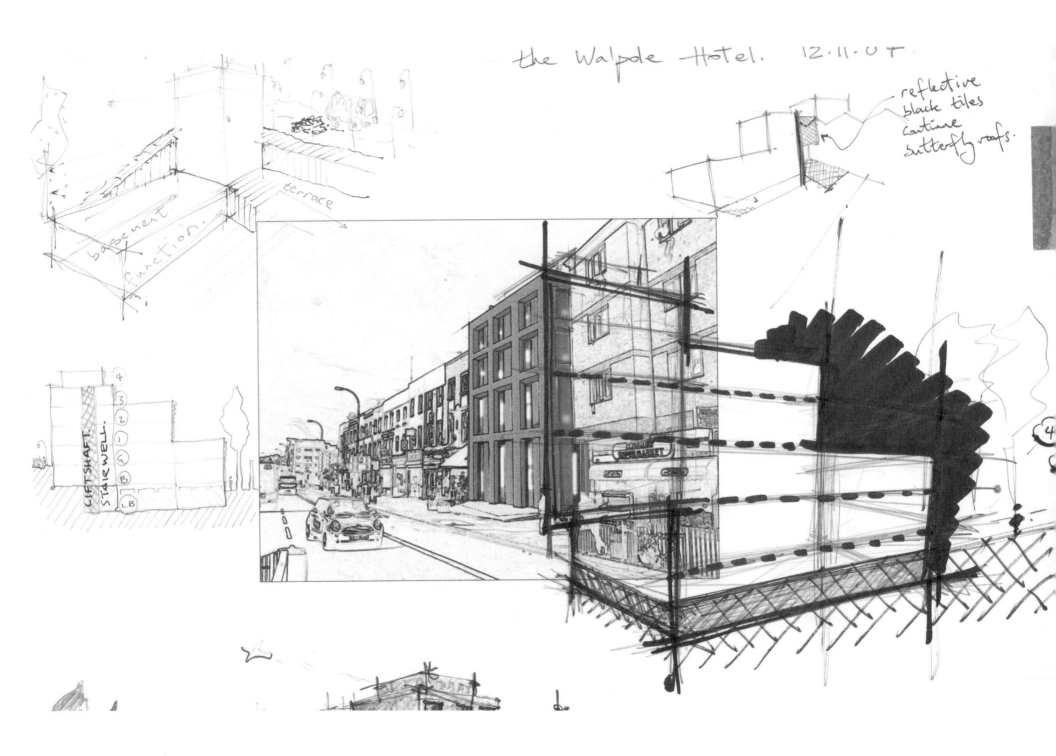

the Walpole Hotel. 12·11·0T·

reflective
black tiles
continue
butterfly roofs.

terrace

basement
function.

LIFTSHAFT.
STAIRWELL.
4
3
2
1
G
B
LB

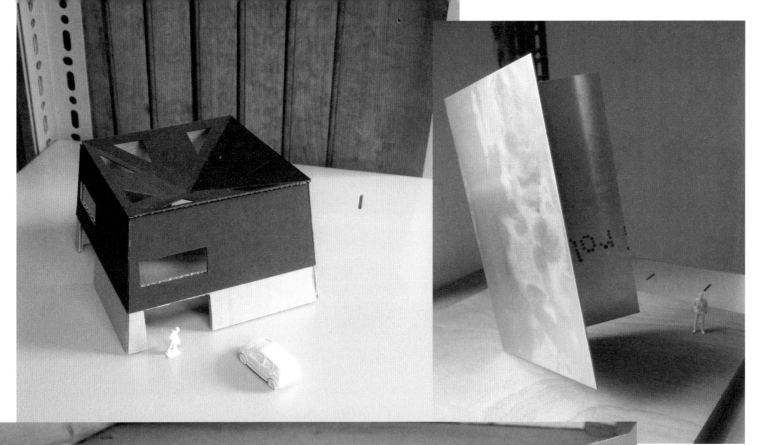

KENNEDYTWADDLE

Kennedytwaddle is a design studio headed up by Gary Kennedy and Chris Twaddle, who met while studying at Duncan of Jordanstone College of Art & Design in Dundee in the early 1990s. Neither of the pair are architects but their work is primarily concerned with the refurbishment and design of buildings.

The result of this 'non-architect' architectural practice is an approach that excites clients and displays distinctly different traits from your average 'serious' architect.

'We work via loose sketching and abstract mark-making to stimulate forms within a space,' says Kennedy, 'and with crude models suggesting materials and volume.'

These methods are realized as collages, overdrawn sketches, drawings and models. The designs reveal the duo's love of interior and set design, while the informal nature and more playful use of colour in their sketches separate their work from that of many architects.

'The fluidity and looseness of our initial sketch designs keep the thought process as free and fluid as possible,' explains Kennedy. 'We work quickly. It could almost be described as slap-dash, and that's good because sometimes a fluke jerk of the hand can open up a whole new and unexpected avenue.'

Kennedy openly 'outs' himself as a devotee of life drawing—a talent mourned by many older architects as a lost art. It is this skill that makes it possible for kennedytwaddle to be so relaxed in their sketch-making. Featured here are various models and collages for residential projects, as well as an overdrawn sketch of the Walpole Hotel, London [196].

20 rue de l'eglise . Auteuil Le Roi .

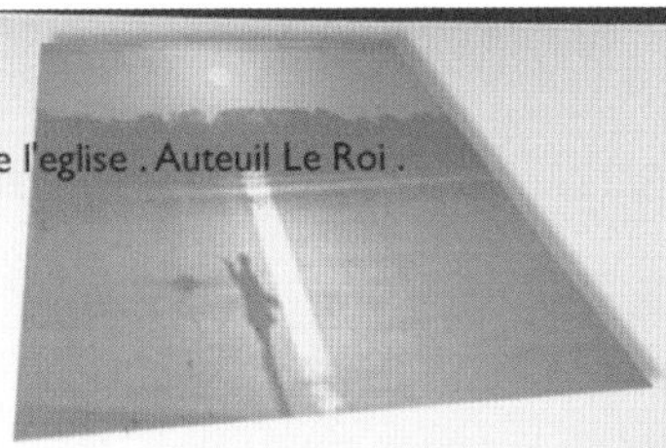

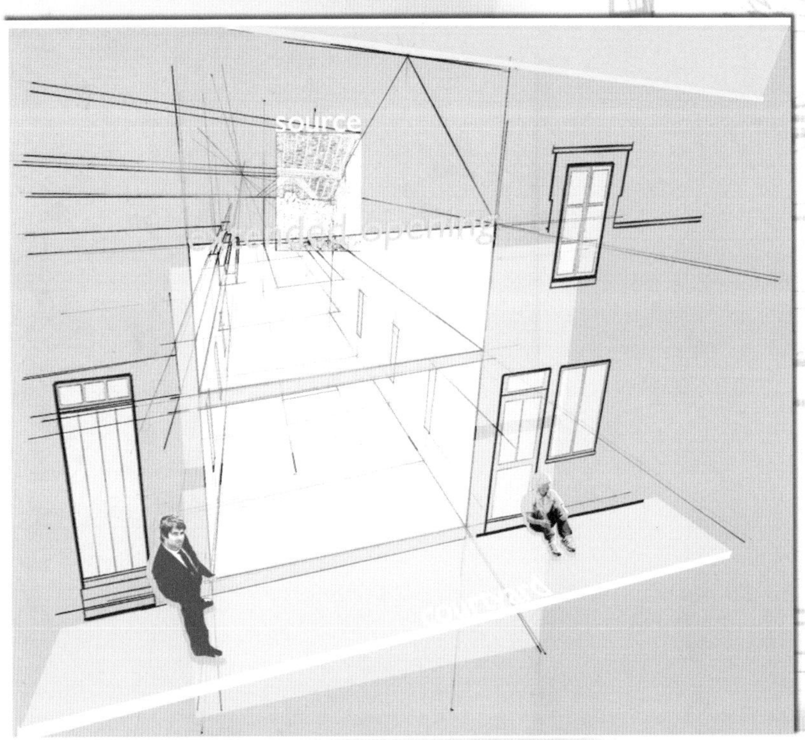

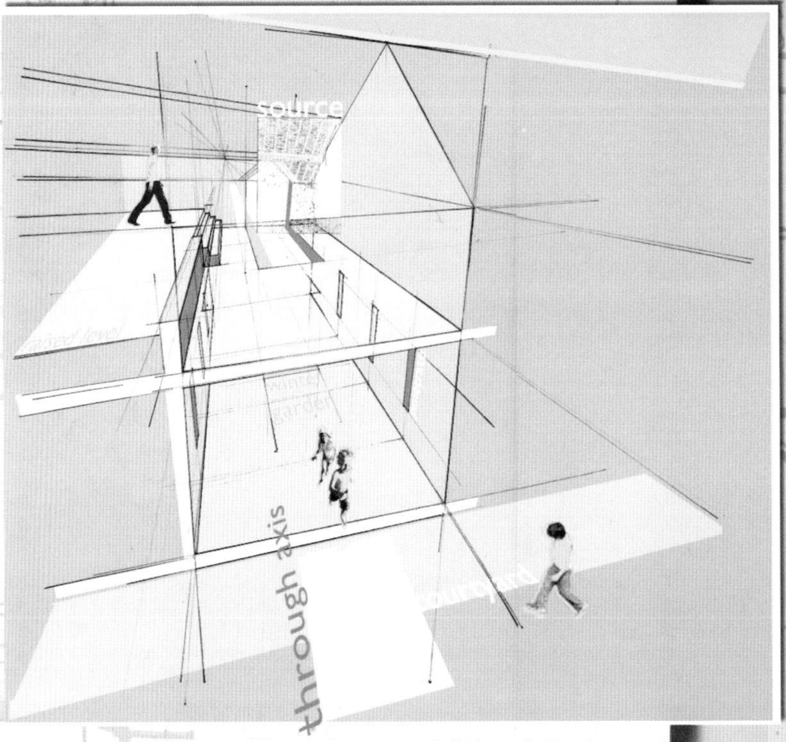

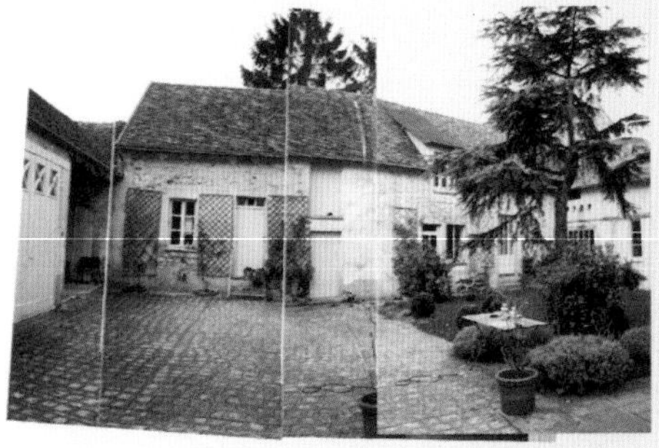

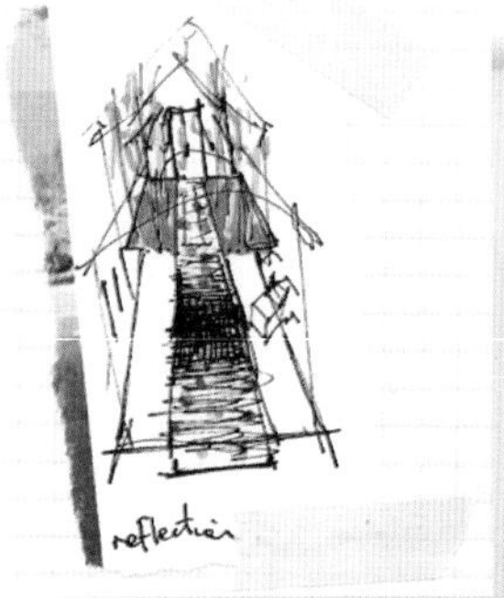

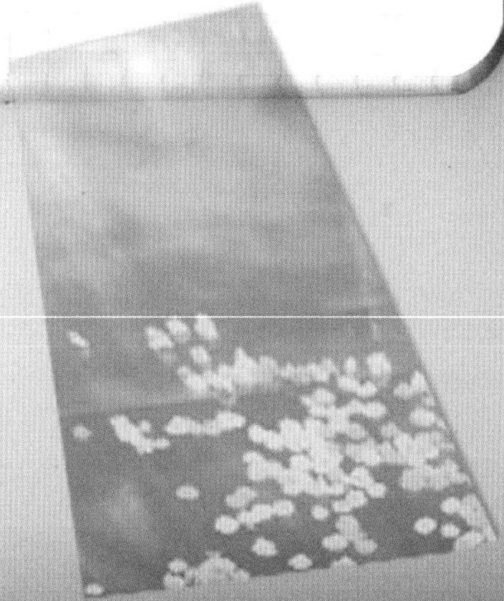

source

der opening

source

through axis

reflection

kennedytwaddle architectural design

20 rue de l'eglise . Auteuil Le Roi .

kennedytwaddle architectural design

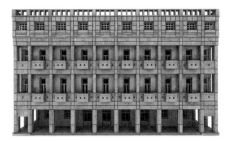

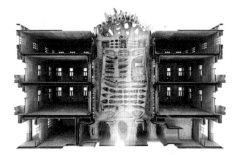

a - a

b - b

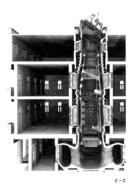

c - c

d - d

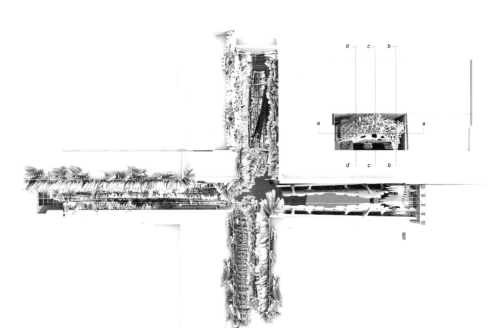

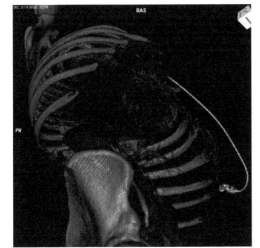

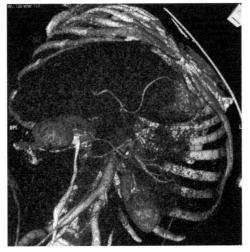

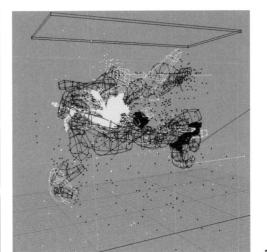

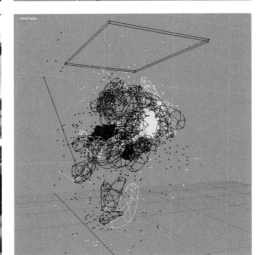

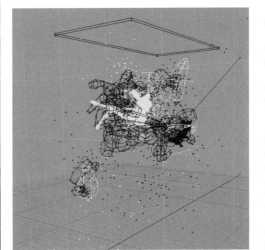

TOBIAS KLEIN

The work of this German-born architect and lecturer can best be described as a narrative design within digital environments, exploring the relationship between actual and virtual in CAD/CAM technologies to 'overcome the dichotomy between craftsmanship and art'.

His Soft Immortality study [201–03] examines the body and the syncretic nature both of the transplant, and of transplanting elements of the body into architecture.

The transplant promotes the idea of a hybrid, natural–artificial mutation within the consciousness; it is an object that fades into a broader acknowledgment of its extended surroundings and meanings.

'The Soft Immortality installation re-creates a virtual body and aims to dissolve the common boundary concept, in favour of a viscous space definition,' says Klein.

'Sculpting virtual-based organs on a scanned real grown bone is butchery in reverse. The non-existance of parts is the difference between the work of the butcher, and that of the artist modelling virtual pos-sibilities. At this point the design reaches out to get hold of the form and starts to shape the virtual into the scanned actual.'

Taking a step into architectural design is Klein's Chapel of Our Lady de Regla, Havana [200]. Located inside an existing courtyard, the chapel design grafts organic mutations onto a formal architectural land-scape. 'This church no longer follows pure abstract algorithms, shapes created from scripted parameters,' says Klein. 'The temple is no longer distorting reality; it is reality that has emerged out of the ritualistic narra-tive virtual.'

201

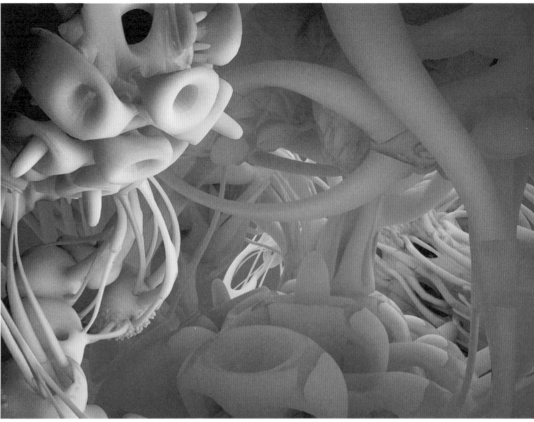

MICHAEL LEHRER

'When I was young, my mother told me that if I didn't make it as an architect, I could always be a painter,' says Michael Lehrer. 'I draw because, for a creator, it is like breathing. Life drawing, which for me is among the most important aspects of my training as a visual thinker, is ongoing training for the eye and the soul. I think it is de rigueur for an architect.'

Lehrer's colourful abstract paintings and beautifully sensitive life drawings are different from his architectural sketching, but in many respects they cover the same ground. Use of colour and an eye for form are apparent in both. 'All my artistic work is about the search for space, light and form,' he says. 'It's a search for three-dimensional space in two dimensions.'

He started life drawing as a child, taking classes at the Barnsdall Art Center in Hollywood, California, part of the Barnsdall Art Park that boasts several Frank Lloyd Wright buildings. Lehrer now holds bi-weekly life-drawing sessions at the his office, to which all his staff, as well as consultants, friends and fellow architects, are invited. 'The live model gives the architects in the room the needed perspective of how space relates to people.'

Lehrer says that when drawing architecturally his projects begin with a very simple loose plan, axonometric or sectional sketches. 'These are really parti sketches, searching for a synthetic form that seems to solve the real problems of the site, the program and the project.'

205

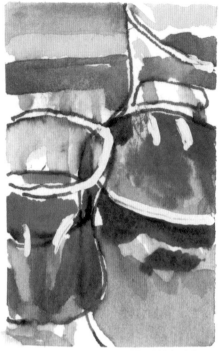

WINE
PEPPERED PORK

VILLANDRY   05 OCTOBER 2001

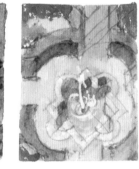

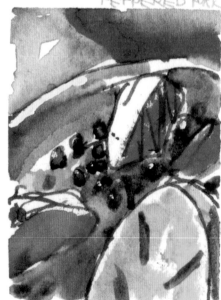

DINNER with BOB @ CHANTILLY

ST. SAVANT · MAISON TAFT · 06-07 OCTOBER 01

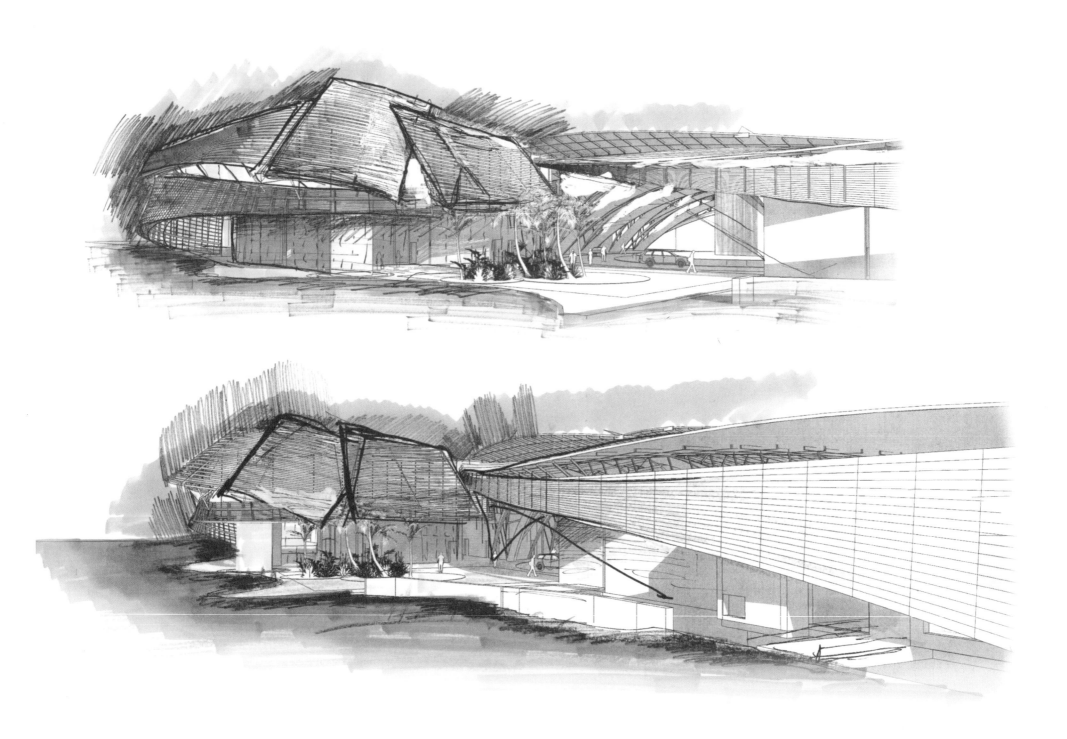

Detail 005
Steel connection to laminate beam

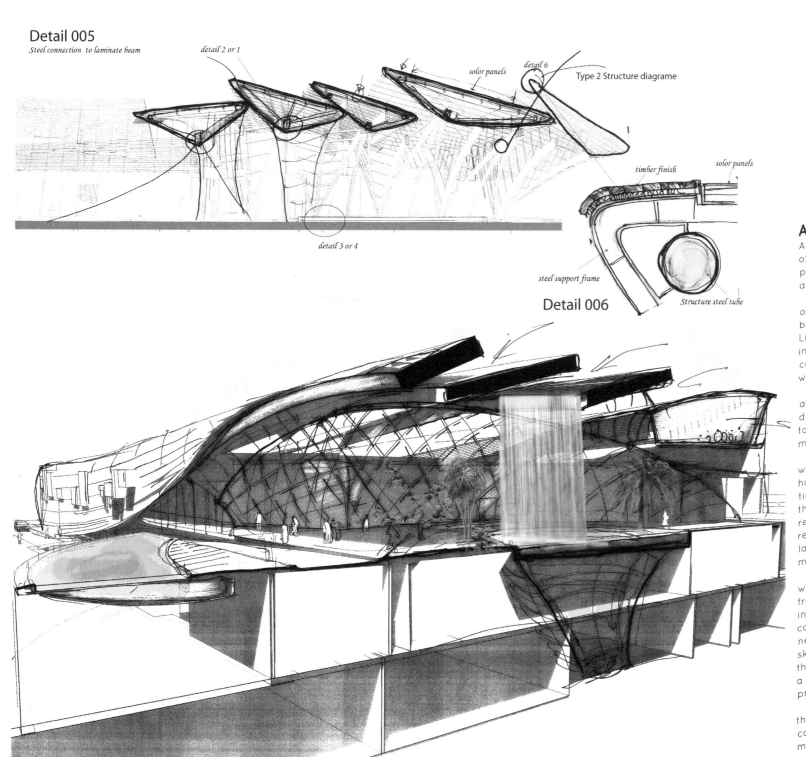

detail 2 or 1

solor panels

detail 6

Type 2 Structure diagrame

detail 3 or 4

timber finish

solor panels

steel support frame

Structure steel tube

Detail 006

ALISTAIR LILLYSTONE

Architectural design is a methodical series of steps that culminate in a coherent project—almost all architects would agree, and Alistair Lillystone of HOK is no different.

'Initially, we ascertain what the scope of the design is and then gather as much background information as possible,' says Lillystone. 'Client aspirations are also important, and, once all this information is collected it gives me a direction and defines what I should start to draw with.'

Usually, Lillystone starts using CAD, creating a measured drawing to work from. This drawing is then printed and used as a guide to start sketching, painting or creating card models from.

'The initial drawing is a good base to work from,' he says. 'The introduction of hand drawing or painting [208–09] is essential, as it is quicker to record the ideas and thoughts one may have, and can be more readily tested. Using this method helps to remove the constraints and adds another layer to the design. Using a card sketch model also helps…as it's 3D.'

Once Lillystone has reached a point where he feels he has gained enough ideas from these methods he draws them back into CAD. 'Once designing back into the computer has been completed it might be necessary to print out the drawings to hand sketch over them again,' says Lillystone. 'Or, the CAD model might be at a point to enable a computer laser-cut model [210–11] to be produced.'

This repetitive method allows Lillystone the flexibility of hand drawing, painting or card sketches, while also helping to maximize the benefits of CAD and BIM (building information modelling).

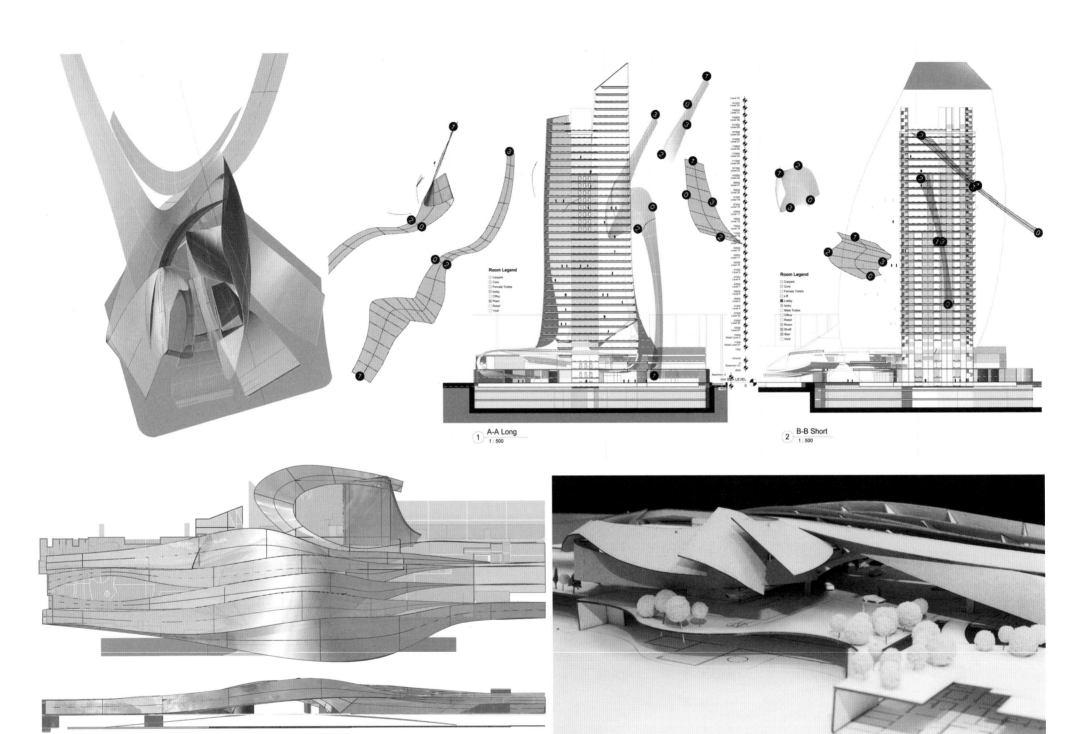

A-A Long
1 : 500

B-B Short
2 : 500

Room Legend
- Carpark
- Core
- Female Toilets
- lobby
- Office
- Plant
- Retail
- Void

Room Legend
- Carpark
- Core
- Female Toilets
- Lift
- Lobby
- Male Toilets
- Office
- Room
- Shaft
- Stair
- Void

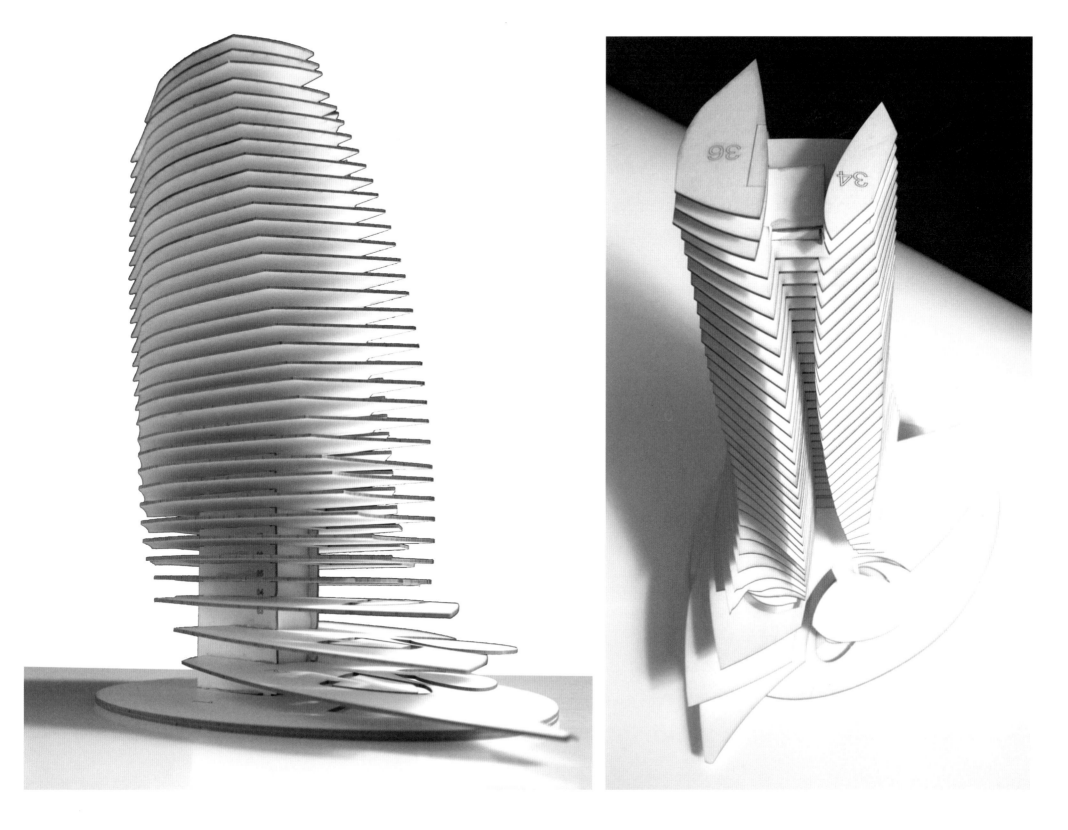

212–213
214–215

CJ LIM

'I am very curious how some designers work exclusively with the computer without initially doing hand-drawn sketches,' says CJ Lim. 'The nuance of the sketch brings life to a project.'

This may sound unusual, coming from a man who teaches at one of the most progressive architecture schools in the world (the Bartlett in London), but while CJ Lim's ideas are radical, his method of expressing them is traditional.

He employs hand-drawn sketches to illustrate initial ideas and conceptualize his architectural narratives for the team at Studio 8. 'I am very much a fountain pen and detail paper person; I can't sketch with a thin pencil or pen!' he says. 'I work fast and sketching is an immediate tool, an efficient way of communicating complex ideas. Sketching allows me simultaneously to be strategic and think poetically. This way, ideas flow without inhibitions or self-consciousness. Our more interesting projects are generally products of the nuances of hand-drawn sketches.'

Studio 8's innovative designs focus on unique interpretations of cultural, social and environmental sustainability programmes. 'After the initial idea has been formalized, we work a lot with sketch models too,' says Lim. 'They come a little later after the hand-drawn sketches, but the two forms of sketching complement each other in the design process. As the design evolves, sketching helps us to edit and strategize the ideas, to prioritize and to discard the thoughts that revolve around the project periphery.'

Upon completion of a project, Studio 8 does a 'big clean up'. Key sketch drawings and models are archived along with the final models and drawings. While the practice has not seen many of its designs built, they are widely exhibited and published.

213

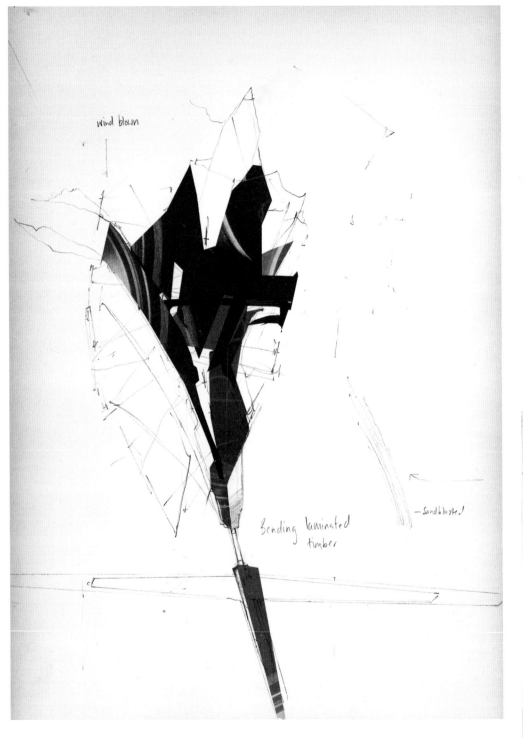

wind blown

Bending laminated
timber

— Sandblasted

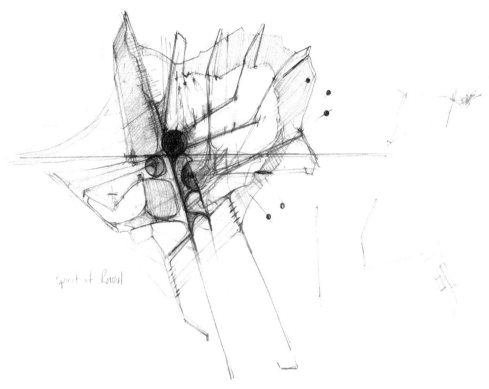

Spirit of Raoul

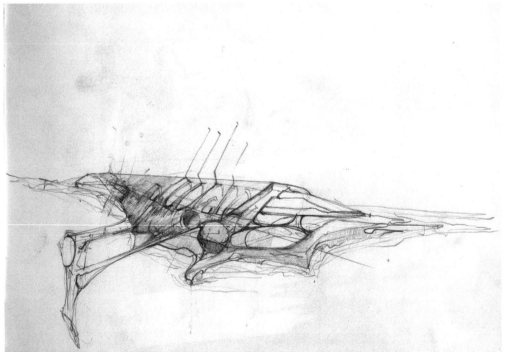

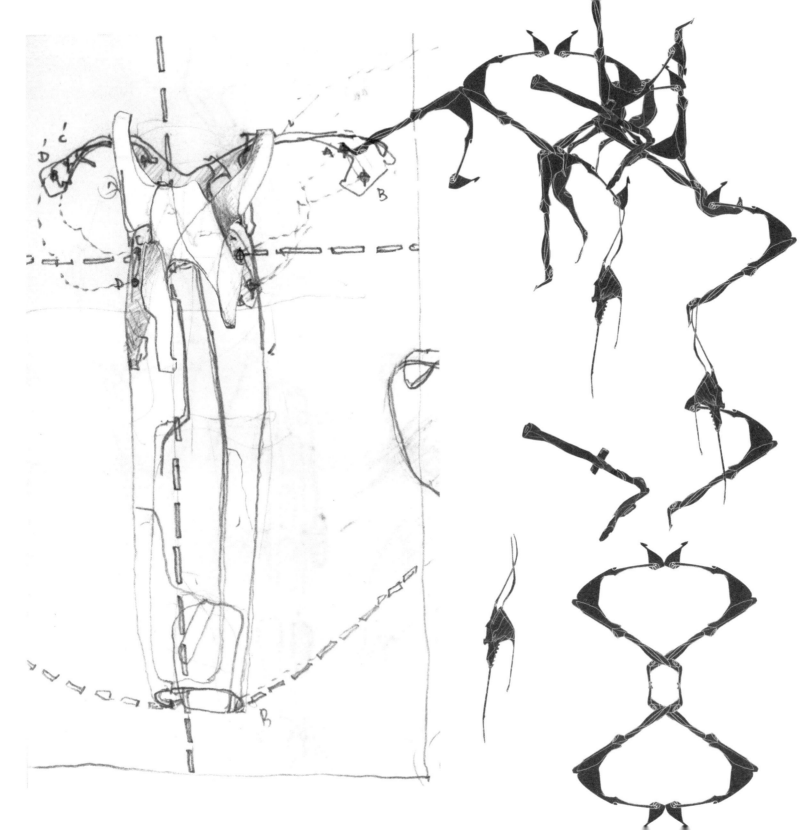

LIQUIDFACTORY

Kate Davies and Emmanuel Vercruysse are architects and teachers. Their practice, Liquidfactory, is a multidisciplinary firm operating at the confluence of art, architecture and performance. 'We are primarily concerned with the event,' they say. 'Viewing a site as a territory or stage for a series of performances, we seek interventions that respond to both their spatial and temporal contexts.'

Beginning with a sketch, the architects capture the 'initial ghost' of the project on paper. These sketches are more about sense and feeling rather than anything practical. They then scan the sketches and rework them both digitally and through collage, after this comes a series of quick models.

'These models are about exploration. For us, design happens in the hand more than the mind,' says Davies. 'The sketch is the closest we can get to the fragility and beauty of an imaginative thought. It serves as a mediator between the flighty and untrustworthy visions of the mind and the brutal and undeniable reality of the made thing. Our aim above all is to catch some of the magic of the initial thought in the final piece.'

The sketches and drawings displayed here act as a blueprint for the project. The architects subsequently begin to think about materiality, by creating working prototypes. However, they always have the initial sketch as a reference point and aesthetic target to drive the made pieces.

'For us the initial sketches are the most precious part of the project; they are half the story. Our whole fabrication process is about capturing the magic of that first sketch.'

JOHN LYALL

'All architects should really be able to draw,' according to John Lyall. 'Hand–eye coordination with a pencil allows for a fairly rapid definition of space and form. The process then charts a journey, making each sketch a stage along the way. This journey cannot be made flexibly or quickly by clicking a mouse on a computer!'

Lyall works in a small sketchbook and from the earliest point in a project likes to prepare and explore 3D concept sketches such as these from a cultural/residential project in Ipswich called Cranfields Mill [218–21]. 'This sketching displays my thought process and enables me to cover a lot of ground very quickly, making swift, early experiments in context and form.' He uses soft pencils or felt tips — for a dash of colour — and believes it is important to include a human figure or vehicle to give the sketch a sense of scale. 'Viewers have to understand the sketch and engage with it; it can't be too vague.'

Lyall is the only member of his practice who does not draw with a computer; therefore, sketching out plans, sections and 3D concepts is vital for the communication of his designs to colleagues, who then accurately plot the architecture in CAD. Illustrative sketches such as those of the dance rehearsal rooms at Cranfields Mill help to explain his design motives. 'My next opportunity for serious sketching comes when the team has developed accurate computer massing models. I then over-draw these "skeletons" to explore forms — fenestration, roof types, details, shadows, materials, etc.' he says.

Lyall also likes experimenting with different artistic mediums, including etching and silk-screen printing. 'By taking one of my hand-drawn sketches through a simple full-tone photographic process and printing it over stencilled patches of colour, I can build up a fulsome "picture" even though it's still a simple sketch at heart.'

219

etched
+
clear glass

etched
glass

Daylight streaming in

Dance House – Studio 3/Ballet

Dance East : College St. / Foundry Lane.

JHC 2003.

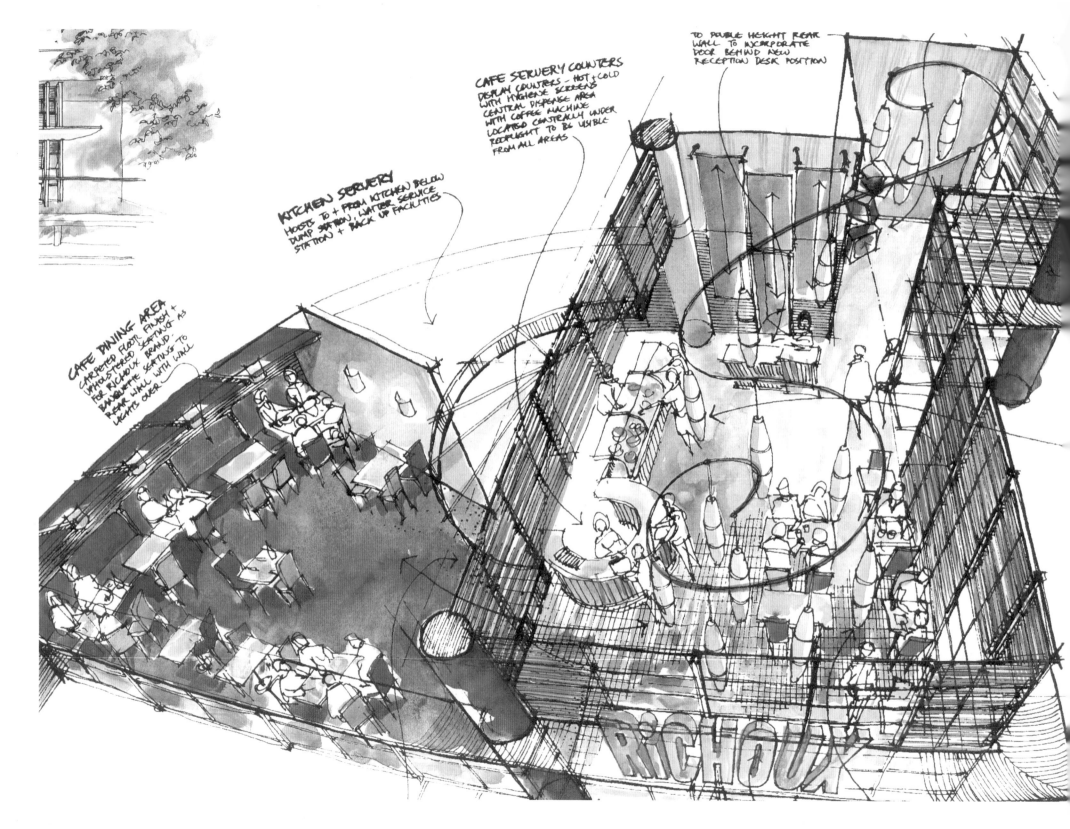

TO DOUBLE HEIGHT REAR WALL TO INCORPORATE DOOR BEHIND NEW RECEPTION DESK POSITION

CAFE SERVERY COUNTERS
DISPLAY COUNTERS - HOT + COLD WITH HYGIENE SCREENS CENTRAL DISPENSE AREA WITH COFFEE MACHINE LOCATED CENTRALLY UNDER ROOFLIGHT TO BE VISIBLE FROM ALL AREAS

KITCHEN SERVERY
HOISTS TO + FROM KITCHEN BELOW DUMP STATION / WAITER SERVICE STATION + BACK UP FACILITIES

CAFE DINING AREA
CARPETED FLOOR FINISH + UPHOLSTERED SEATING AS FOR RICHOUX BRAND BANQUETTE SEATING TO REAR WALL WITH WALL LIGHTS OVER

RICHOUX

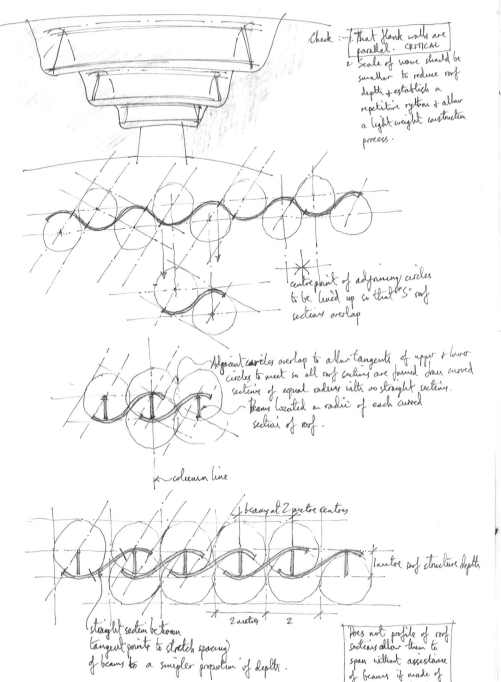

Check : 1. That flank walls are parallel. CRITICAL

2. Scale of wave should be smaller to reduce roof depth + establish a repetitive rythm + allow a light weight construction process.

centre point of adjoining circles to be lined up so that "S" roof sections overlap

Adjacent circles overlap to allow tangents of upper + lower circles to meet so all roof sections are formed from curved sections of equal radius with no straight sections.
— Beams located on radii of each curved section of roof.

← column line

beams at 2 metre centres

1 metre roof structure depth

2 metres   2

straight section between tangent points to stretch spacing of beams to a simpler proportion of depth.

Does not profile of roof sections allow them to span without assistance of beams if made of rigid frame structure.

44

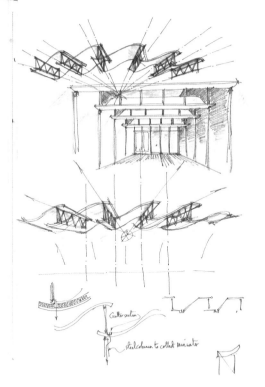

Gutter section

steel column to collect rain water

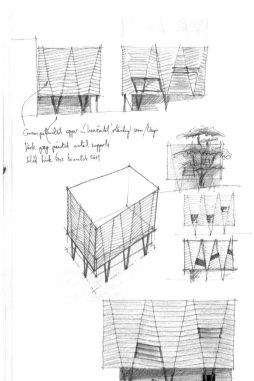

Green patinated copper in horizontal standing seam / trays
Dark grey painted metal supports
Solid brick base to match SGH

MACKENZIE WHEELER

'Ideas invariably start in the sketchbooks, whether they are good or bad.... There should be nothing precious about a sketchbook,' says Rupert Wheeler, of Mackenzie Wheeler. Excerpts on this spread include designs for the Richoux restaurant at the Museum of London [222], Vesta Rowing club [223, main image and top right] and West Thames College [223, bottom right].

'The idea is free to develop and may well change completely while in the sketchbook. It's good to sleep on it for a while, "let it cook for a few days", because once it is in the book it is in your head and you can test it out against things you come across on a day-to-day basis.'

Many of Wheeler's sketches form part of a sequence, where an idea for a project is being worked through in a fairly intense manner. The result is a stream of consciousness that can flow around between conflicting or similar ideas. On these occasions Wheeler can get through many pages in an evening. 'This is my favourite use of sketchbooks,' he says, 'where you start with no preconceived idea of what you will end up with.'

A lot of Wheeler's sketchbook is given over to the detailed design of elements and many such sketches go directly to metal-workers, joiners, etc., who then base their shop drawings (plans that show how an object is to be built or assembled) on them. 'Such sketches are also vastly preferable for clients, as they give a much better feel as to what the client will be getting [certainly moreso] than some bland detail from a CAD office,' explains Wheeler. Illustrative sketches such as those of the swimming pool at Feltonfleet School in Surrey [224], and the bar/restaurant at the Marriott Hotel on the left bank in Paris [225], give clients a great insight into the design.

'I often refer to past sketchbooks when recalling a similar problem that has been tackled before. They are all indexed to assist this process. The long-term value of these sketches as a diary of works conceived and completed is priceless.'

223

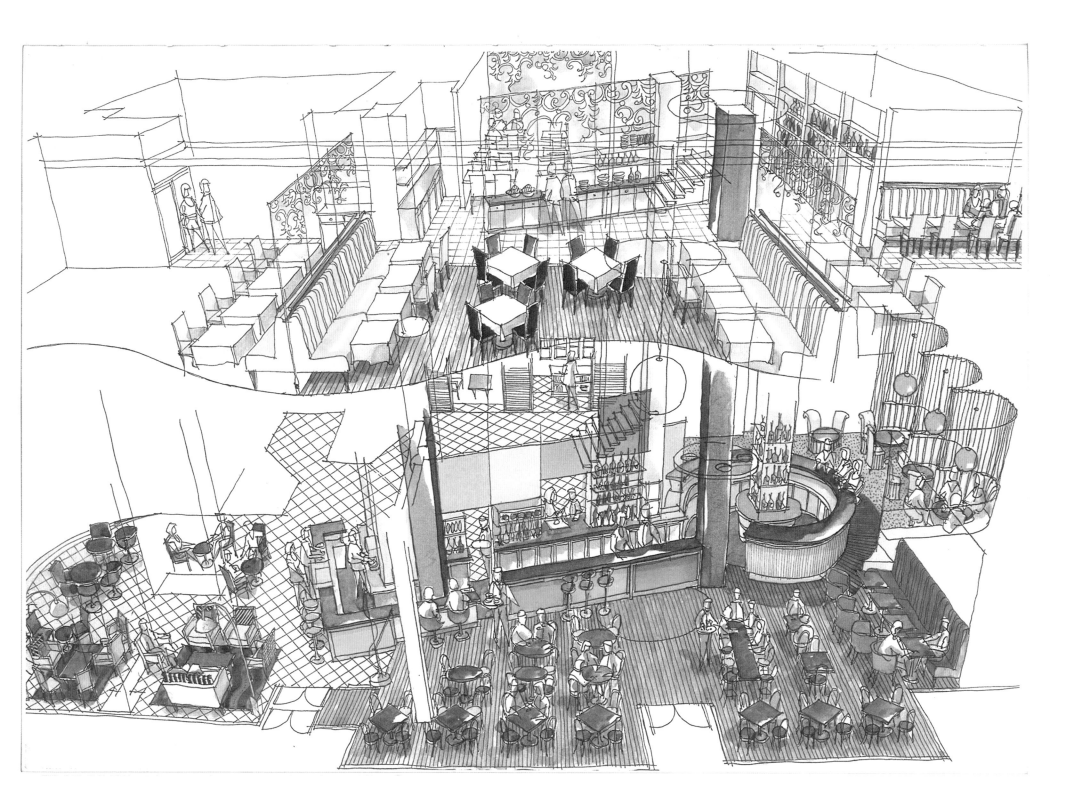

BARRIE MARSHALL

'All of our architectural projects start with an idea rather than any drawing. The idea somehow simultaneously evolves out of an understanding of the practical constraints—brief, function, size, site, cost, client aspiration—and a more abstract concept of what imagery the building may express,' says Barrie Marshall, principal at Denton Corker Marshall.

'The initial thought process quickly starts to connect idea with reality. Is the building singular, articulated, permeable, recessive, expressive, sensuous, etc.? How do we want the building to be perceived?' At this time Marshall starts to sketch, to try to catch an 'essential image' of the building's external form. Initially described as rough, the sketches take on a more advanced look when the concept is first presented to the client.

Marshall describes the sketch not as a method of 'testing' what the building will look like but as a depiction of an idea that he already knows will look good as a building. 'What I'm trying to emphasize is that I don't really use the sketches as a means of developing a design form—that comes from the initial discussions. Sketches help refine how the building will appear or work.'

From first presentation to agreement with the client, the sketches are used as inspiration and a reminder of the true essence of the design. 'I work on the assumption that there is always a sketch, an image that defines the building, because through all the complications and constraints, as a design develops it is easy to lose sight of the strength of a concept and of what the final building should evoke.'

227

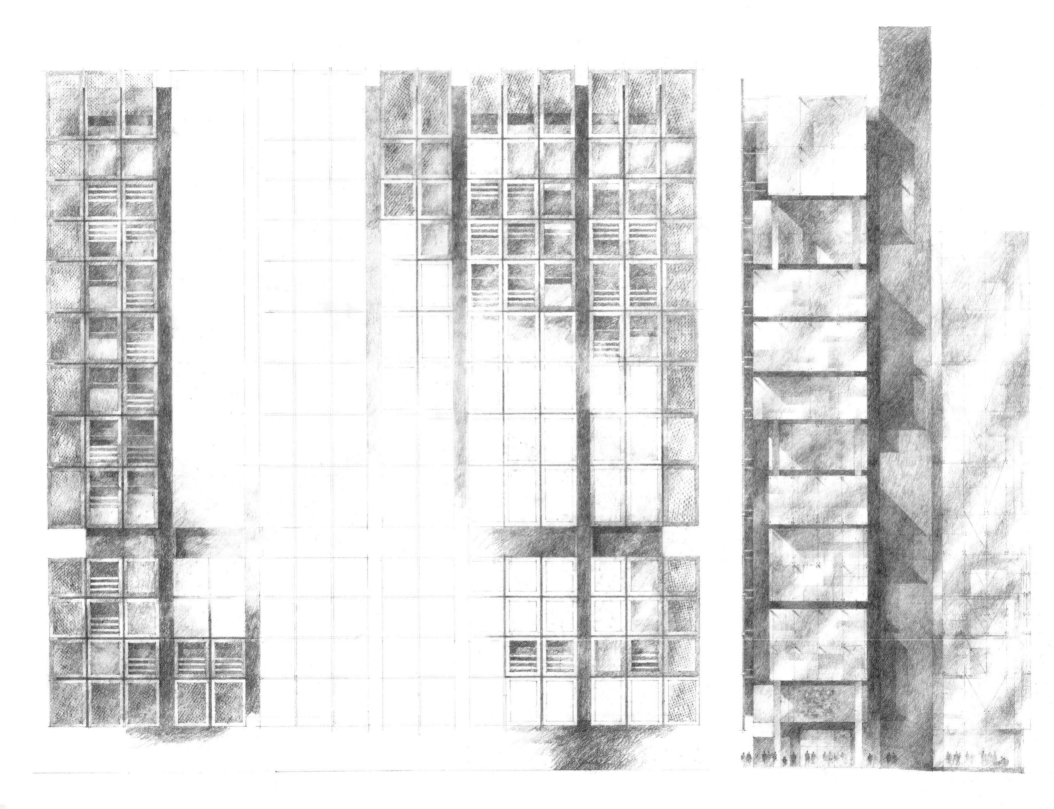

WA Perf. Arts centre

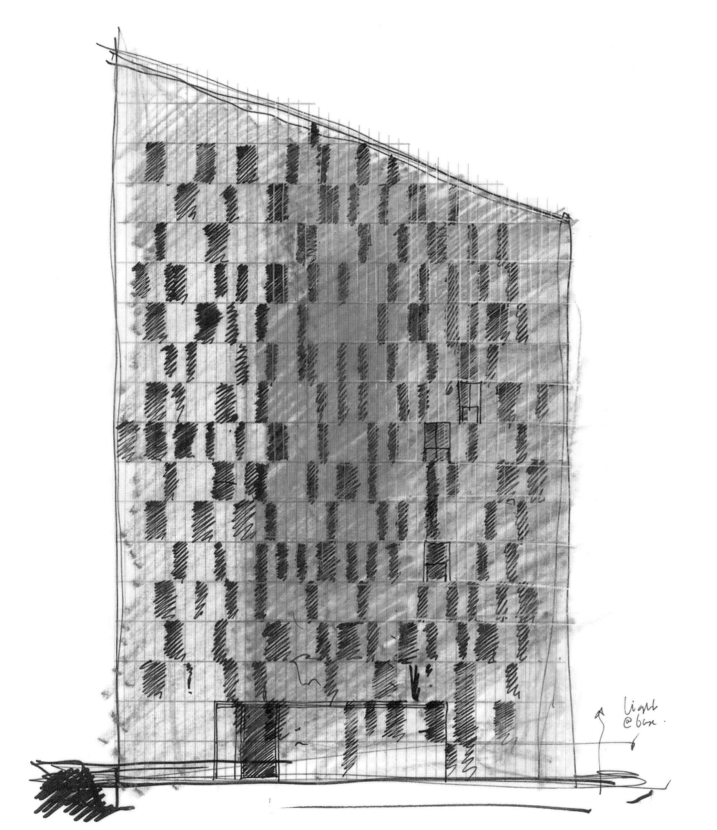

light
@ base.

STEPHEN McGRATH

Stephen McGrath's work explores themes of scale, resonance, motion and geometry—conditions that create the cycles of our environments. 'Cities and open spaces, and particularly places discovered while travelling in Japan, hold memories of delicate qualities of light, of transparency and translucency, materiality, time, decay, the visible and the invisible; places that at once conceal and reveal,' says McGrath.

McGrath has painted throughout his architectural career and this has played an integral part in the development of his ideas both at university and in the professional environment. Initially, his ideas are illustrated in sketch form with the prevalent use of colour. 'Sketching is a very quick method,' says McGrath. 'Conversely, sometimes paper cutting is used to examine rhythm, form, language and scale. Paper cutting is very slow and deliberate.'

Sketching and paper cutting provide a basis for exploring ideas in different ways. These methods mean that a new project can be approached from diverse perspectives at the same time. 'The thought process is helped by working at different speeds,' explains McGrath. 'Hand sketching can often be very intuitive in real time. The more deliberate manipulation of cut paper slows the mind and opens an alternative realm of thought.'

'In some cases the initial sketches inform the design of a building's façade with rhythm and texture.' says McGrath. 'However, sometimes this [initial sketching] process helps to eliminate unhelpful ways of approaching a new project.

'I am continually looking for new methods of making the first mark on paper.'

233

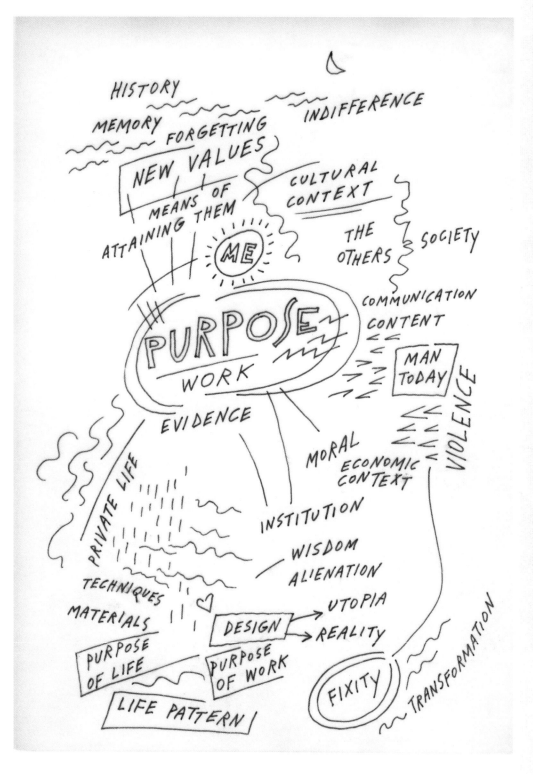

HISTORY

MEMORY FORGETTING INDIFFERENCE

NEW VALUES

MEANS OF CULTURAL
ATTAINING THEM CONTEXT

ME THE SOCIETY
OTHERS

COMMUNICATION
CONTENT
PURPOSE
MAN
WORK TODAY

EVIDENCE VIOLENCE

MORAL
PRIVATE LIFE ECONOMIC
CONTEXT

INSTITUTION

WISDOM
ALIENATION

TECHNIQUES
UTOPIA
MATERIALS DESIGN
REALITY
PURPOSE
OF LIFE PURPOSE
OF WORK FIXITY TRANSFORMATION

LIFE PATTERN

PICCOLA
PENNELLATA
INFORMALE

LANCETTE SECONDI
IN ORO VERO

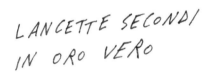

OPPURE
GEOMETRICA

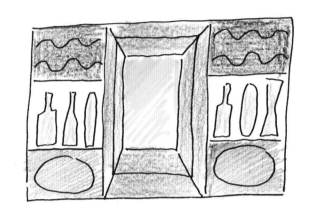

ARAZZI CON
DECORAZIONE
ARCHITETTONICA

ALESSANDRO MENDINI

Architect and designer Alessandro Mendini says: 'Fragments are the key. Projects, visual alphabets and different disciplines are freely mixed together in order to provide an impression of emotions. Our oeuvre is a continuous combination of parts, and the overall image is the subject of our work. For this reason, we present individual projects as fixed fragments in a mobile system. They are the tangible and partial materials of an abstract flux of ideas.'

Atelier Mendini employs a staff of twenty architects and graphic and industrial designers. The Atelier has a special department for project research and experimentation in materials. It has worked for clients in over thirty nations and is currently providing consultancy in city planning for several cities in Korea.

Mendini's eclectic style absorbs influences from multiple genres and schools of design. However, its defining element is the use of colour. His sketches, whether for a museum or a hat stand, involve bold form and exciting combinations of shapes. In addition, his design method often involves diagrammatic sketches, surrounded by descriptive notes and key words, or inspirational ideas.

'The designs are the linguistic components of an ongoing puzzle that is never completed,' says Mendini. 'The sense lies in the progressive utopian hypothesis of reaching an impossible synthesis; it lies in this expanded, centrifugal movement that has no end. The message of our work lies in this atmospheric dust, this polyphonic rhythm, a throng of figures full of contrasts.'

235

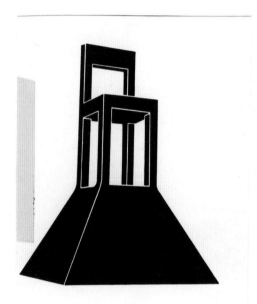

L18 GIU. 1984

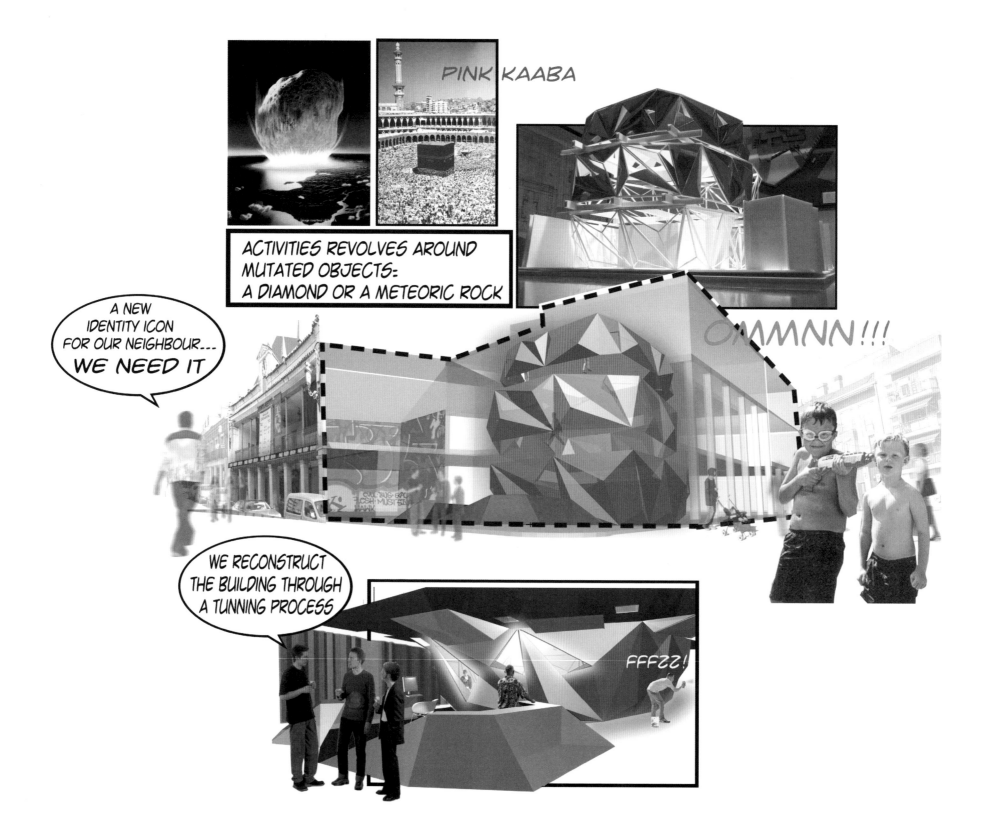

MI5 ARQUITECTOS

'First of all, we like to immerse ourselves in the context in which we are to intervene,' say the architects of Spanish practice Mi5 Arquitectos. 'We collect a lot of material and references, we talk and talk about it for a long time.'

From there, the practice goes straight to 3D computer modelling and digital photomontages. Very specific imagery, nothing abstract, to ensure that the 'cocktail' of form and function they have come up with works.

The practice often uses the comic strip as a narrative system to group and sort its material. It thinks that this pop iconography is communicative and conveys something of the work environment and decision-making processes of the office.

'The comic strip also gives our clients the chance to redescribe themselves from a make-believe standpoint, a process that we call "social-fantasy".

'We try not to respond to projects with preconceived ideas. Each situation calls for strategies and languages that we like to call "hyperspecifics". We believe the results will be understood as a material "super-expression" of the context.'

Mi5 does not work in the conventional linear process. Instead the practice generates images as quickly as possible and operates by trial and error.

'Sometimes we advance and other times we move backwards. We work like detectives. Once we have the clues, they are arranged, and we return to discuss the precision required to solve the puzzle in each case.

'What we reject completely is the idea of growth from a single sketch that then becomes a model and then, like a mannequin, receives the evening gown. Architecture is more unique and intricate than that.'

239

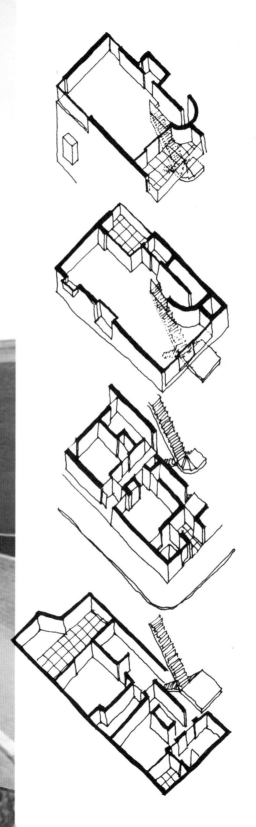

NAGAN JOHNSON

'It is rare that a scheme is devised entirely by the individual, so initial sketches are used for office communication, as well as problem solving,' say the architects of Nagan Johnson. 'The fast nature of the sketch allows easy correlation between the many demands that have to be accommodated within a design.'

The practice's first designs always begin with freehand drawings in pencil or pen on tracing paper. The plan may be the initial generator of a scheme but sometimes a more abstract, diagrammatic approach is taken. 'There are times when an idea is more to do with a section or a 3D form, which can be effectively articulated in a sketch,' say the architects.

Sketching starts the design process and helps to crystallize Nagan Johnson's ideas. It enables poor ideas to be rejected, while the better ones are considered further.

'We would expect to arrive at close-to-final solutions using sketches. At the stage where a design is complete, it becomes difficult to tell the original sketches from the later, due to the fluidity of the process. Some conceptions are cul-de-sacs and others are only slight deviations from the original idea.'

While being as computer literate as the next practice, Nagan Johnson believes that CAD is both a blessing and a curse. 'We have found that our best designs do not originate from the screen. However, we will often use the computer as a collaborative tool to embellish freehand sketches. It is a means to an end.'

243

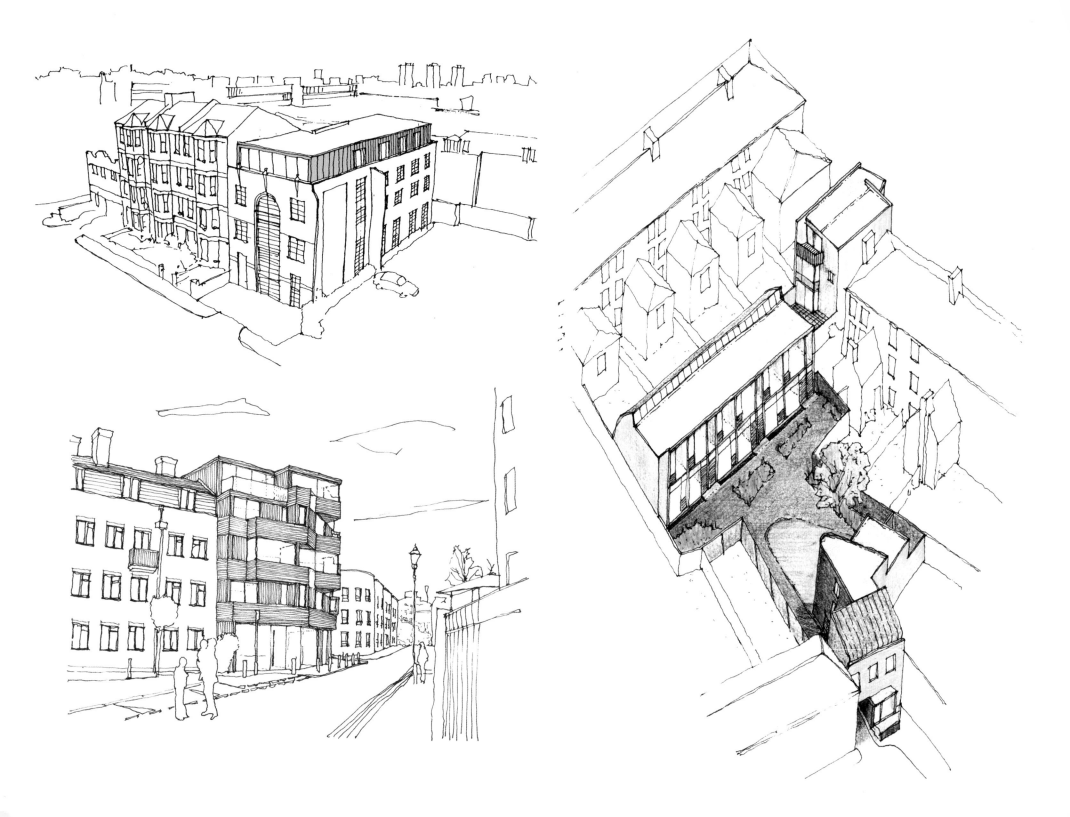

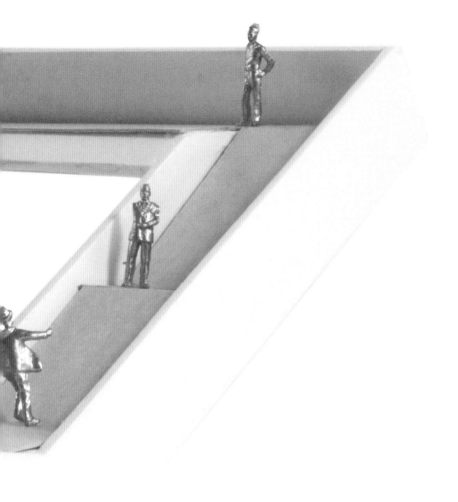

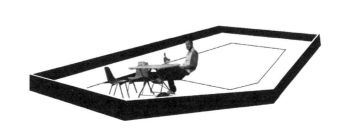

O+A

Dutch practice O+A rejects the notion of a brilliant architect making a doodle, which ends up becoming a building. 'We find these sketches to be the result of false romanticism,' says partner Auguste van Oppen. 'Our design process is a laborious one, where ideas and space evolve into a concept in the midst of a tremendous amount of work. This may appear to be rather inefficient but in-depth research drives the design process much more than designing itself.'

O+A is interested in creating a systemic architecture 'which actually does something'. The practice views the first sketch not as a single artefact but as an agglomeration of information and spatial studies.

Many different techniques are employed in getting to the essence of the brief: spreadsheets, physical and digital models, sketches, lists, documents highlighted by third parties, and so on. The models shown here develop the idea of an urban beach and elevated walkway on the River IJ in Amsterdam [246–47], while the following pages feature a design for the Casanova 2009 housing competition [248–49].

'Paradigms tend to shift as a design progresses. A client may well discover new possibilities or limitations, and our own assumptions made earlier on in the design process may not be valid after all,' says Van Oppen. 'Being able to fall back on a wealth of information and ideas enables us to keep giving authentic answers to changing demands. It also provides a fruitful source of inspiration for additional ideas later on.'

'We belong to the first generation of architects educated entirely in the information age. A consequence of this is that the traditional architectural sketch is employed more as an explanatory tool on the building site than in the office itself. Quick doodles are still made but mostly as a prelude to digital versions.'

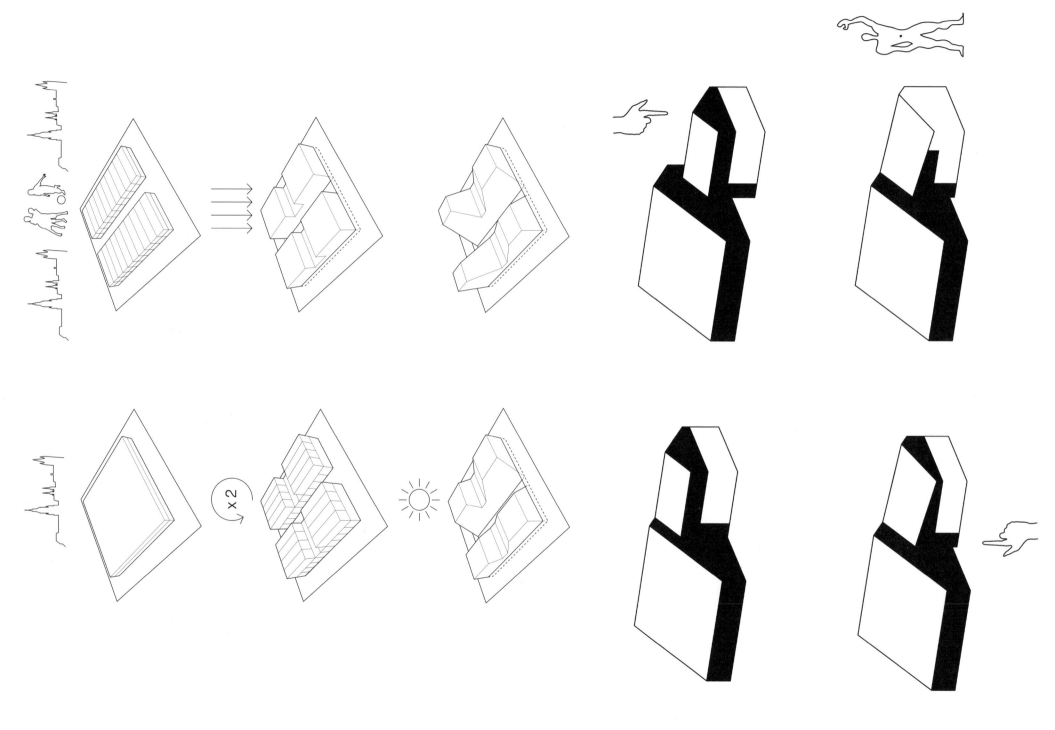

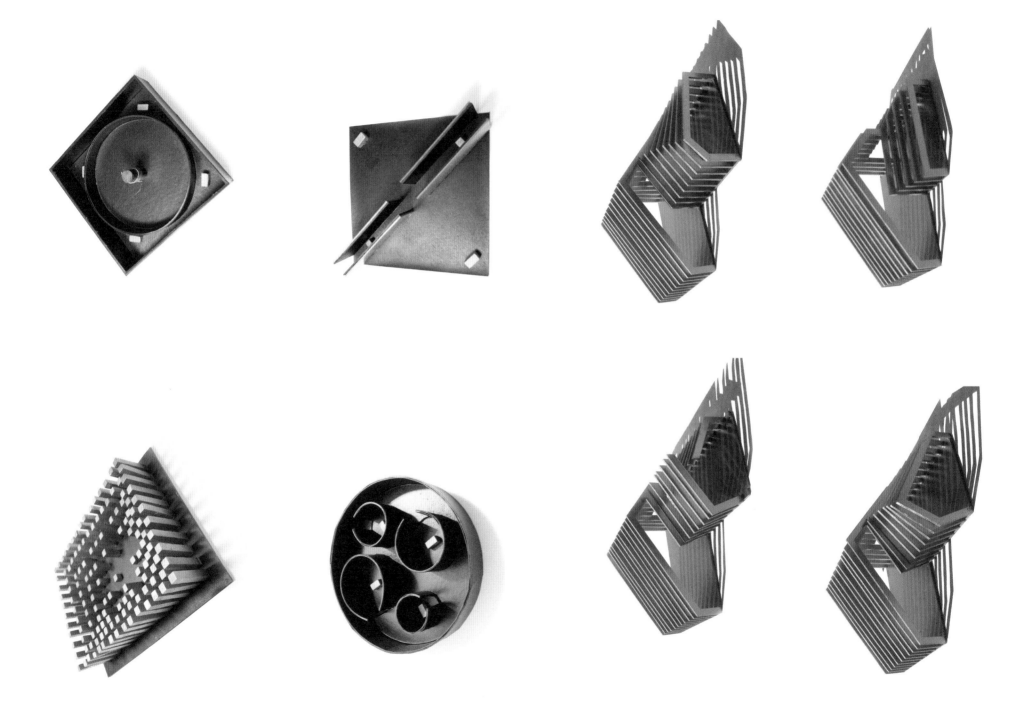

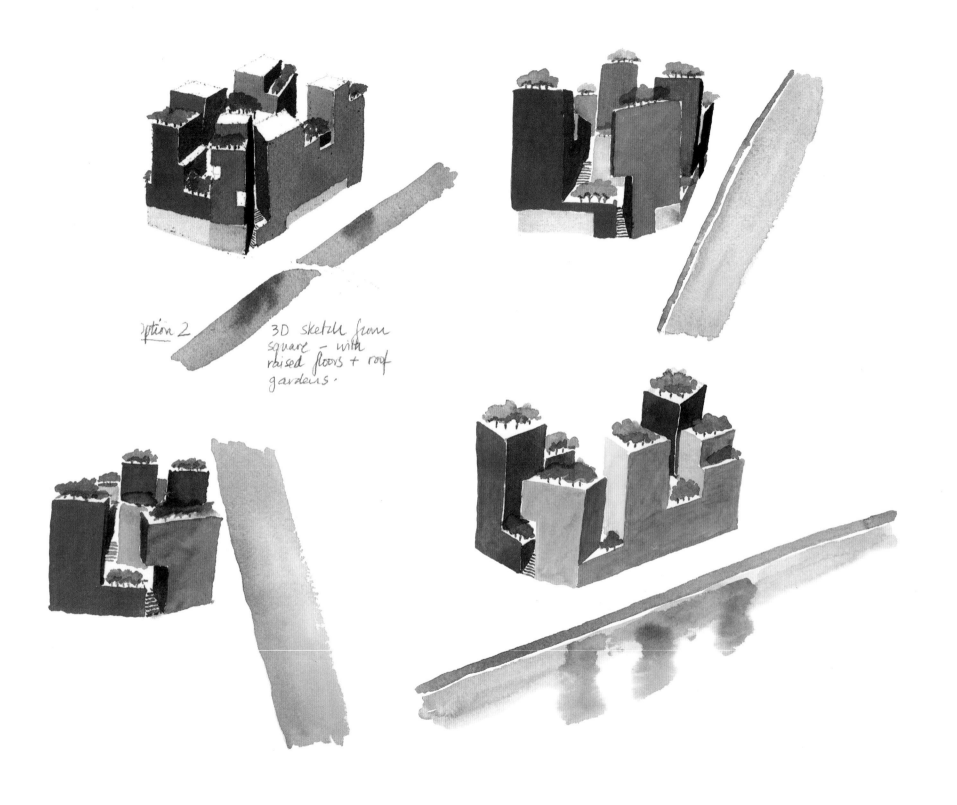

option 2   3D sketch from
square — with
raised floors + roof
gardens.

O'DONNELL + TUOMEY

O'Donnell + Tuomey see sketches as representing a continually developing developing story, a kind of conversation. 'We see the design process as a continuum from initial design to construction details,' says Sheila O'Donnell. 'There is no point at which "initial sketches" are complete. We continue to make them throughout the design—sometimes they are of details, sometimes the overall concept—as a form of checking against the initial concept.'

O'Donnell and her colleagues use freehand pencil sketches in plan, section and 3D in conjunction with accurate site drawings and cardboard site models. The pencil sketches are based on these site drawings, and alternative sketch models are made and tested on the site model. O'Donnell also uses watercolours to explore 3D forms and to develop the relationship between the site and the proposed building.

'We use drawing as a means of thinking, and, early in projects, different kinds of thinking are required,' says O'Donnell. 'The pencil plan sketches made over the site plan are a means of feeling our way into a place. The watercolours allow ideas to be condensed and distilled—because of the nature of the medium it isn't possible to show detail but it is possible to represent the hierarchy of intention—while the context is reduced to a kind of abstraction.' Here, watercolours detail ideas for the Timberyard housing scheme in Dublin [253] and mixed-use urban blocks in Amersfoort, the Netherlands [252].

Plan sketches are used to test the brief requirements: to discover essential connections and to introduce a sense of geometry, structure and dimension. 'We believe in the primacy of the plan; in the pattern and form it gives to building. We seek a certain rigour, so we are always thinking in plan from the outset but in parallel with other types of sketch, and models.'

253

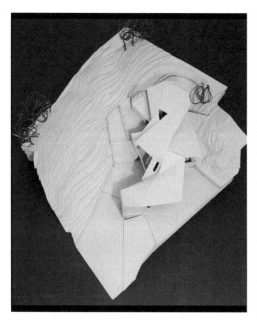 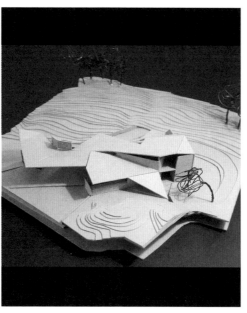  

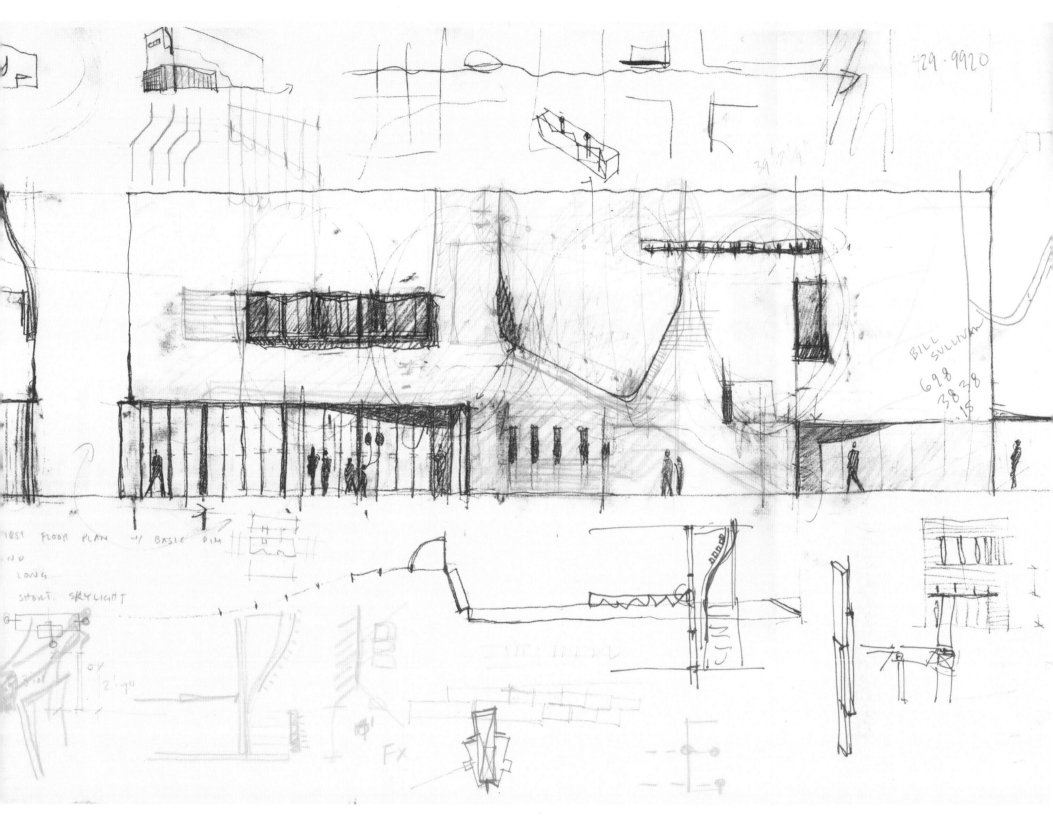

429.9920

BILL
SULLIVAN
698
3838
15

FIRST FLOOR PLAN w/ BASIC DIM

NO

LONG.

SHORT. SKYLIGHT

2'9"

Fx

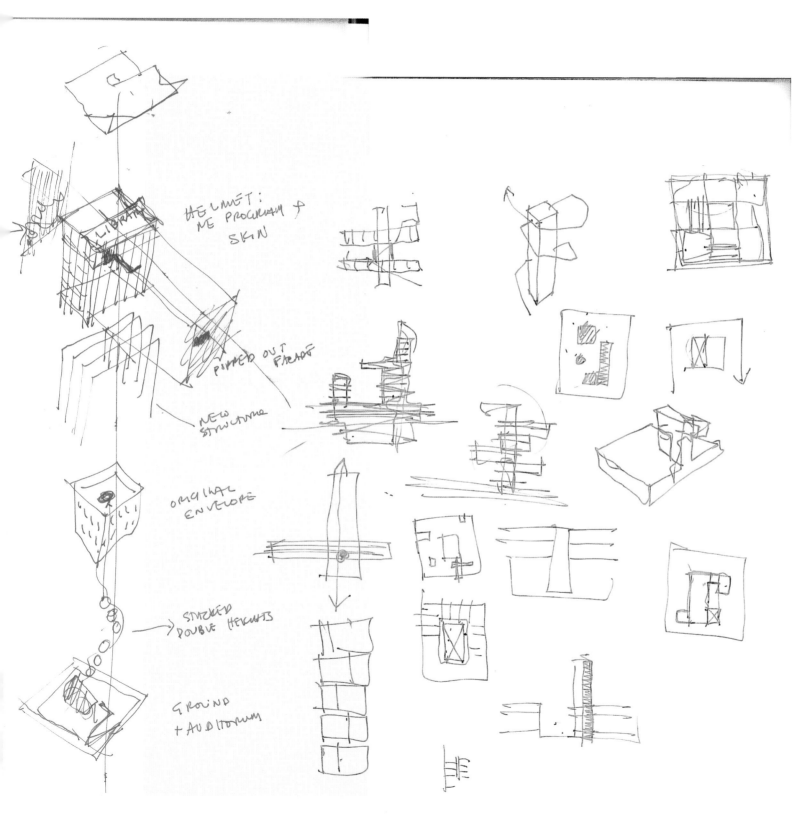

HELMET:
THE PROGRAM &
SKIN

LIBRARY

POPPED OUT
FACADE

NEW
STRUCTURE

ORIGINAL
ENVELOPE

STACKED
DOUBLE HEIGHTS

GROUND
+ AUDITORIUM

OFFICE DA

Boston-based design firm Office dA is led by partners Monica Ponce de Leon and Nader Tehrani. The firm's work ranges in scale from furniture to architecture, urban design and infrastructure—all with a focus on craft, detailing and precision.

Taking on a wide range of projects encourages the practice to use different media to inform its work. 'We sketch, we compute, we build models, we animate. Our process is not linear and as such we use varied techniques to speculate on different possibilities: motion, animation; figuration, models; subjectivity, perspectives etc.' Here, Helios House, Los Angeles, is sketched over a digital drawing [256], while designs for the University of Melbourne originated as computer sketches [256, bottom left].

The architects seize on the challenges unique to each project—the peculiarities of a site, requirements of the brief, or cultural specifications, for example—as the catalysts for transformation in architecture. An investigation of the potentials of materials and construction techniques, sometimes imported from fields outside architecture, is the foundation for every design. Much of the firm's research is dedicated to an exploration of how to improve on contemporary modes of construction, investigating both industry standards as well as evolving technologies derived from digital manufacturing processes. However, when all the methods and materials have been investigated Office dA will often fall back on sketching to test its ideas.

'Designing is a projective task, testing out ideas through specific media, and in turn interrogating the medium itself as a mode of design speculation. Suffice to say that we work iteratively, using the process of drawing, modelling and animating to layer information, and test scenarios—and eventually something is built.'

257

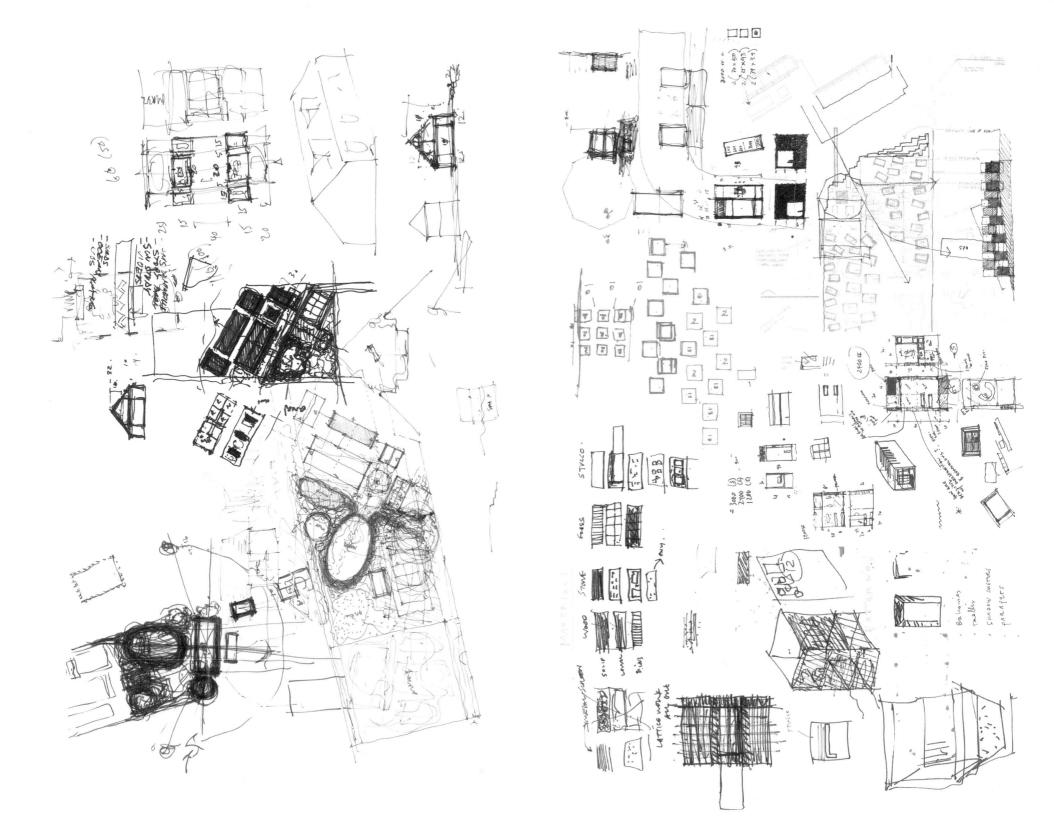

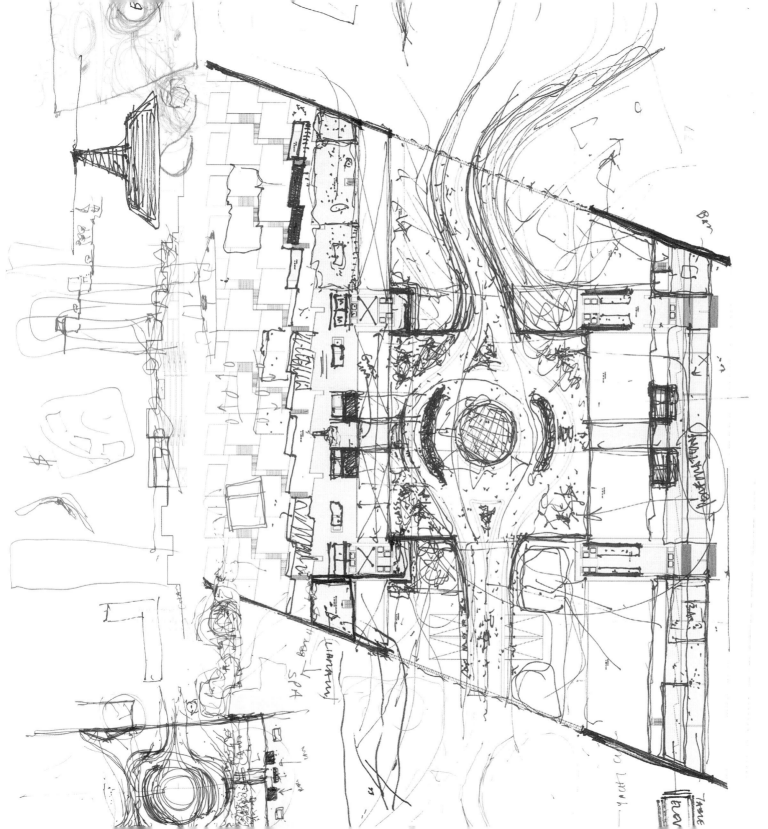

CHAD OPPENHEIM

Chad Oppenheim—founding principal of Oppenheim Architecture and Design—is a young but highly successful architect based in Miami, Florida. He has gained a name for himself as an exciting designer, and his work ranges from single residential houses to multi-storey condominiums and a billion-dollar hotel resort in Las Vegas.

Many of these projects have been published as designs and are still in construction, soon to dramatically change the skyscape of Miami and the UAE in particular (see Marina and Beach Tower, UAE [258]). However, for all his West Coast charm, and the super-slick computer-generated imagery used to promote his latest multi-home residential projects to prospective buyers, Oppenheim likes to get back to basics when starting on any new design: 'Sketching is the cornerstone of all of my designs. I start with a blank page and draw what I feel encapsulates the meaning, the story behind a new project.'

Different stories evolve from different places: Oppenheim does not have a signature style. His projects connect to their surroundings and his sketches rough out how this will happen, right from the very beginning.

For instance, Oppenheim's design sketch for San Silencio, Port of Caldera, Costa Rica [260, far left] is organic and flowing. 'The architecture undulates harmoniously with the contours of the slopes and cliffs, synchronizing with the topography and the rhythms of the environment,' he says. The Corniche in the UAE [261] is conceived as, 'a totemic response to programmatic desires, emerging elementally from the circular footprint of the site as a stacked assemblage within a diaphanous membrane'.

259

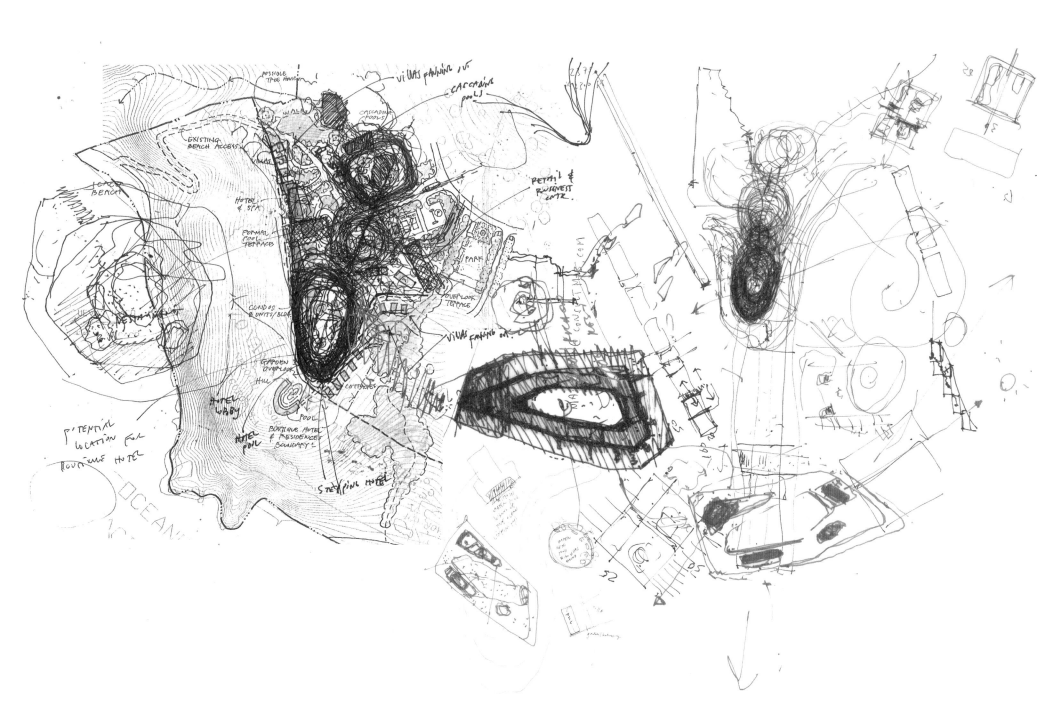

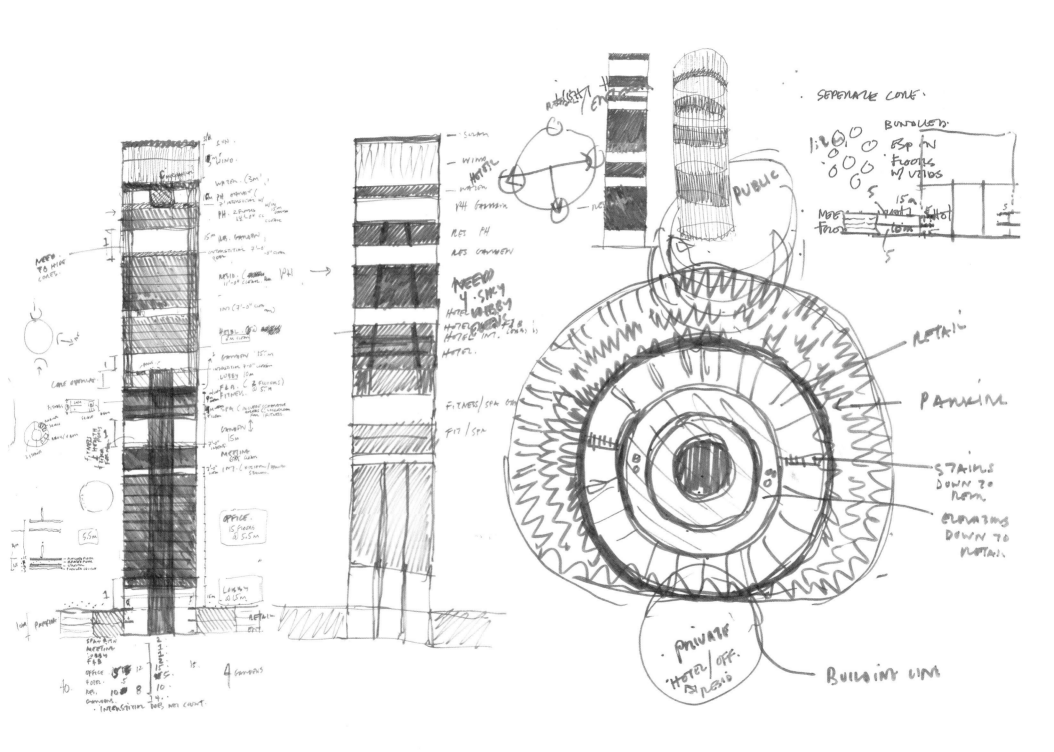

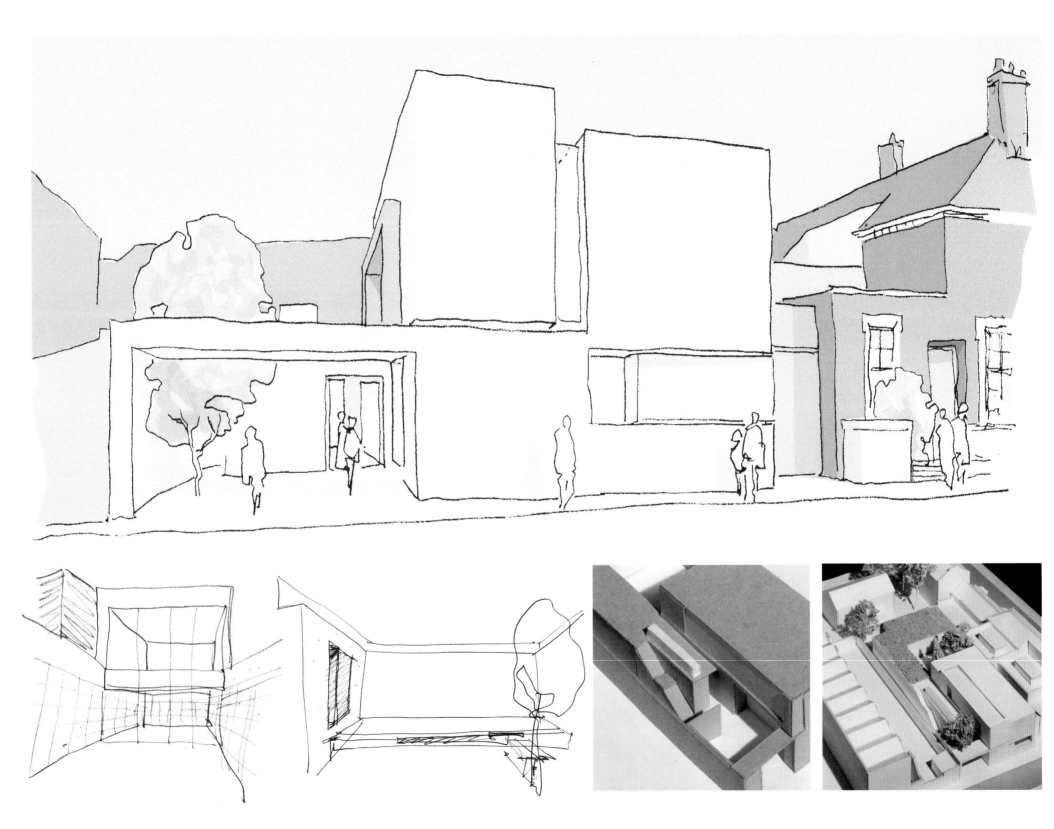

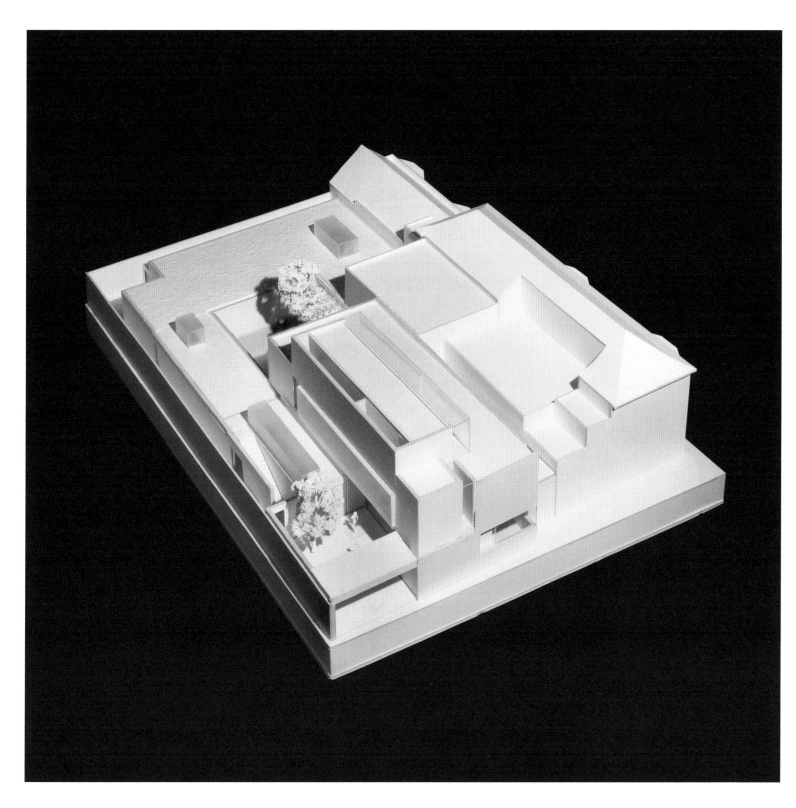

TERRY PAWSON

'Ideas, like projects, spring from within a wide spectrum of possibilities and there is no single way of illustrating an idea,' says Pawson, principal of the practice bearing his name. 'However, the first stage in our design process is invariably one of analysis, assessment and study, to try to understand the key concerns set out within the brief and to look for those other issues that may be equally important but have not yet been identified.'

Pawson's first ideas tend to materialize as freehand sketches [262], which he describes as 'cartoon-like diagrams', illustrating principles that begin to inform the project development. Often these sketches go on to be transformed into a model [263]. At other times, these sketches may be a reference image, a painting, a place, or another building: abstractions are eventually subsumed within the process of drawing and modeling as the project begins to coalesce. The pictures on these pages show the Vernon Street house.

Any kind of drawing or creative production is an iterative process, Pawson believes. 'Sometimes, it is necessary to draw the same thing repeatedly in order to extract or synthesize an important essence, the drawing refining and confirming the design approach each time it is done.'

This freehand sketching, analysis and discussion seek out the individuality within each site and brief; and try to synthesize something that is special and individual. Pawson says: 'We do not look for either formulaic or formalistic answers but see the design process like Michelangelo, who when sculpting, looked to release the figure already trapped within the stone.'

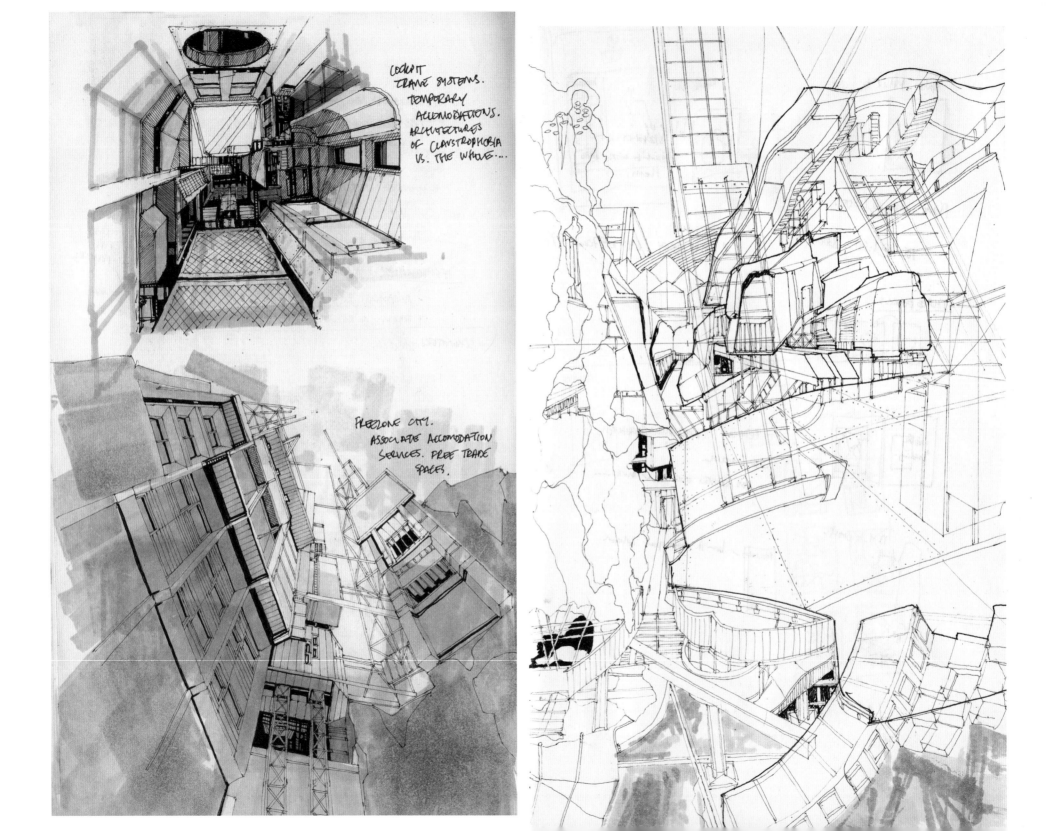

COCKPIT
CRANE SYSTEMS.
TEMPORARY
ACCOMODATIONS.
ARCHITECTURES
OF CLAUSTROPHOBIA
VS. THE WHOLE....

FREEZONE CITY.
ASSOCIATE ACCOMODATION
SERVICES. FREE TRADE
SPACES.

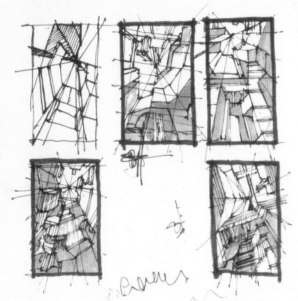

MIGRATION OF WORKERS - BROWN STONES AND "HAND ME DOWN" BUILDINGS.
UN RENOVATION, SLUM TOWN SURROUNDING THEY AREA.
A "NAIVE" ARCHITECTURE SURROUNDS THE GREAT PINNACLE OF
MODERNISM AND SUPPLANTS IT. NEW CHAMBERS ARE BUILT INTO
THE GROUNDS. ITS DEFENDS ITSELF. AGAINST ATTACK.

LUKE PEARSON

A graduate of a Master's course in architecture at the Bartlett, London, Luke Pearson quickly attracted attention in design and artistic fields alike. His work was shown in the Royal Academy of Art's annual Summer Exhibition soon after he graduated MArch.

Pearson's sketches have a dark industrial feel, but there is far more to them than the initial 'techno hit'. 'I generally build up a series of concepts at varying levels of abstraction, through quick pen drawings, while also investigating how I can start to create a visual language that will shape and direct the project,' he explains.

He investigates the boundaries of different media too, using Copic Wide Markers on different surfaces to create bleed effects similar to watercolours. Thin paper allows the marker pen to bleed through a number of leaves, 'to start to build up a dialogue between the pages of the sketchbook through the physical nature of the paper'.

Pearson is both an architect and an artist. His MArch allowed him to explore the worlds of computerization and hand drawing to the fullest. 'I admire the production of a quick but convincing drawing of a space through the movements of the hand,' he says. 'In a world where the notion of digital manufacturing as an investigative tool is starting to take hold on college education and theoretical practice, my working methods embrace the simplicity and at the same time myriad possibilities of the interface between hand and pen and substrate.'

265

BLACKWATER.

BEWARES FOR HIRE...

FREE ZONE, MILITARISED...

GROWS AROUND INDUSTRIAL PRACTICAL CHEAP
LABOURS...

TESTING ENGINES.

FRAMEWORKS.

DISINTEGRATED RUINS.

TOWN PLANNING ES MUM.   p: 28, 30, 59....
OBSERVATIONS ON CONTEMPORARY ARCHITECTURE...

THE SECRETARIAT.
"FUTURE FROZEN SOLIDLY IN THE FORM OF THE PRESENT"
→ TOO TRUE.
EXCAVATIONS? REVEALING THE ANACHRONISMS. → THE ICEBERG
THE MATTE-SPACE
BELOW?

FROM THE GROUND UP : ⇒   GANDY.
UN IN RUINS.
CONCEPTS FOR AN UNFROZEN FUTURE.

MINIMISED.   IMAGINARY FIELDS.   HACKING INTO
A TEMPORARY.   SUPPLANT   THE FROZEN
"SIMULACRA"   FUTURE
OF AN ARCHITECTURE
MOVING FORWARD.   podium?

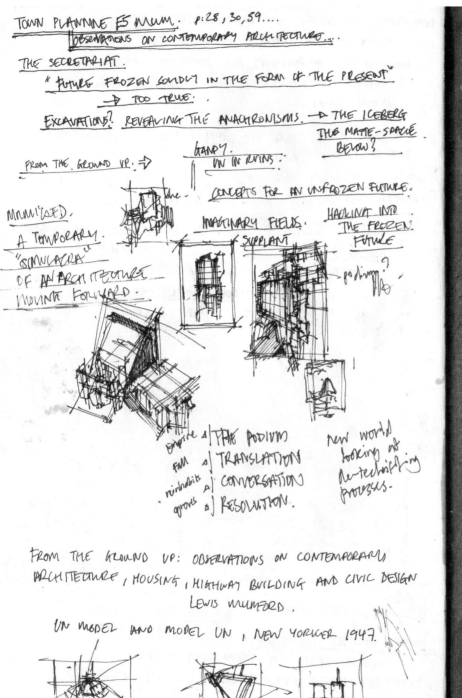

PODIUM
TRANSLATION   new world
CONVERSATION   looking at
RESOLUTION.   de-technifying
                     processes.

FROM THE GROUND UP: OBSERVATIONS ON CONTEMPORARY
ARCHITECTURE, HOUSING, HIGHWAY BUILDING AND CIVIC DESIGN
LEWIS MUMFORD.

UN MODEL AND MODEL UN , NEW YORKER 1947.

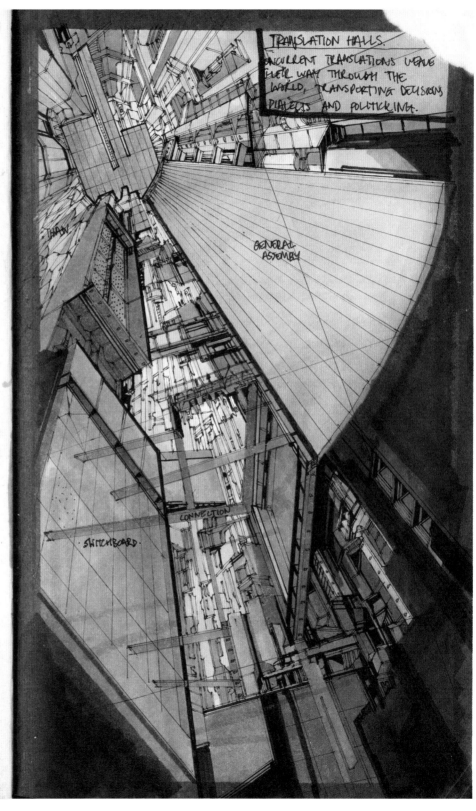

TRANSLATION HALLS.
CONCURRENT TRANSLATIONS WEAVE
THEIR WAY THROUGH THE
WORLD, TRANSPORTING DELUSIONS
DIALECTS AND POLITICKING.

THAW

GENERAL
ASSEMBLY

CONNECTION

SWITCHBOARD.

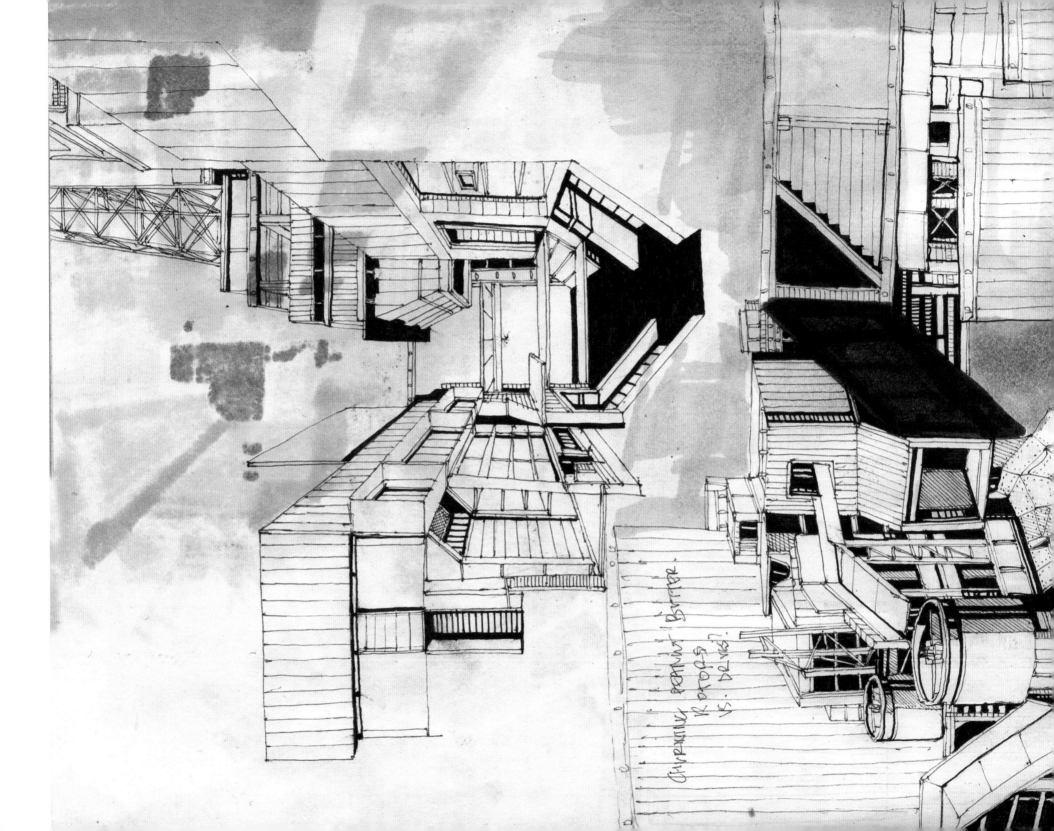

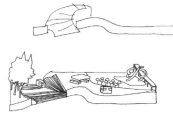
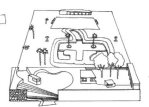

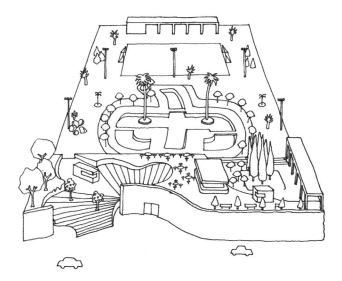
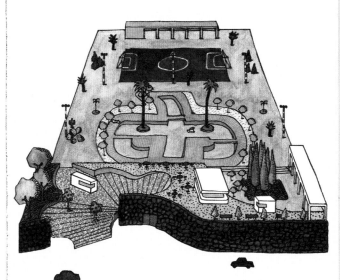

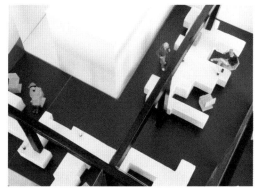

POINT SUPREME ARCHITECTS

Point Supreme Architects was founded in Rotterdam in 2007. Partners Konstantinos Pantazis and Marianna Rentzou were joined by Beth Hughes in 2009, and the practice is now based in Athens.

'We generally create collages to illustrate our ideas and physical models to test their application in space,' says Pantazis. 'We believe in the combination and use of opposing techniques. Each project demands work in different techniques and each type of illustration communicates differently. The simultaneous use of collage, model, sketch, painting and render for each of our projects offers the ultimate result.' Collages help the practice to be both abstract and precise at the same time, while physical models provide a fast volumetric result. 'These first moments and illustrations are the most critical ones. They are spontaneous and free from constraints, which is very liberating, and therefore carry the most creativity,' explains Pantazis.

Shown here is a design for a competition run by Benetton to design the company's headquarters [270], and sketches for the Emileon Sports Center, Agrinio, Greece [271]. On the following pages Point Supreme sets out a manifesto for 'greening' Athens [272–73] and, a reworking of the Eiffel Tower for a competition in Dubai [274–75].

'All the subsequent design adjustments that come from refinement and development are constantly evaluated against the first illustration. There is a give-and-take process between the imaginary, which is extracted from the first illustration, and the real, which is dictated by the constraints [such as limitations imposed by materials and budget, and by the physical site]. Given that the power of the first impulsive idea is usually unbeatable, the success of the design is dependent on how close we can stay to the very first illustration,' says Pantazis. 'However, projects gain richness and depth through development so the translation of the initial illustration into reality does not have to be literal, it is important to capture the intent and energy of the initial moves.'

271

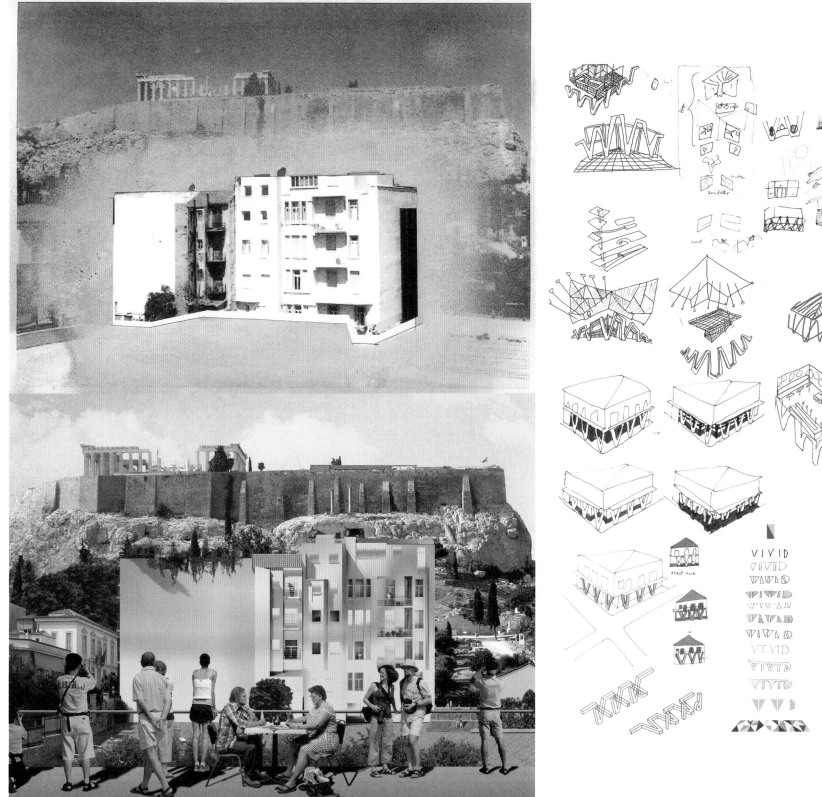

PAUL RAFF

Paul Raff calls his sketches 'gestural drawings' and it is easy to see why. These crude doodlings could not be easily turned into built form. However, they do show the first inklings of a design idea; the almost primitive marks of an architect doing what his instinct tells him.

'My gestural drawings often show not a building form but a flow or connection or other physical idea of some sort,' says Raff. 'They open up imaginative possibilities rather than locking them down. Sketches of details have been seminal to many of the innovations in my projects. I have often had younger architects working with me who think it's crazy to be drawing construction details when we don't have plans or massing worked out. They eventually see how it drives deeper to thoroughly thought-through architectural designs.'

From these initial sketches Raff expects to have a strong sense of direction, a feel for the driving forces of a project. He says he also lets things evolve in an open-minded way throughout the process, expecting it to develop considerably from the first sketches.

'When a specific project poses significant geometric challenges, which they often do, we are quick to use computer drafting and modelling to explore them,' says Raff. 'However, we also like sketching and rough little physical models to express ideas, especially because it's inspiring to have them sitting around the studio as we work.'

Raff explains that later, 'All our sketches and drawings are archived. Our models kick around the studio for years till they eventually fall apart.'

277

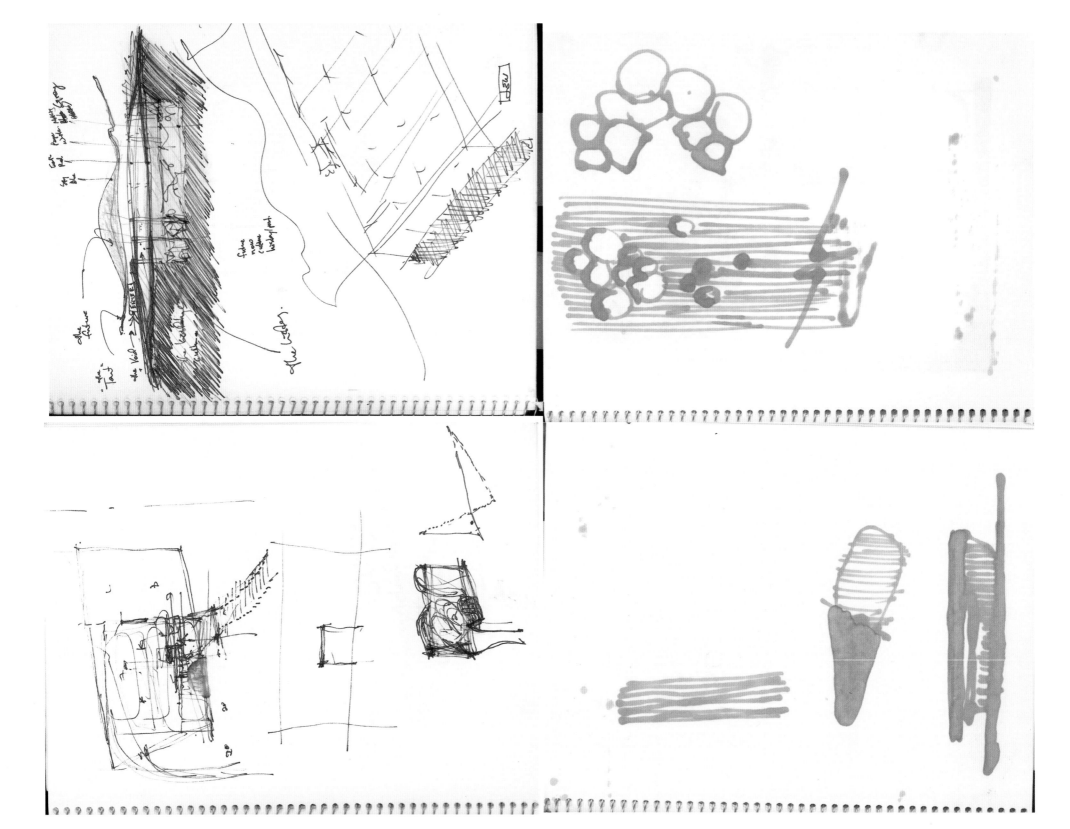

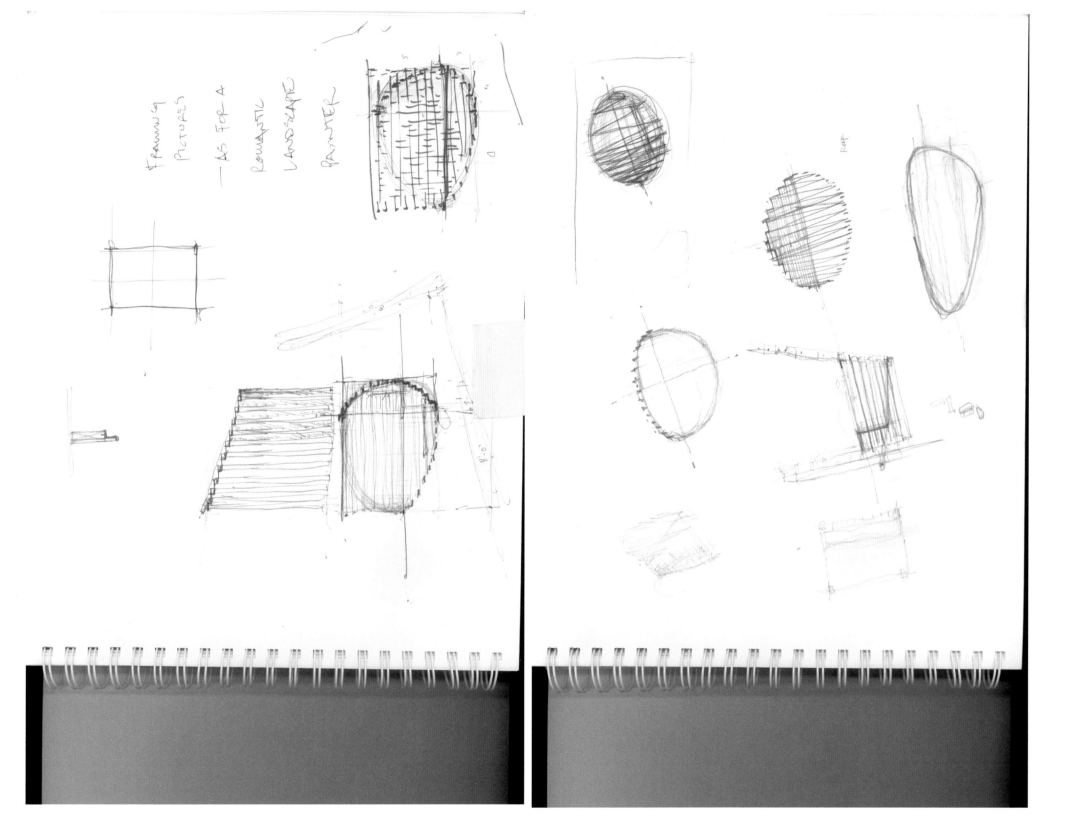

FRAMING
PICTURES

— AS FOR A
ROMANTIC
LANDSCAPE
PAINTER

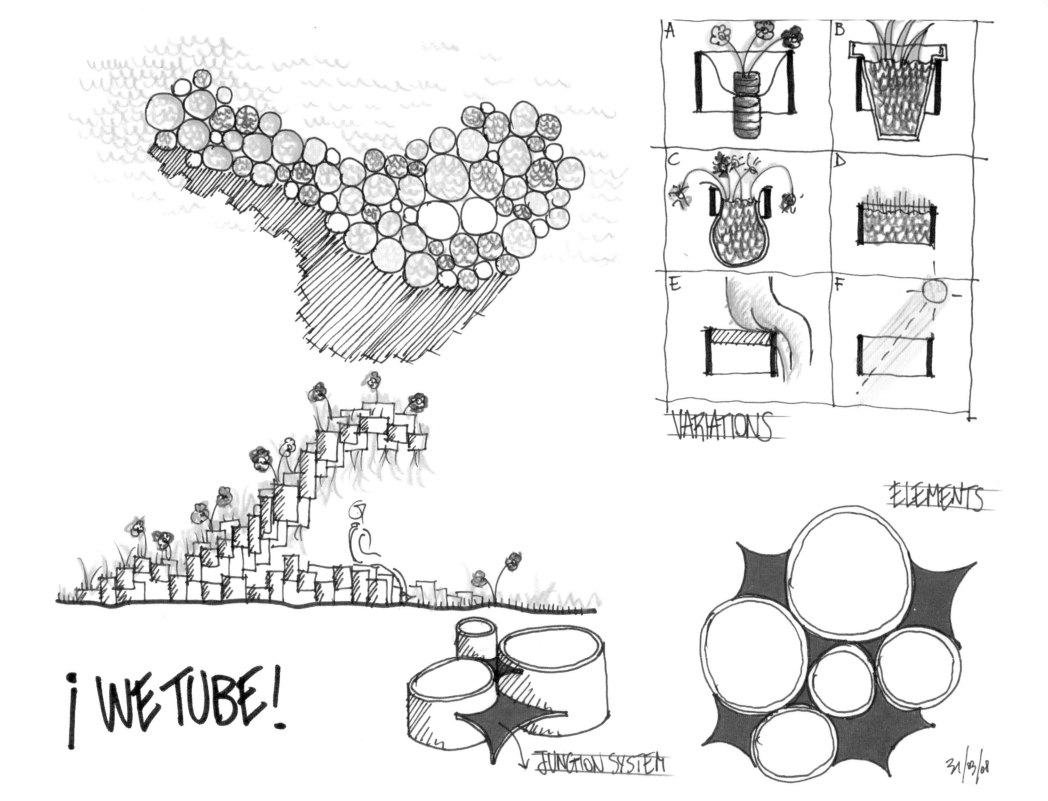

¡ WE TUBE !

JUNCTION SYSTEM

VARIATIONS

A   B
C   D
E   F

ELEMENTS

31/03/08

CARLO RATTI

Established in Turin, carlorattiassociati is strongly connected with partner Carlo Ratti's research programme at the Massachusetts Institute of Technology, and makes the connection between digital technology and architecture one of its main focuses.

This fascination with all things digital, however, does not preclude Ratti and his associates from using simple sketches to advance their ideas. 'If it is true that, as Mies [van der Rohe] said, "Architecture is the will of an epoch translated into space,"' says Ratti, 'we would use the following time / design line: zeitgeist → idea → concept sketch → diagram sketch → design sketch → design maquette → design → space. This line contains many feedback loops, hence we feel the process allows us to translate an idea into physical form and constantly go back to our initial hypotheses.'

The practice starts by discussing concepts for projects and then uses diagrams and sketches to illustrate them. 'We expect to get rather close to the final design in our sketch concepts,' says Ratti. 'Probably 80% of our original design sketches get carried through to the completed design.

'However, from the architectural point of view, one of the main issues after the digital revolution is the way in which the design process is influenced by new technologies. We say: "La civilisation digitale cherche et trouve son expression architecturale" [The digital civilization seeks and finds its architectural expression] (apologies to Le Corbusier).

'The answer? Augmented Architecture—the field of architecture of Augmented Reality—a concept that has grown up over the last fifteen years to suggest interconnections between the digital world and the real one.' Ratti's Augmented Architecture calls into question the traditional processes of architecture, working above all on themes such as reconfigurability and interactivity. It is comforting to know that he still works towards these goals using sketches. Here, designs for a study entitled We Tube [280–81], while over the page is a design for the Cloud, a lit observation deck for the 2012 Olympics, in London [282–83].

281

woon.
eind dag.

ROCHA TOMBAL

'In our office we enjoy freedom of expression. During a brainstorm people use the technique they prefer to express themselves,' says Ana Rocha, of Rocha Tombal. 'Myself, I am not a computer person. I studied architecture at a time when we had to be able to hand draw everything. We were forbidden to use computer drawing for presentations because "the computer didn't think."'

Rocha believes that when you sketch you come into intense contact with the space. 'The dream, still floating in your mind, comes out entirely through your hand.' By drawing you discover the challenges of the project—and projects such as the transformation of a water tower into living space [284 top, 285] require thinking through thoroughly.

'We draw in order first to discover the problems, before we start working on the solutions,' she says. 'Doing this by hand, not only through a plan but especially through a perspectival drawing, connects you to all stages, from dream to solution, from conceptual space to detailed space, all in one single thought.' (See various illustrations of housing schemes [284 bottom, 285–86, 287 bottom]).

'I often see young architects drawing plans systematically with the help of the computer, but not thinking "in" the space they are designing. Those I call drawings without a soul, without their own life.'

Rocha Tombal uses digital technology to achieve quick results, but specifically for production drawings. 'Often architects are forced to "produce" fast plans, a façade, sections, technical drawings etc.,' says Rocha, 'but there's no time for connecting those elements together as one work. That's the moment where hand sketching can really improve the sensibility of the design, and give a new chance to experiment.'

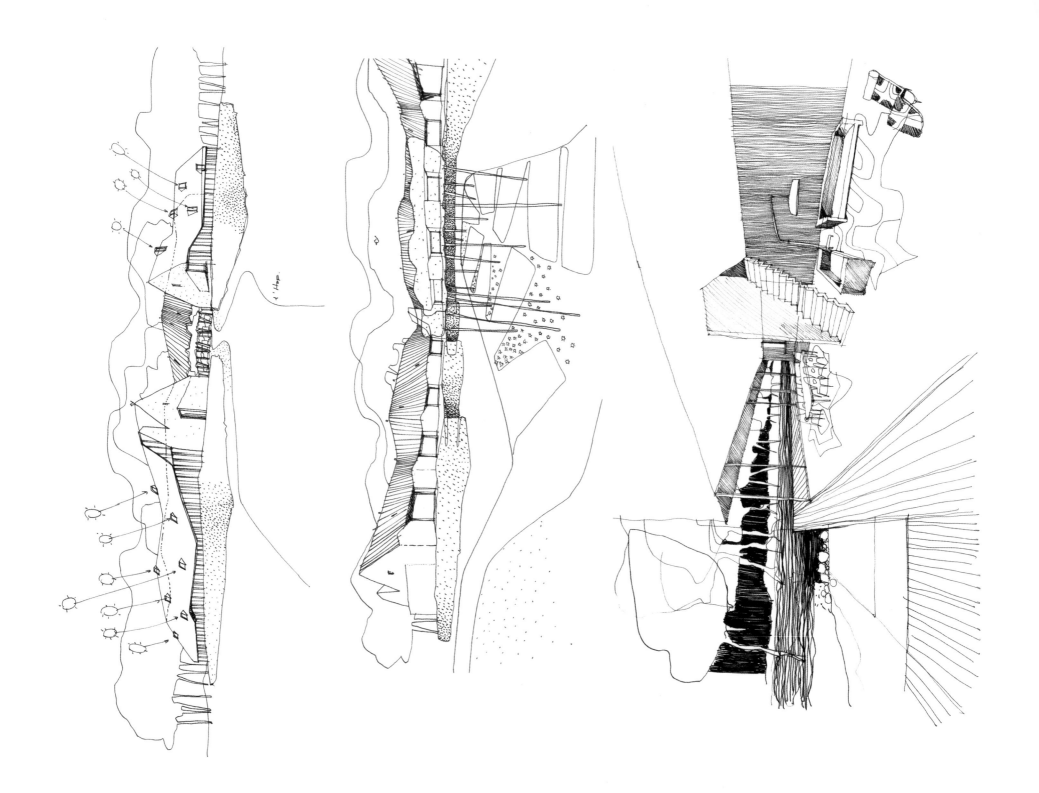

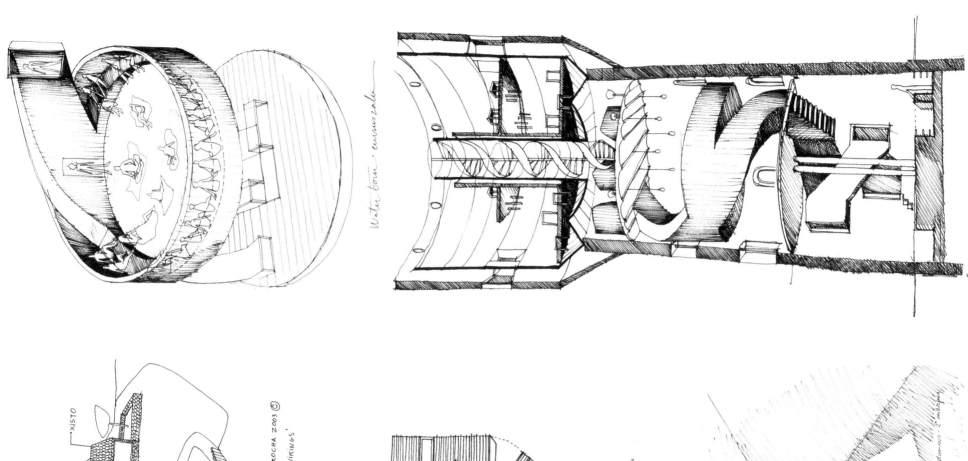

Water tower · concar^{...}

ANA ROCHA 2003 ©
'THE VIKINGS'

ANA ROCHA 2003 ©
'ZINC MONOLITH'

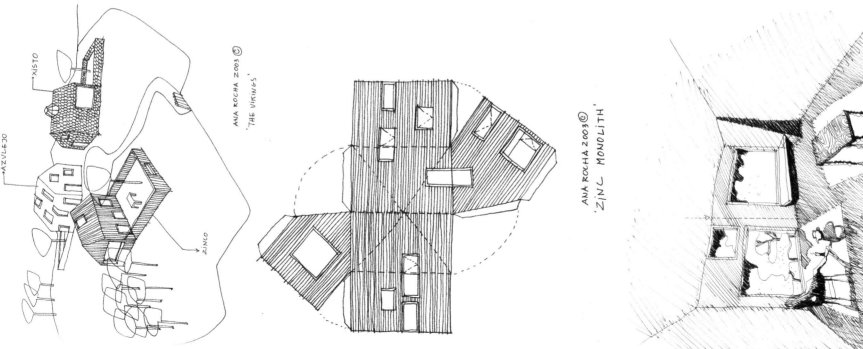

XISTO

AZULEJO

ZINCO

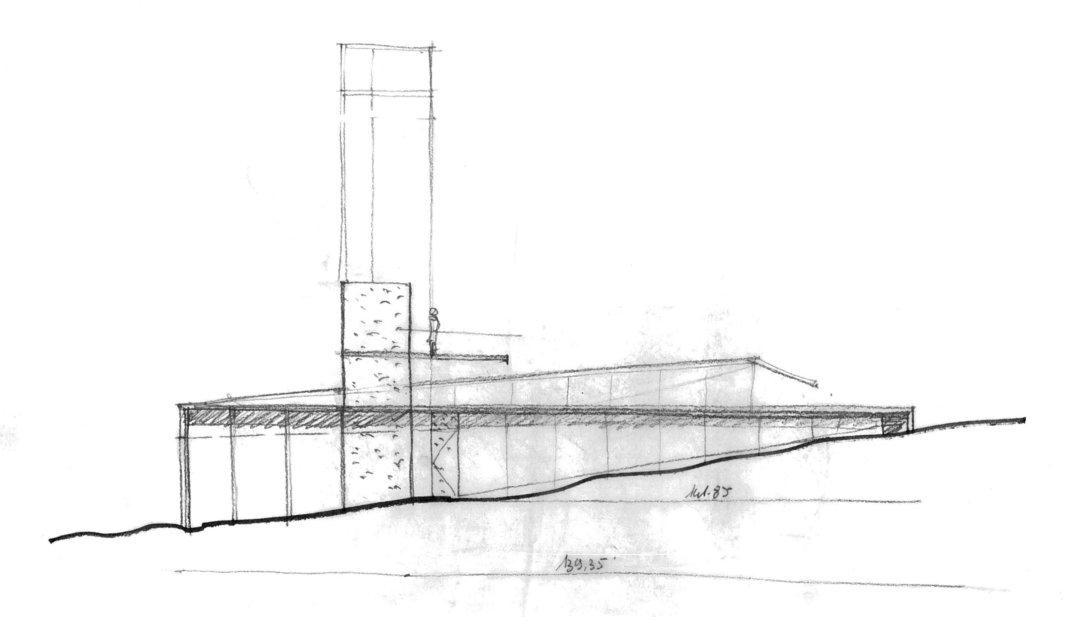

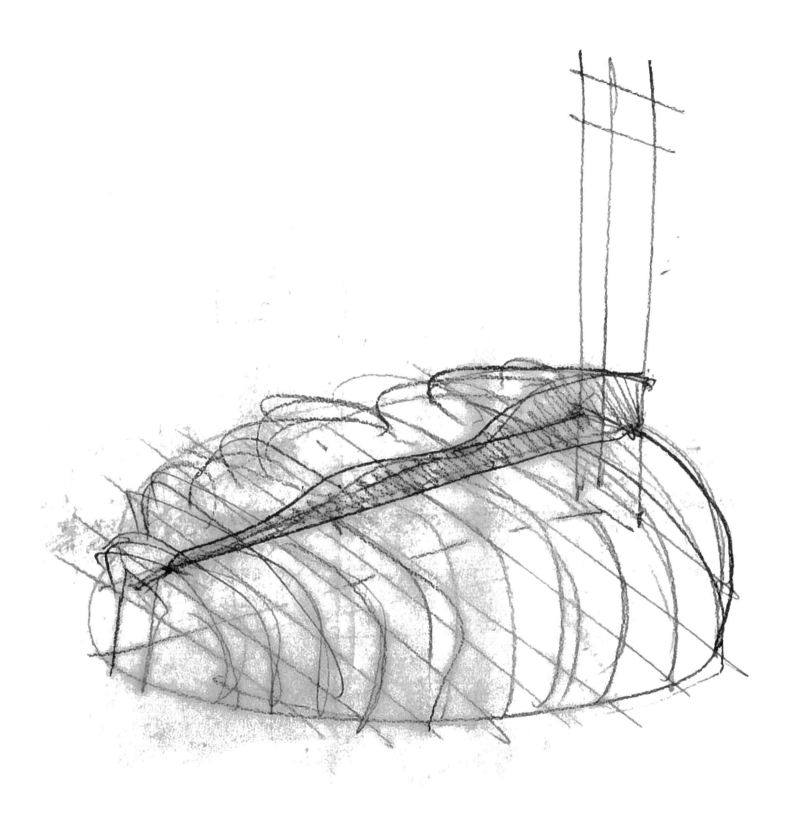

MARC ROLINET

'I put on a wall the different photos of the site, images, feelings (sketches or texts made on-site) and then I brainstorm with my team,' says Marc Rolinet, founder of Rolinet & Associés. 'Here, many small sketches and some small paper models are created.

'I then isolate myself, go to the mountains or somewhere else quiet, to select the main ideas and make draft drawings with simulations of spaces and volumes. I have to put myself inside the spaces, inside the building to feel the project. If I can't feel the spaces, the light, the interaction that I established as fundamental when I was on the site, we start all over again, and again, and again.

If satisfied with the initial concept, Rolinet starts a second phase of the debate with his team, with all drawings, sample materials, etc. surrounding them. 'I believe that the computer should be used only as a support to handmade drawings. And, during these initial stages I don't accept drawings made using computers because they limit the creative process.'

As the concept is so thoroughly explored (it probably takes longer than any other part of a Rolinet project) moving the design on from this point is relatively simple. 'It's the testing process that takes a lot of time. It's the fun part. It's when we try to formalize one thought, one feeling or a storm of ideas,' he says.

'For me, the phase of conception is never complete because we are creating, doing sketches and even small models of construction details, spaces, or sometimes furniture, all the time. This is the beauty of design.'

Sketches featured are of the Chapelle des Diaconesses, Versailles [288–89], and a Lisbon office building [290–91].

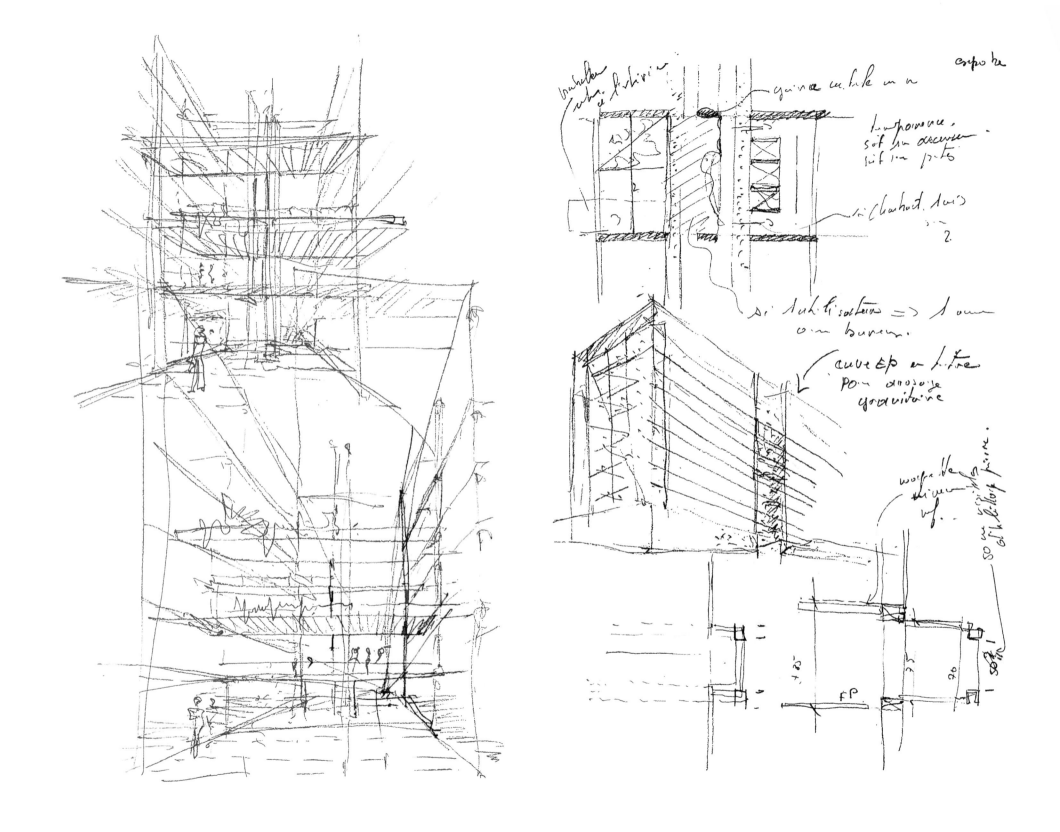

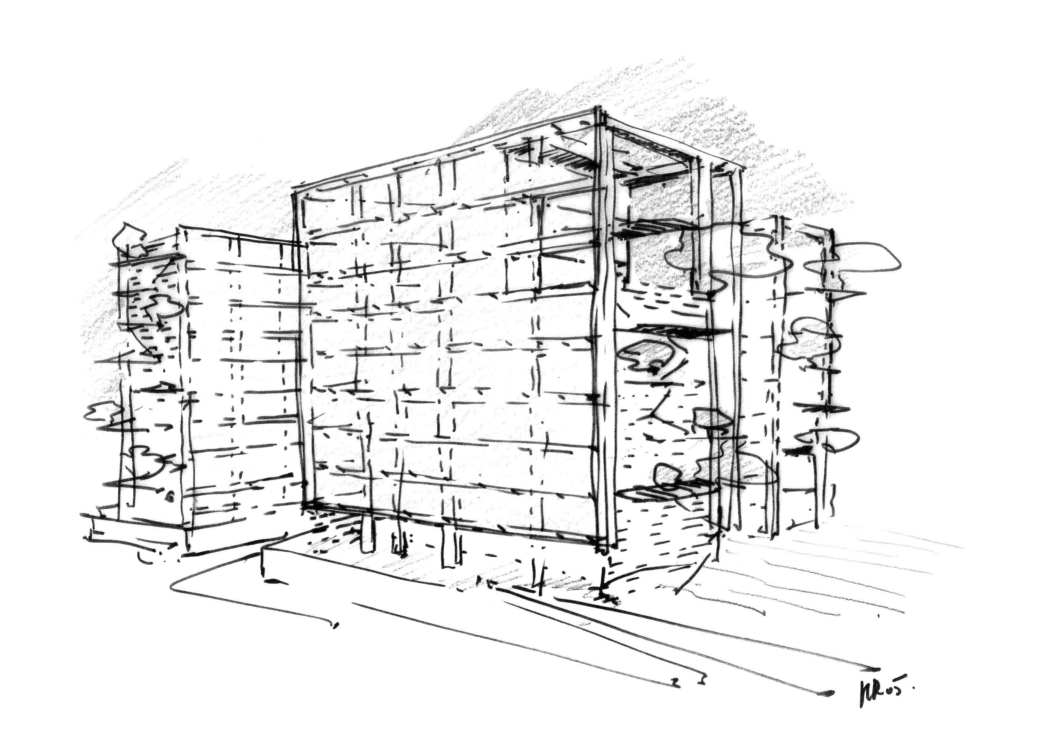

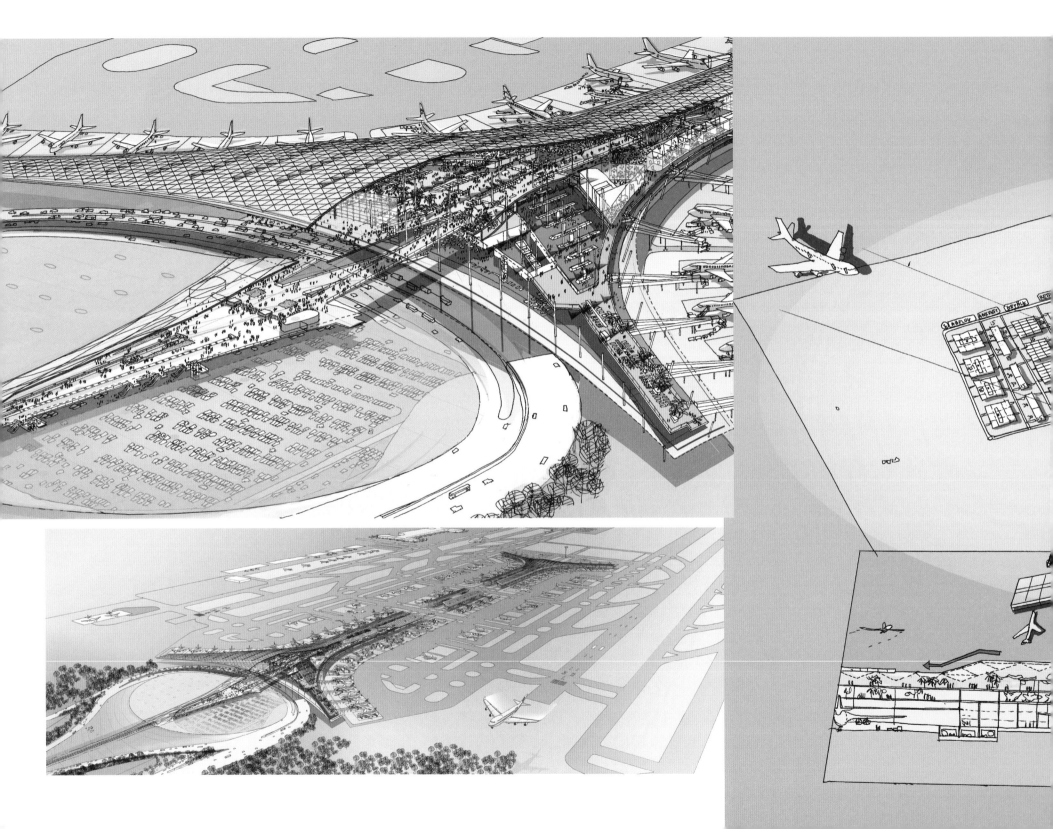

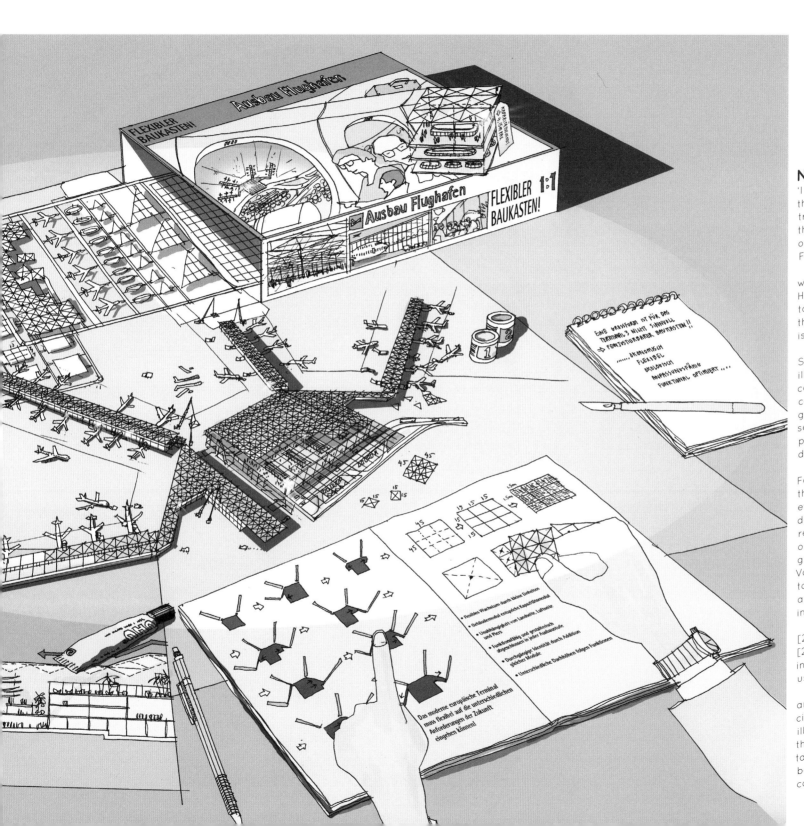

NARINDER SAGOO

'I carry a pen wherever I go. I draw on anything, anywhere—but I do like drawing on tracing paper, which comes in rolls and is the cheapest and least precious material in our studio,' says Narinder Sagoo, partner at Foster + Partners.

Norman Foster once asked Sagoo why he drew on this throwaway material. His answer: that it removed any pressure to produce a work of art. 'It relieves you of thinking about how to draw, and so the mind is focused on what to draw.

'I believe drawing is a language. Sometimes sketches are a "quick chat", an illustration of a thought or a discussion over coffee, and sometimes they are longer, more considered dialogues—more like paragraphs than sentences,' says Sagoo. 'In that sense sketches weave throughout the design process, informing decisions, direction and discourse in many ways.'

Drawing takes on various guises in the Foster studio—a reflection of the changes that architects see year on year. 'I still draw every day, but often those drawings are developed by my colleagues into digital renderings and paintings,' says Sagoo. 'As our projects increasingly spread across the globe, the way we communicate changes. Various parts of the world respond differently to the way we traditionally express ideas as architects—Americans like sketches, clients in China generally want CGIs.'

Here, Sagoo's drawings of Beijing Airport complement his 'Airport as a Kit' sketch [292]. Over the page, one of Sagoo's drawings has been coloured up by a colleague, using digital painting techniques [294–95].

'We have a responsibility to study and think about cultural and historical associations, and the social context of graphic illustration. We then respond accordingly. If that means we have to let go of our personal tastes and the norms we are used to then so be it. I think this strengthens our ability to communicate through drawing.'

293

10

always in the shade

Walking to the forest Retreat

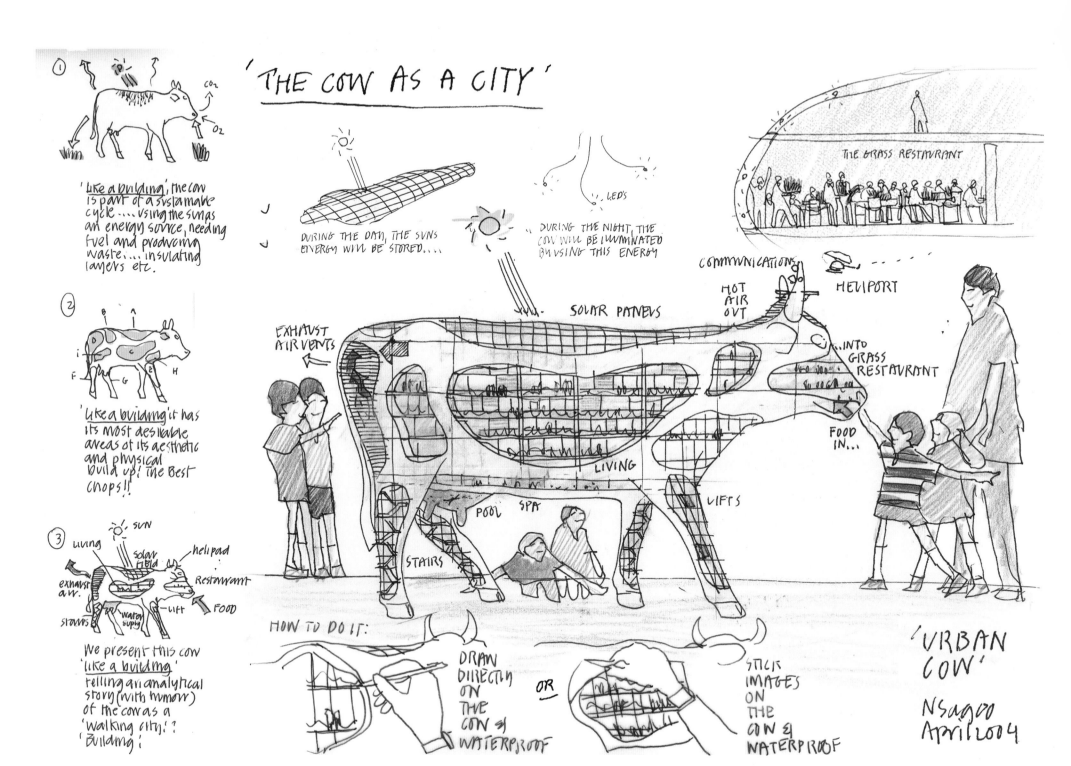

'THE COW AS A CITY'

1 'like a building', the cow is part of a sustainable cycle.... using the sun as an energy source, needing fuel and producing waste.... insulating layers etc.

2 'like a building' it has its most desirable areas of its aesthetic and physical build up! The Best chops!!

3 We present this cow 'like a building' telling an analytical story (with humour) of the cow as a 'walking city'! ? 'building'!

sun
living
solar field
helipad
exhaust air
Restaurant
stairs
water supply
lift
FOOD

DURING THE DAY, THE SUNS ENERGY WILL BE STORED....

LED'S

DURING THE NIGHT THE COW WILL BE ILLUMINATED BY USING THIS ENERGY

THE GRASS RESTAURANT

SOLAR PANELS

COMMUNICATIONS
HOT AIR OUT
HELIPORT
...INTO GRASS RESTAURANT
FOOD IN...

EXHAUST AIR VENTS

LIVING
LIFTS
POOL   SPA
STAIRS

HOW TO DO IT:

DRAW DIRECTLY ON THE COW & WATERPROOF

OR

STICK IMAGES ON THE COW & WATERPROOF

'URBAN COW'

Nsagoo
April 2004

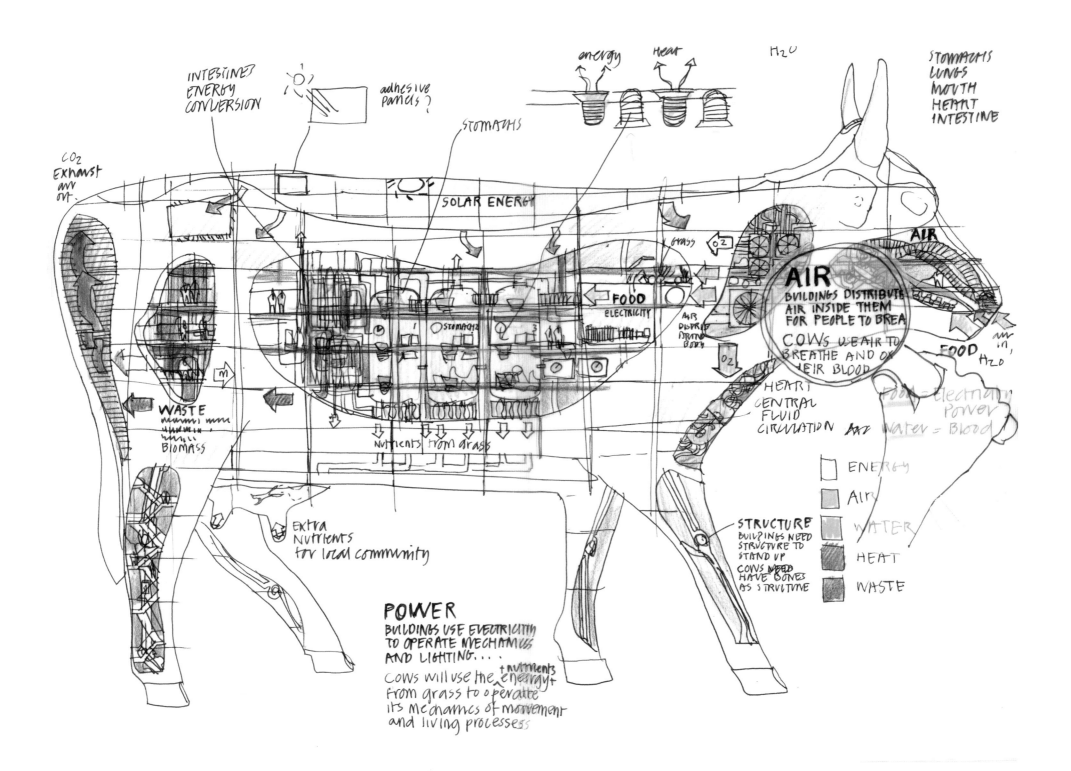

INTESTINES
ENERGY
CONVERSION

adhesive
panels?

energy   Heat H_2O

STOMACHS
LUNGS
MOUTH
HEART
INTESTINE

STOMACHS

CO_2
Exhaust
air
out.

SOLAR ENERGY

grass   O2

AIR

AIR
BUILDINGS DISTRIBUTE
AIR INSIDE THEM
FOR PEOPLE TO BREA
COWS USE AIR TO
BREATHE AND O
IEIR BLOOD

FOOD
ELECTRICITY

STOMACH 2

AIR
DISTRI
BUTING
BODY

O2

FOOD
H_2O

WASTE

BIOMASS

HEART
CENTRAL
FLUID
CIRCULATION

Food=Electricity
Power

Air   Water = Blood

Nutrients from grass

ENERGY

Air

WATER

HEAT

WASTE

Extra
Nutrients
for local community

STRUCTURE
BUILDINGS NEED
STRUCTURE TO
STAND UP
COWS NEED
HAVE BONES
AS STRUCTURE

POWER
BUILDINGS USE ELECTRICITY
TO OPERATE MECHANICS
AND LIGHTING....
COWS WILL USE the +nutrients+
energy
from grass to operate
its mechanics of movement
and living processes

After Focus 9.
20 July 2004

KEN SHUTTLEWORTH

Ken Shuttleworth has been passionate about buildings for as long as he can remember. Nicknamed 'Ken the Pen' at university, he uses sketching as a means of continually refining and exploring his ideas and expressing them to others.

'When I was studying at Leicester Polytechnic people called me that. I used to do twice as many drawings as anybody else so they used to say I had water-cooled pens, because I drew very fast.'

Shuttleworth has sketched some of the world's most recognizable recent buildings, including Barcelona's Collserola communications tower, Chek Lap Kok Airport in Hong Kong, the Swiss Re building in London (popularly called the Gherkin) and one of Europe's tallest skyscrapers, the Commerzbank tower in Frankfurt. Sketches featured here are of new designs for the Kings Reach Building, London [299] and details for the Kite Tower, Leeds [298].

Shuttleworth formed Make in 2004, and has since assembled around him a team of talented architects who can work well with him. 'Architects are trained to be individuals, they're trained to be artists. But in reality you can't do it on your own. It has to be done as part of a team.

'I always wanted to be an architect, right from childhood. I was always fascinated by it. I used to draw houses and castles and that sort of thing from the age of 5 or 6.'

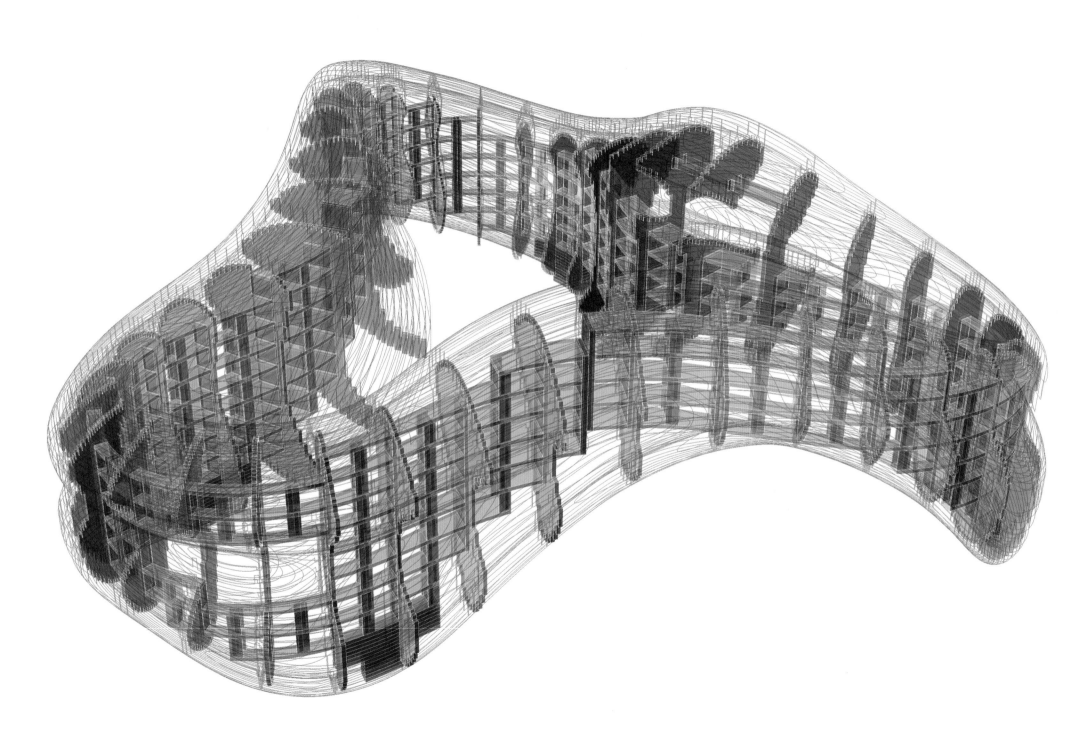

DANECIA SIBINGO

Younger than many of the other architects in this book, Architectural Association student Danecia Sibingo is one of a new generation of truly computer-literate designers, who see the use of intelligent software as a means of composing ever more exciting and unusual architectural proposals.

For this particular project, Driftwood Pavilion [300–01], Sibingo created the concept using a computer-generated script, which manipulated the movement of lines in a continuous parallel fashion, resulting in beautiful drawings that were used to form the final plan.

'My interests revolved around carving, eroding and layering on this project,' says Sibingo. 'Inspired by images of the Jordanian city of Petra, I sought to achieve a sensuous and overwhelming spatial effect. And by scripting I felt I had better control of what I wanted to create and achieve.'

Sibingo's scripted line drawings were subsequently modelled in the design program Rhino, where the project's sculptural and architectural affinity with driftwood was enhanced. 'The fluidity and undulation of the lines brought a feeling of curiosity, journey and discovery within the sculpture's spatial parameters,' says Sibingo.

Some of the imagery that went into designing Driftwood Pavilion has subsequently been shown at the end-of-year exhibition at the Architectural Association in London. Studies have also been sold at a contemporary design auction.

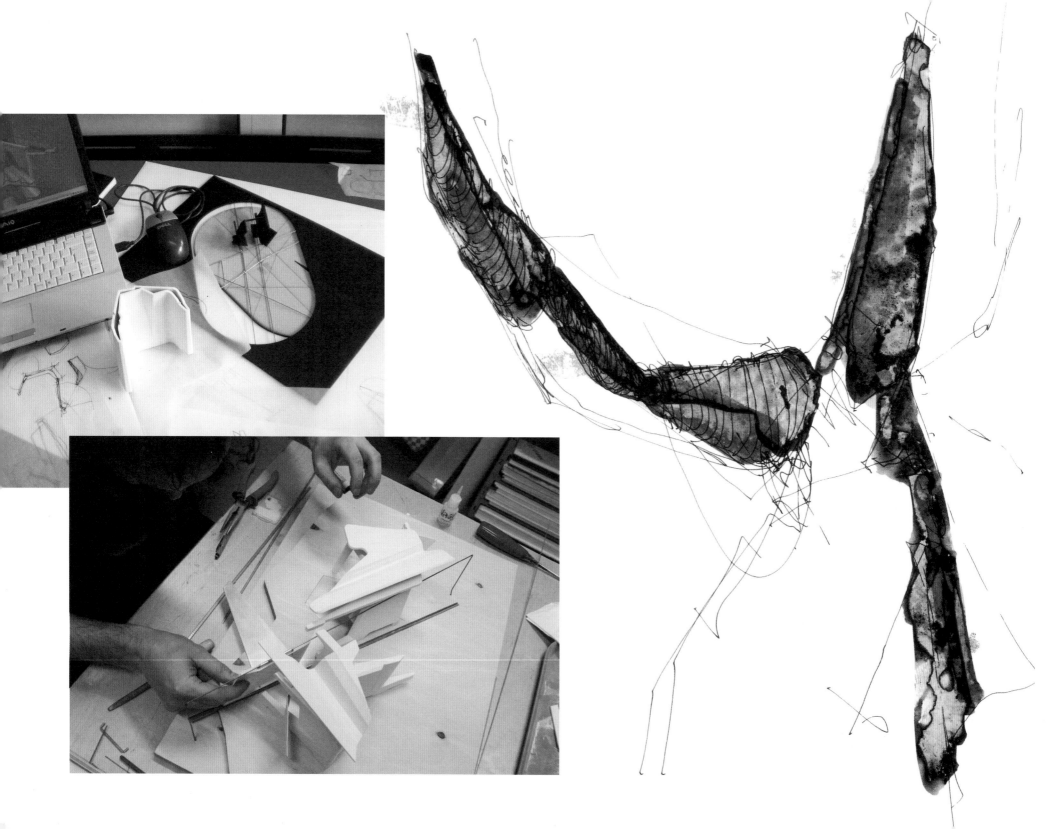

302-303
304-305

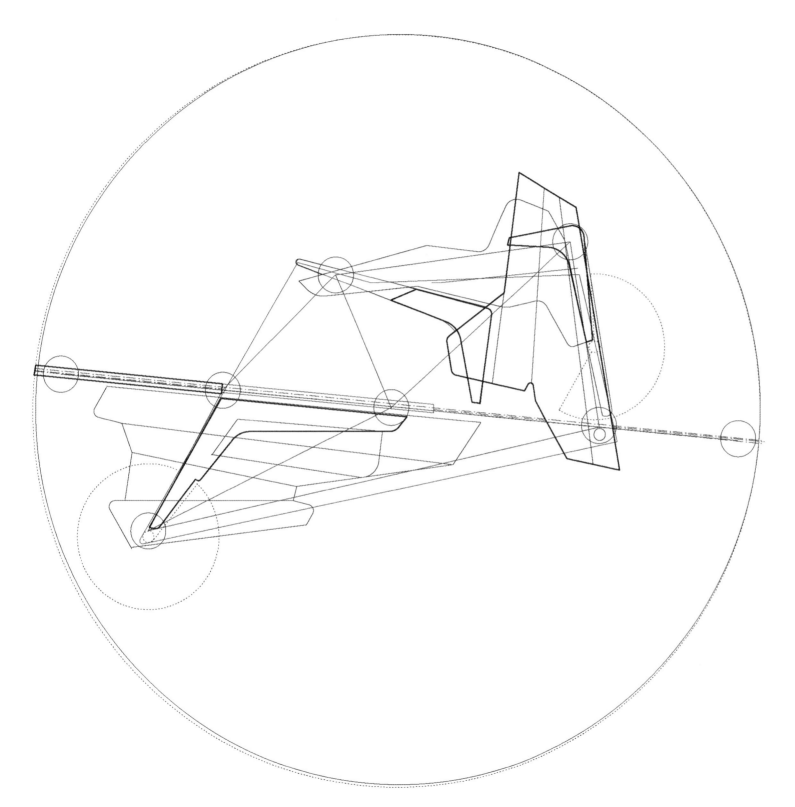

SIXTEEN*(MAKERS)

Sixteen*(makers) is a multidisciplinary practice that works at the threshold between the ideal and the real. Consisting of a group of academics (Phil Ayres, Chris Leung, Bob Sheil and Emmanuel Vercruysse) and one former student (Nick Callicott)—all from the Bartlett School of Architecture in London—the practice takes on design experiments that blur the boundaries between architecture and science.

'We enjoy architecture as a fluid and dynamic discipline, where a multitude of imposed and passive ingredients design its physical and tactile character,' explains Bob Sheil. 'Central to our method is the production of speculative prototypes to discover, evolve and adapt ideas, some of which begin as a hunch or curiosity.'

This experimental approach means that sixteen*(makers) works more like a manufacturer or product designer than a typical architectural practice. While sketches are part of the armoury, they sit alongside simplistic doodles, 3D models and scaled prototypes—all simultaneous experiments to solve a single challenge or problem. Shown here [302-05] is a selection of stages and tools employed during the design of 55/02, a shelter for the Keilder Water and Forest Park, Northumbria.

'We are great believers in the tacit knowledge that is acquired through working with materials and learning from experts,' says Sheil. 'In recent years we have developed an understanding of digital and analogue manufacturing processes, environmental behaviours, time-based realities, responsive systems and design that adapts to change.'

For more than two decades, the skills of the team at sixteen*(makers) have evolved through experimenting with techniques—from the handmade to the digitally crafted. Our attitude is often described by the phrase "design through making", a motto that says design does not end when making begins.'

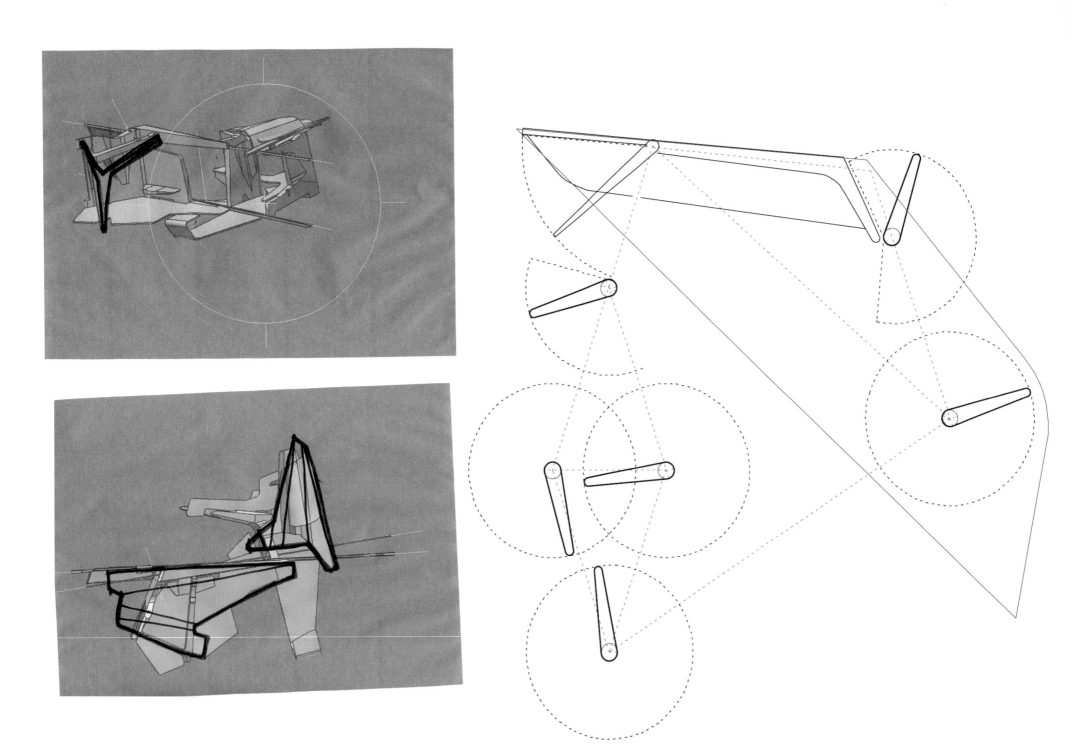

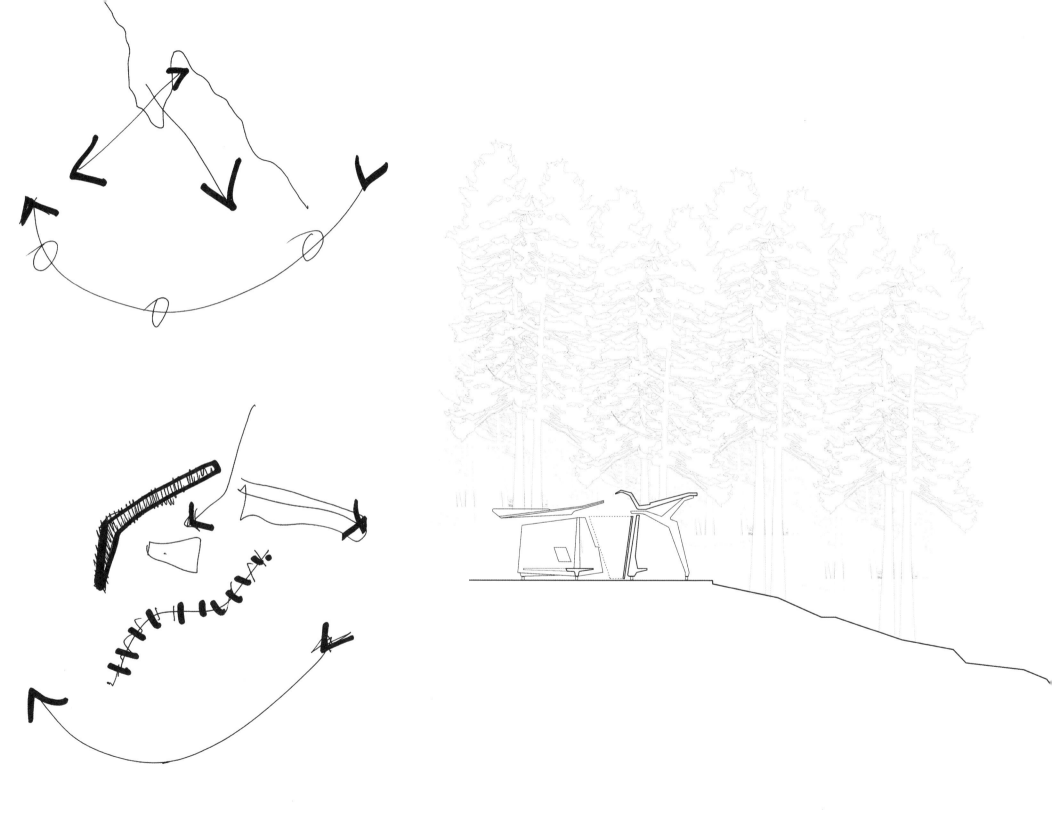

Manual

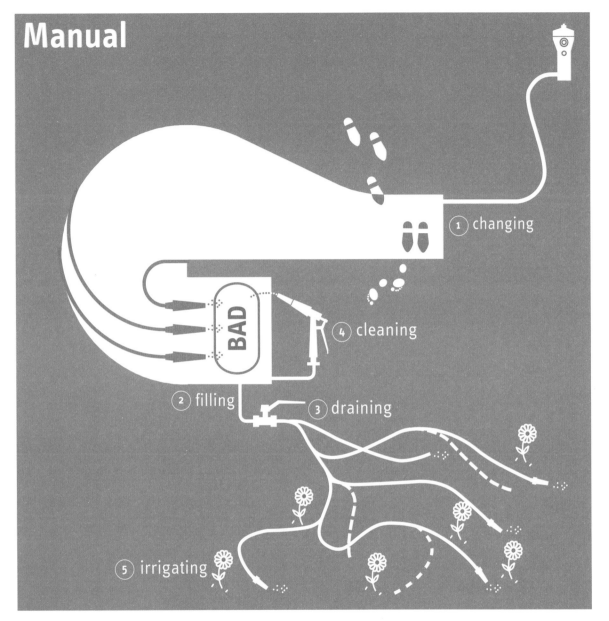

1. changing

2. filling

3. draining

4. cleaning

5. irrigating

BAD

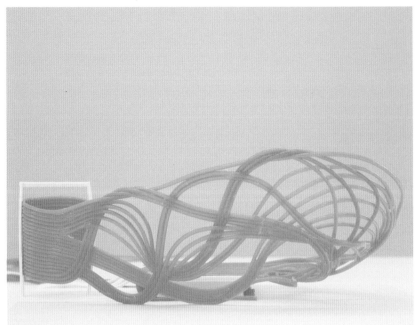

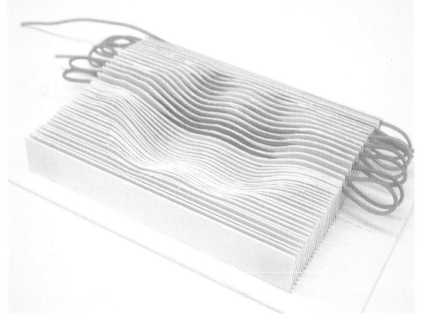

infrastructure

bath

natural resources

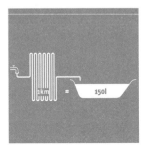

1km = 150l

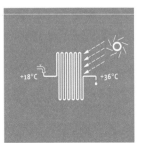

+18°C   +36°C

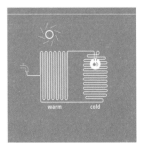

warm   cold

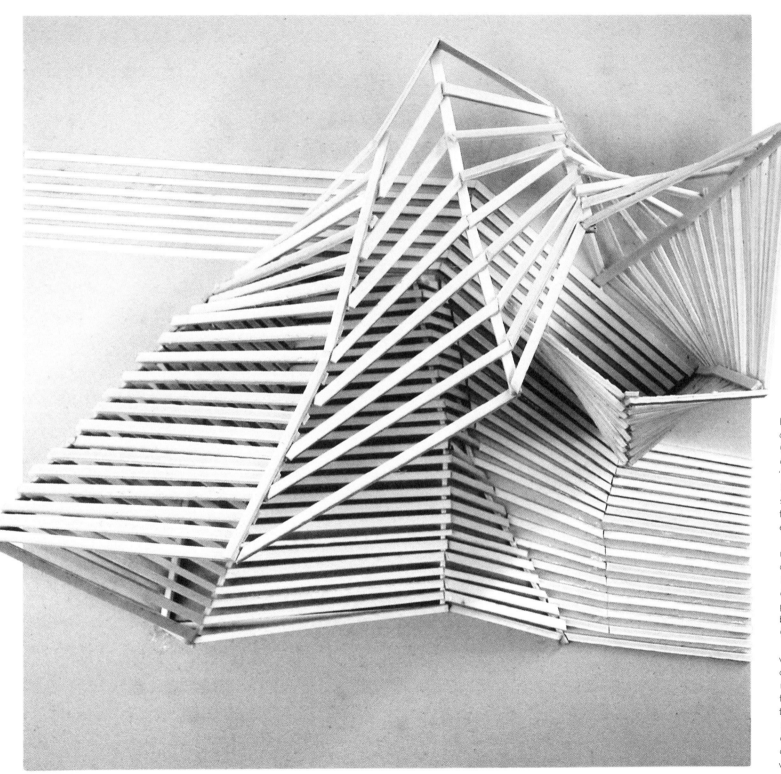

SMAQ

'Freehand sketches, on the one hand, allow for a very "haptical" and tactile approach to a site, on the other hand, they are a means to articulate early intuitions about a possible strategy,' says SMAQ partner Andreas Quednau.

'The pencil's flow makes the brain work. Models work along the same lines, though when adding the 3D aspect they are also a way to test and evaluate the first ideas.'

SMAQ uses a combination of free-hand sketches (see California project LA Water [308–09]), models, CAD-drawn diagrams and collages (see BAD(bath) [306–07]). The practice's diagrams work mainly on the 'conceptual sharpening' of a project. 'They may be drawn as manuals, as story-boards or as children's book illustrations,' says Quednau. 'Trying to tell the concept or the story to outsiders forces us to use different methods of storytelling.'

Quednau sees the various methods and media playing separate roles. 'The hand-drawn sketches may be a warm-up phase but, some lines detected by the initial "haptical" approach may become the spine of the project. The diagrams are a testing ground, but sometimes...point to the project's essence. Collages...unfold a narrative.'

As Quednau and his fellow architects work, he describes their output as 'a cloud of different ideas or scenes that will get connected and pushed further when drawing the paths, cycles or usages that connect them'. Collages then sum up and illustrate the project, they set the scene. 'Working on the collage means rounding up the story, from close-up material choices to far-reaching views into the urban context.'

307

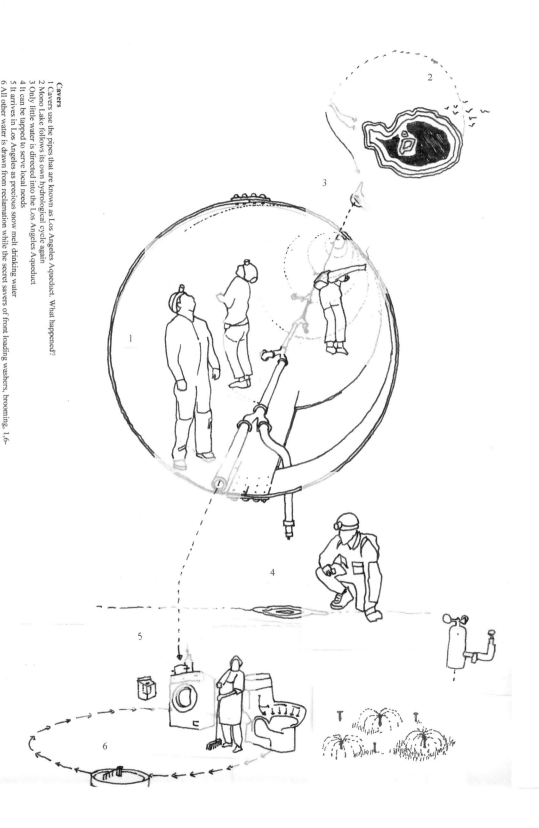

Cavers

1 Cavers use the pipes that are known as Los Angeles Aqueduct. What happened?
2 Mono Lake follows its own hydrological cycle again
3 Only little water is directed into the Los Angeles Aqueduct
4 It can be tapped to serve local needs
5 It arrives in Los Angeles as precious snow melt drinking water
6 All other water is drawn from reclamation while the secret savers of front loading washers, brooming, 1.6-gallon toilets, weather controled pattern sprinkling have reduced the flow to a reclamation manageable seize.

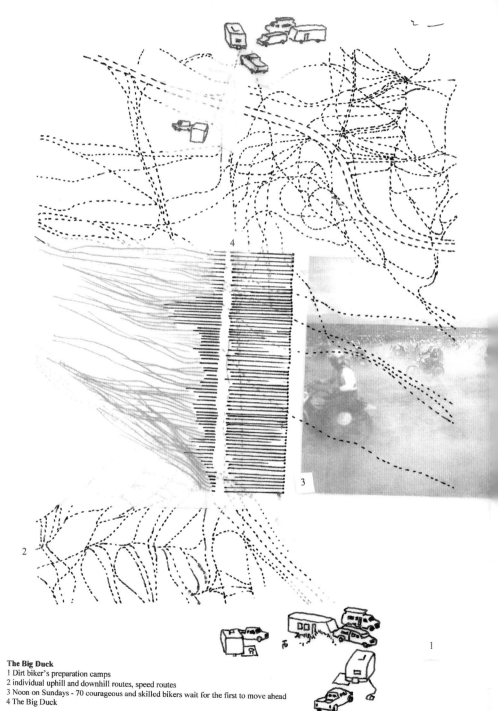

The Big Duck

1 Dirt biker's preparation camps
2 individual uphill and downhill routes, speed routes
3 Noon on Sundays - 70 courageous and skilled bikers wait for the first to move ahead
4 The Big Duck

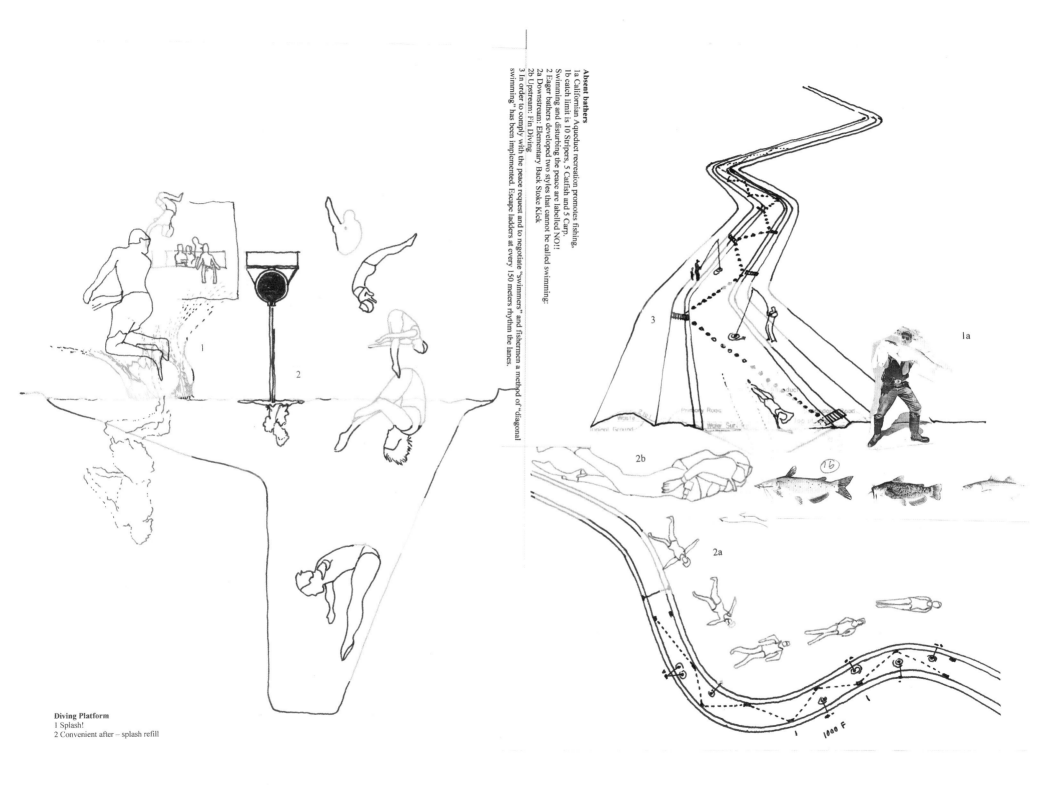

Absent bathers

1a Californian Aqueduct recreation promotes fishing,
1b catch limit is 10 Stripers, 5 Catfish and 5 Carp.
2 Eager bathers developed two styles that cannot be called NO!!
Swimming and disturbing the peace are labelled swimming:
2a Downstream: Elementary Back Stoke Kick
2b Upstream: Fin Diving
3 In order to comply with the peace request and to negotiate "swimmers" and fishermen a method of "diagonal swimming" has been implemented. Escape ladders at every 150 meters rhythm the lanes.

Diving Platform
1 Splash!
2 Convenient after – splash refill

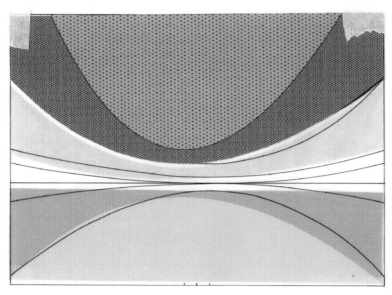

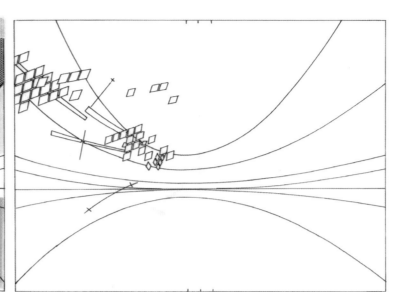

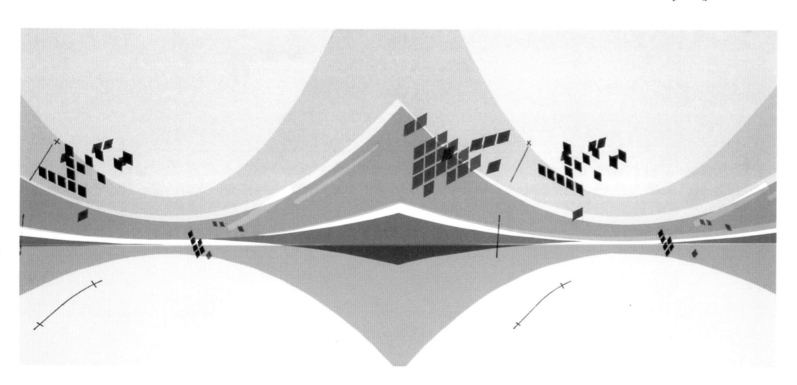

SMOUT ALLEN

Mark Smout and Laura Allen are lecturers at the Bartlett School of Architecture, University College, London. Their work follows two routes: architectural competitions, where the particular rigour of brief, site and programme provide the basis for new investigations, and conceptual design projects that test out the agenda and methodology of the design research practice.

Smout Allen focuses on the dynamic relationship between the natural and the man-made, and how this can be revealed to enhance the experience of the architectural landscape. 'Our work as teachers gives us the freedom to short cut the architectural process,' says Allen. 'And, quite often means that the sketch is the end result, not a means to further a design. As such, our sketches take on a whole new level of importance.'

Their theoretical work develops into beautiful and incredibly elaborate layered sketches that feature both historical and geographic representations, combined with architectural elements.

'Sketches can become very complex, overdrawn and reinterpreted' says Allen. 'This is my style. Mark tends to be more precise but we both like to explore the boundaries and possibilities of projects.

'With this in mind, our drawings aren't confined to methods of architecture,' explains Allen. 'They are used as a viewing device, rather than an encoded document that constructors will decipher.'

The pair constantly theorize about their works, filling notebooks, making models and doing technical drawings. Smout Allen's book Augmented Landscapes (2007) explains how they see the world—as a series of hybrid environments, a neo-nature that mankind continually manipulates [310–13].

311

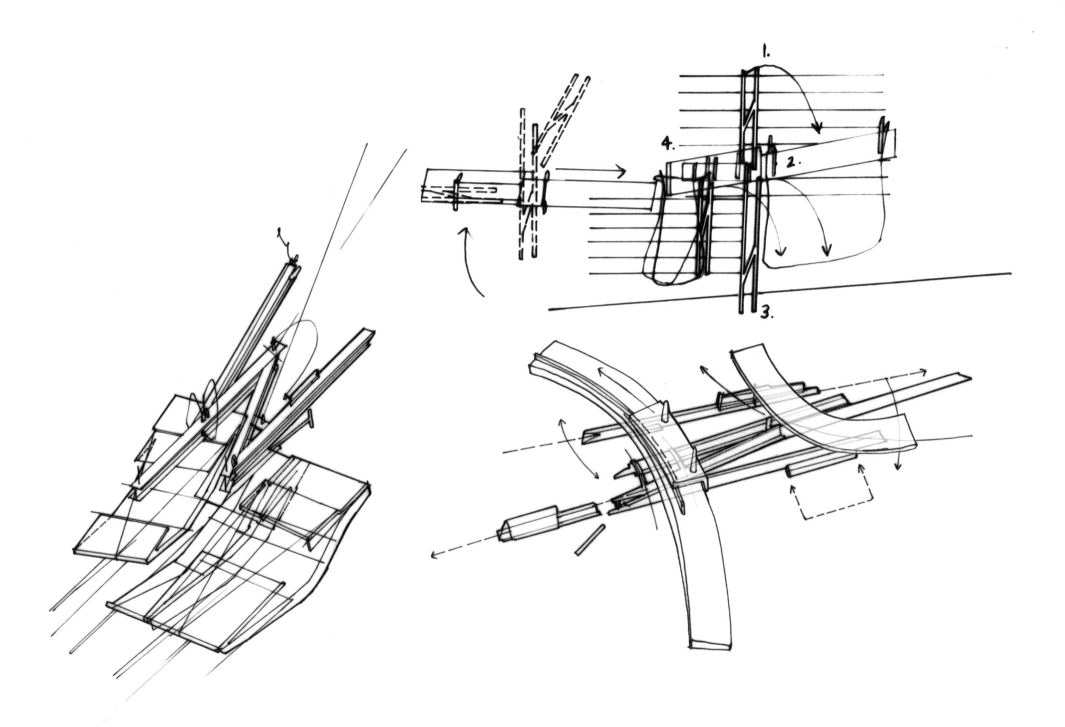

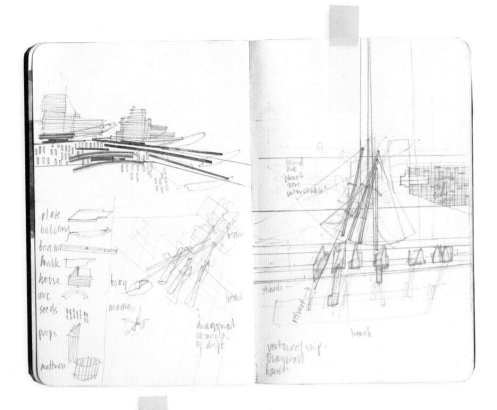

plate
balcony
beam
hulk
house
arc
seeds
props

buoy

marker

diagonal
at angle
of drift

vertical ship
Draysail
branch

matthew

trench

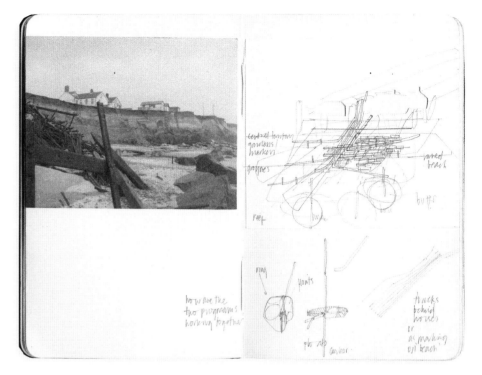

central torsion
cantilevers
markers

groynes

raised
beach

reef

butts

ring

boats

flip slip

anchor

how are the
two programmes
working together

tracks
behind
houses

or
as marking
up beach

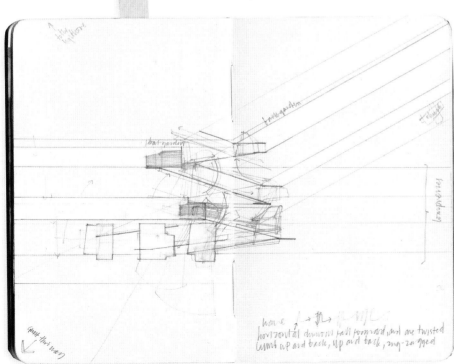

roof garden

boat garden

living dining

frame

horizontal columns fall forward and are twisted
climb up and back, up and back, zig-zagged

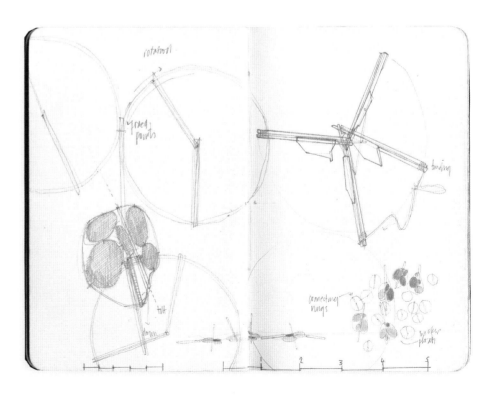

rotation

fixed
points

bending

tilt

connecting
rings

NEIL SPILLER

Neil Spiller is Professor of Architecture and Digital Theory at the Bartlett School, London and a practising architect. For the last ten years he has been working on a major theoretical project entitled _Communicating Vessels_, which now includes hundreds of sketches and drawings [314–17].

The project seeks to create new relationships between architecture, landscape, space, time, duration and geography. 'Such ideas produce a very rich, formal and surreal architectural language, bursting with potential,' says Spiller. 'The project is a speculation, through drawings and words, about the continuing impact of advanced technology on the future of architecture, particularly in relation to virtuality, remote sensing and biotechnology.'

Spiller sketches by hand at his drawing board. In fact, the board often appears within the images themselves, its marked and scalpel-scored surface being scanned through the paper and used as a backdrop to Spiller's surreal world.

Working predominantly in pen and ink, he often draws details of characters or mechanical entities, before digitally placing them onto manipulated backgrounds. Sketches are worked on for about 30 minutes at a time, but the drawings will often be built up of numerous elements superimposed upon one another over time.

'Once they're complete, I don't like to look at or consider the drawing in its raw state,' says Spiller. 'The combination of sketching and scanning material has impressed upon me the cleanliness of the digital world. I like to see my pictures as completed scanned images, like photographs. To view the actual drawings again is to relive the hours spent, the agonies of mistakes....'

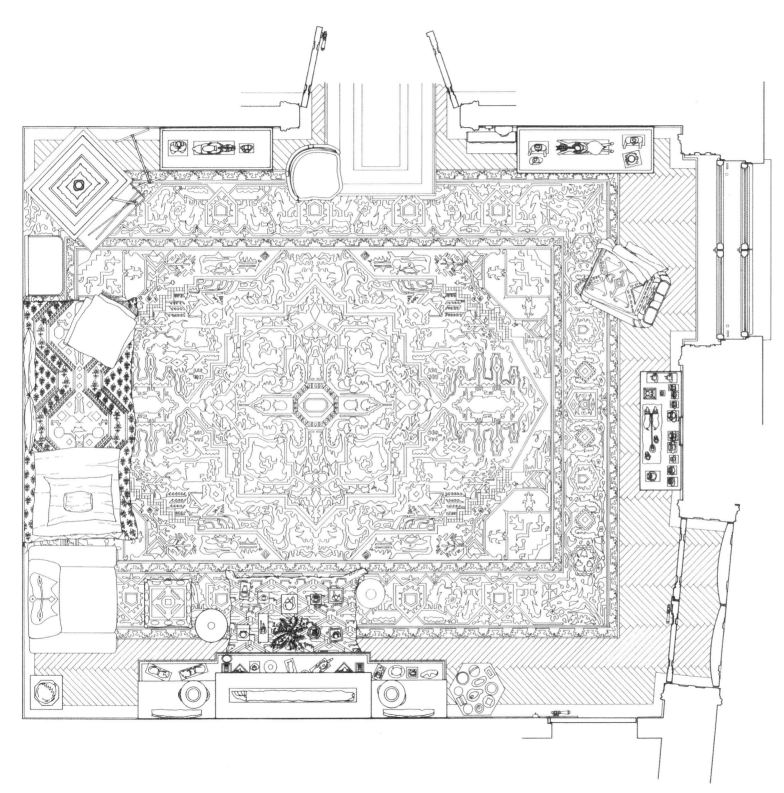

NATALIJA SUBOTINCIC

These images are a set of draft drawings that reconstruct Sigmund Freud's Consulting Room and Study at Berggasse 19 in Vienna, a space that no longer exists.

Natalija Subotincic, associate head and professor of Architecture at the University of Manitoba, Canada, was struck by the spatial nature of Freud's thinking as observed in his letters and drawings, and wanted to look into the actual spaces he inhabited. 'Freud collected over 2,300 antiquities and placed them in these two rooms—his working environment,' says Subotincic. 'Since these places constitute the founding space of psychoanalysis and are embedded with Freud's own psychical "constructions", it was my intention to draw the rooms to further study them.'

She drafted 1:10 scale drawings [318–21] of the walls of the bare rooms and then slowly began moving in all of the furnishings. Referencing various published catalogues of the Freud's collection and photographs of the rooms, Subotincic then placed each item on the appropriate shelf in the right room. Early under-drawings were freehand sketch constructions and were completed with coloured mylar leads.

'I found myself continually piecing together disparate parts in order to assemble and construct the whole. The process of "drawing", much more than simply scrutinizing a photograph, literally let me build my own relationship with the rooms and their contents. In effect, the drawings allowed me to enter into and wander around the rooms.

'I am currently involved in an in-depth reading and "interpretation" of the drawings. I hope to speculate upon the nature and meaning of the world Freud created within these rooms.'

319

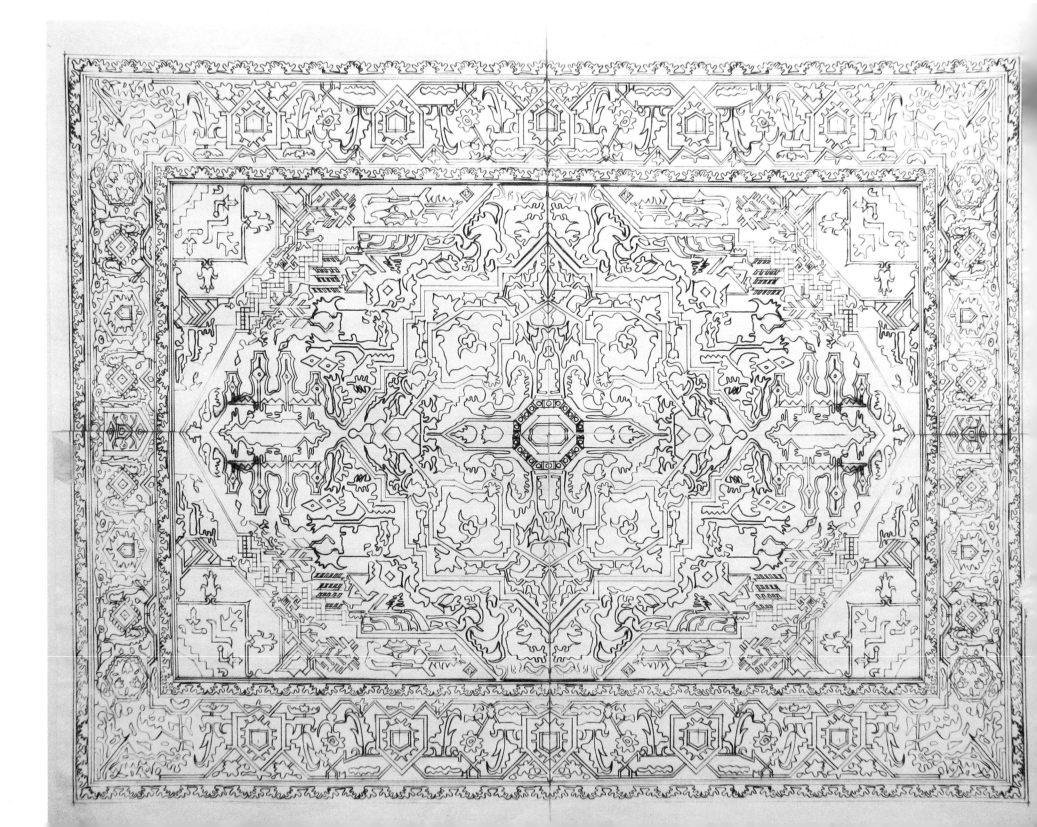

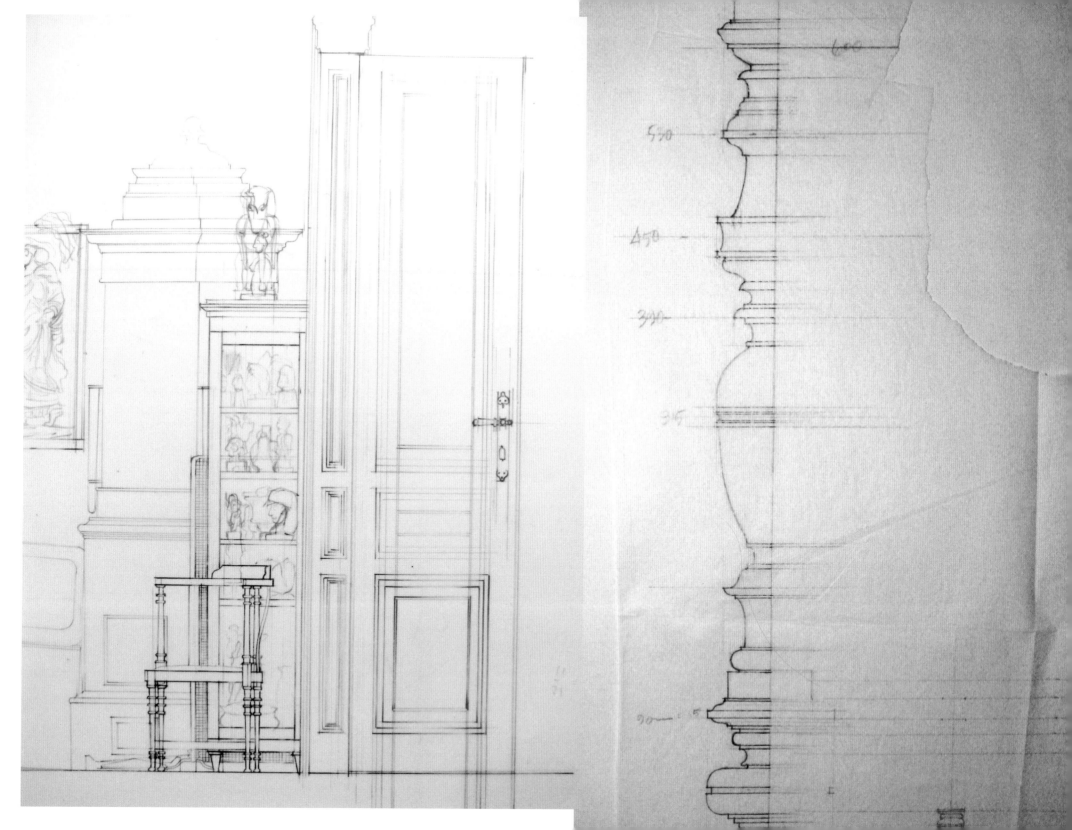

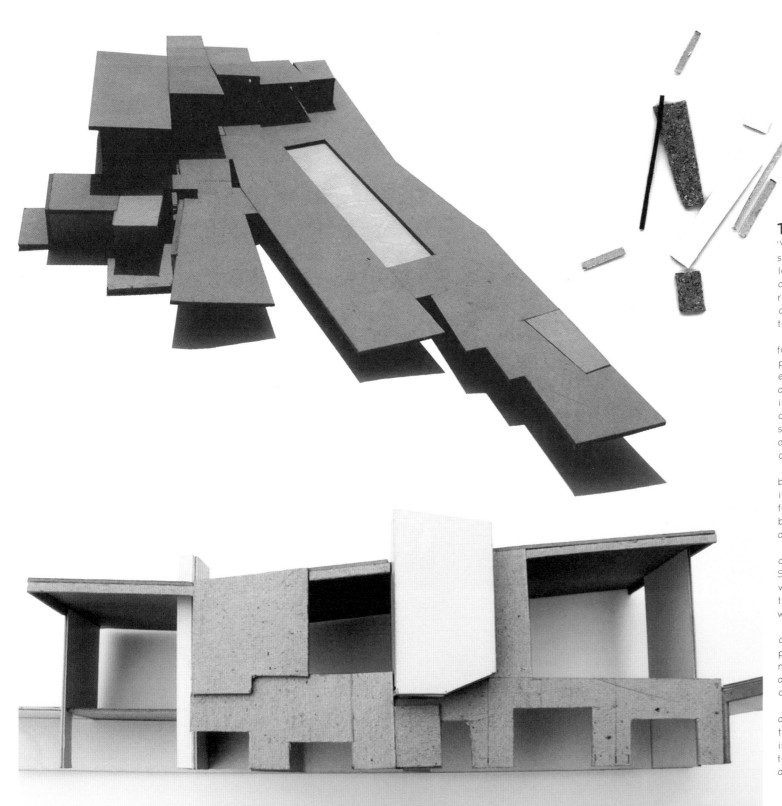

TOH SHIMAZAKI

'We aim to create timeless architecture by seeking spatial solutions, with integrity and lasting meaning for its users. You will find our designs imprint themselves on urban and rural locations, showing feeling for a location and its inhabitants,' say London-based architects Toh Shimazaki.

The practice uses different methods for initiating design, depending both on the project and how they, the designers, feel at each stage. Toh Shimazaki often work with a mixture of media and approaches, including collage, text, pencil sketches, hand- and computer-drawn perspective sketches and sketches manipulated with a scanner, as well as models manufactured from card, plaster and wood.

The OSh House, Surrey [322–23], has been modelled, sketched and collaged to interrogate and crystallize the design. On the following pages, three other projects have been treated differently in their conceptual design [324–25].

'These diverse methods make us discover ideas and/or specific details,' say Toh Shimazaki. 'We try not to know the result when we are designing initially. These methods take us to a place of unknown and discovery, which is very exciting.'

The practice believes initial sketches are never quite complete. As the project progresses ideas evolve. Drawings and models are used to keep the project's focus alive and as such each sketch, model or collage is an artefact in itself.

'As every design process is a journey of discovery, it is not necessarily about keeping the original design going till the end. Rather, it is more about working on an idea throughout to enrich the proposal. This carries on even after the completion of buildings.'

323

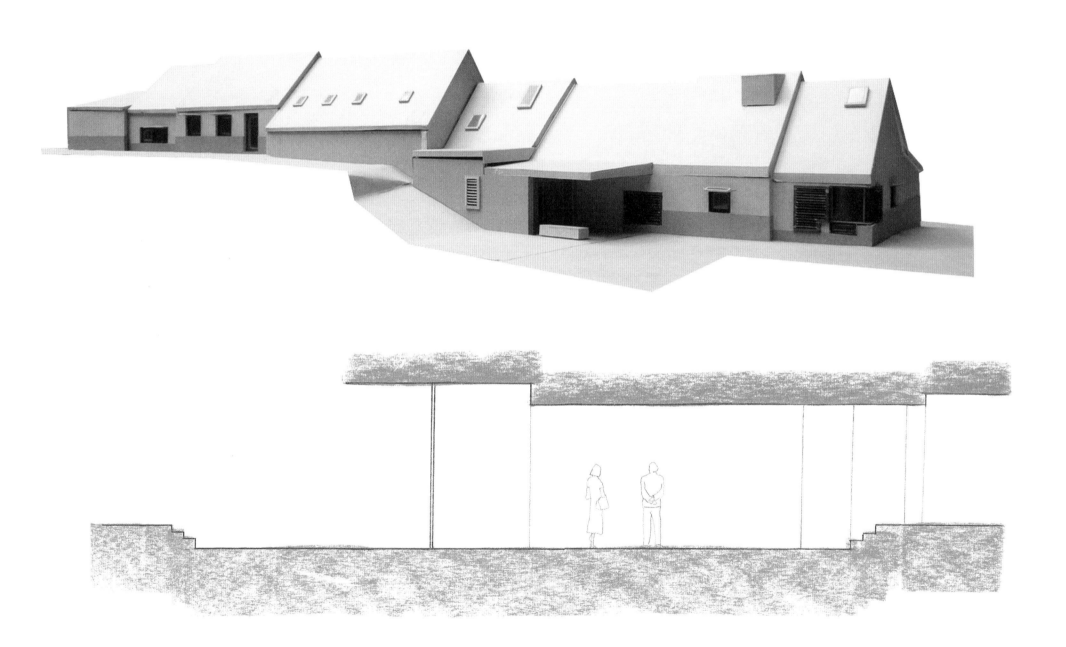

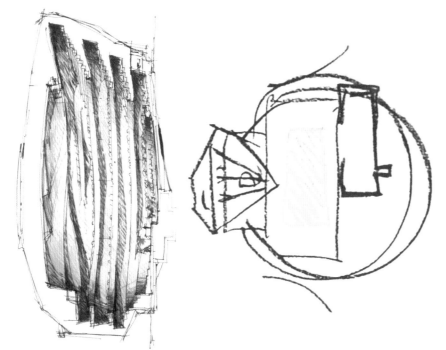

RAFAEL VIÑOLY

'I draw constantly because I enjoy it,' says Rafael Viñoly, principal at Rafael Viñoly Architects. 'I use pencil, thick pens, charcoal and watercolour, and I like to work large-scale because I think it teaches you to control proportion, and makes you think about dimension and form so much more. Small sketches are exercises in self-indulgence.'

Viñoly talks about having a dialogue with his initial sketches, interacting with them and realizing what they say to him on an intellectual level. This may sound strange but he believes that you cannot start a sketch with a preordained idea in mind. He goes on to flesh out the ideas that develop in watercolour, inks and charcoal.

Here, a vivid circular painting [326] is a concept for a World War II memorial monument; next to it is an elevation for the Kimmel Center, Philadelphia [327], while over the page is a dramatic charcoal rendering of an elevation of the Stanford University Medical Center, California [328–29].

'Those first sketches are me looking for an idea,' Viñoly says. 'They are scribbles that aim to find the right route for a project to take. It is fundamental that you have this dialogue with your work; you interact with the drawing, with your thoughts and with memories of sketches and ideas past in order to draw out the next idea. Sketching is not part of the thought process, for me it is the thought process.'

To this end, he is troubled by the cut-and-paste mentality of 21st-century society. He sees young architects simply borrowing ideas from multiple sources and stitching them together. 'This piecing together of ideas, creating collages without any real originality is creating architecture that looks like that too,' he says. 'People, from schoolchildren upwards need to learn to draw again: to slow down and appreciate the beauty of thinking with pencil and paper.

'Most of my buildings look like the original sketch. This is because they are born of a clear concept, an idea that has come from thinking and listening to what my mind, memories and sketch pad are telling me.'

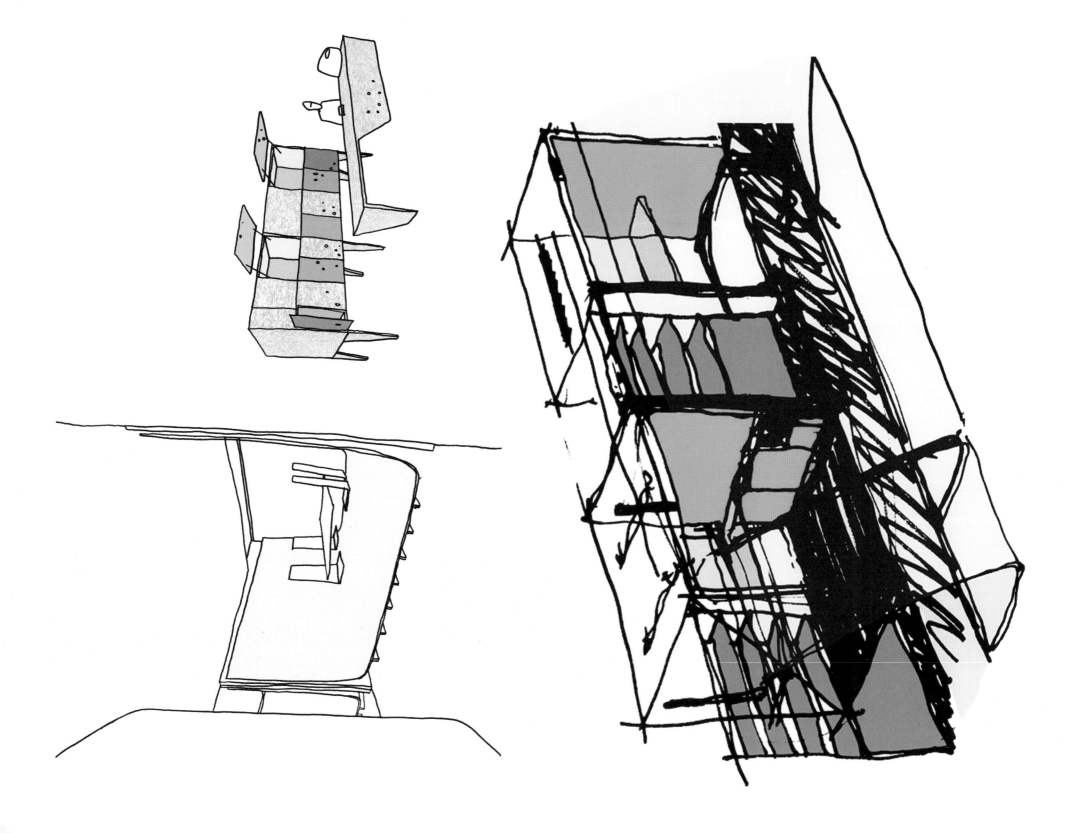

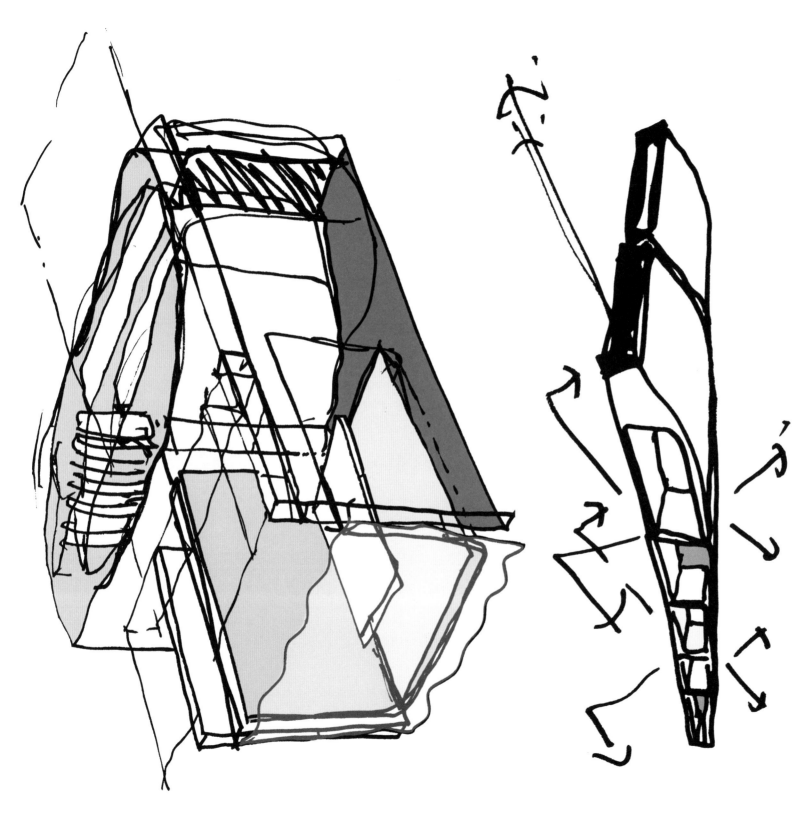

WALKER BUSHE ARCHITECTS

'Our favoured drawing tools are a very fat pencil with a soft lead for the first stages, followed by black felt-tip marker pens of varying thicknesses,' say the architects at Walker Bushe. 'Generally the pens become thinner as the design becomes more established and detail is required to test the initial design premise.'

Over-drawing on one another's drawings is encouraged. In studio design team meetings the architects work collaboratively, as the practice believes that the language of sketch drawing is separate but parallel to linguistic description: they can contribute suggestions that were not apparent before the sketch was made.

During the early design stages, architects at Walker Bushe also make rudimentary card models, some of which are given textural detail. These are deliberately made fast and rough to invite 'happy accidents'.

'All of our schemes are developed using sketches as the start point for exploring ideas and instigating design dialogues,' says Walker Bushe. This system allows the practice to deal with the major design moves (the solutions to know parameters) using only a few sketches, and then to move on and explore areas that may prove to be fertile territory for continued development. This combination often helps the practice reach the optimum solution to a problem.

'The more rapid and "semi-automatic" the sketches are, the more likely it is that the resultant ideas will throw up solutions offering more potential for further design development. Also, the more "sketchy" the initial presentation is, the more a client can feel that they are able to contribute to the early design process without damaging what could otherwise be a fully developed and complete scheme.'

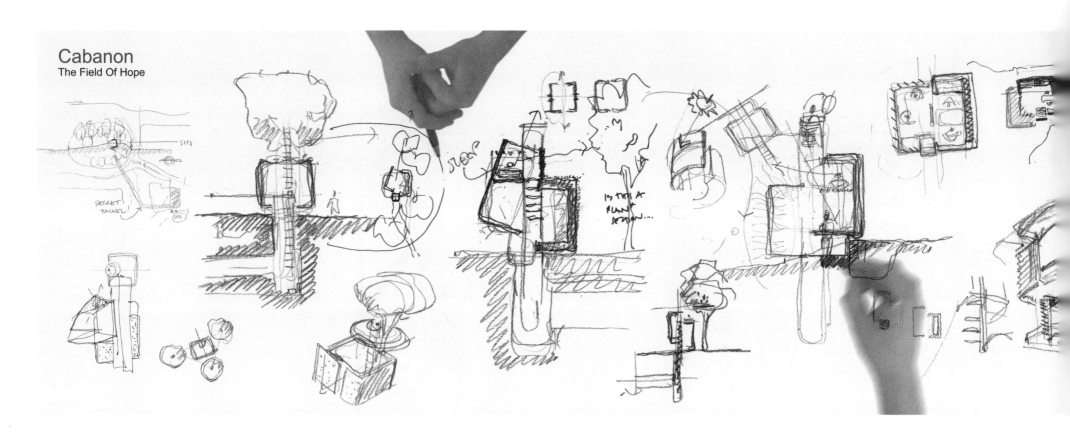

Cabanon
The Field Of Hope

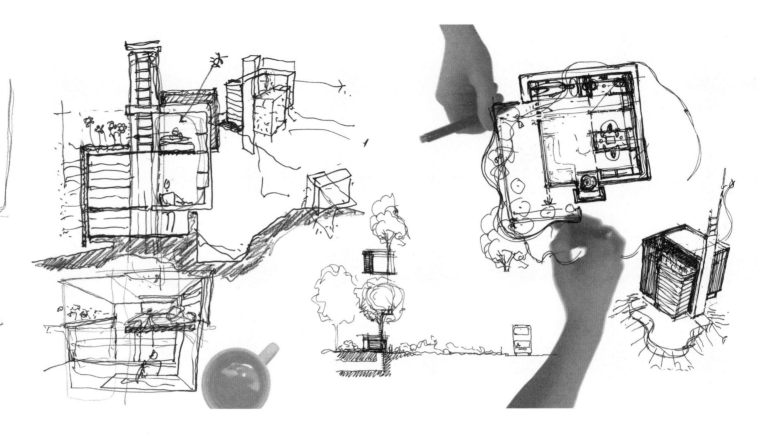

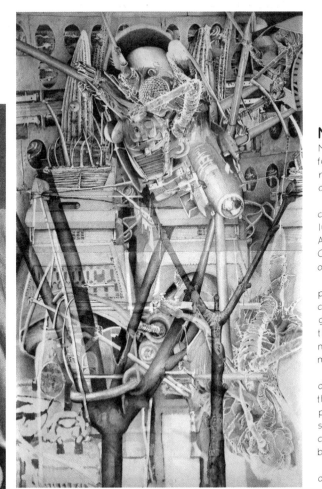

MARK WEST

Mark West's 'form-eruption' drawings transform the way that we perceive sketching, by re-examining the very source of the lines architects draw.

'Graphite is the crystalline form of carbon and is used industrially as a dry lubricant,' says West, Associate Professor of Architecture at the University of Manitoba, Canada. He goes on to explain that the nature of graphite is to be 'wet and slippery'.

West describes drawing as a kind of pulling: pulling your hands through a lubricant. The feeling, he says, is a bit like moving grease around with your fingers, although all this takes place in an 'infra-thin' space, and microscopic, translucent layers cling to the minute surface landscape of the paper.

In a 'form-eruption' drawing, the fundamental act is a clarification of the images that arise from the interplay between pencil and paper: shapes suggest themselves, West explains, 'exactly as they do…in clouds'—forms that are captured and honed by the interested eye.

These figures are not only seen, but also felt. The frictive quality of paper, combined with the caressing, gliding character of graphite allows the sketcher to sense the shape of the pencil point ('first a cone, then a truncated one, then a chisel that sloppily erodes towards a ball-point, now too far gone…now sharpened to a point and so forth') as it interacts with the relief of the paper—developing form through feel. But the relationship is fragile. Anything too wilful or forward will collapse the illusion: the architect will end up merely making marks on the paper and the compelling aura of potential surrounding the illusion will be lost.

'In this way, the final image both contains and obscures the many previous forms and images that constitute the morphogenesis of the picture,' explains West. 'They are "in there", yet no longer visible as themselves. The author of such a drawing holds a secret knowledge of the drawing's inside story. The drawing is felt to be more alive because of its inner geology, its hidden layers and past incarnations.'

335

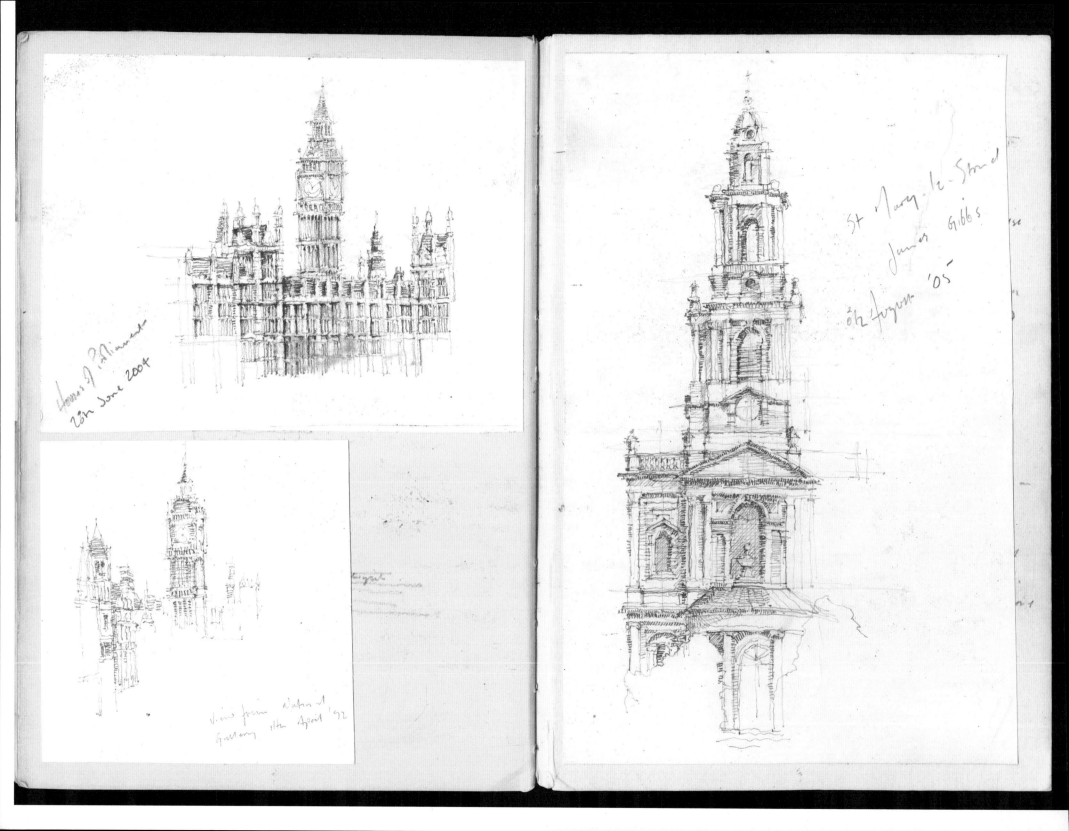

Houses of Parliament
29th June 2004

View from National
Gallery 14th April '92

St Mary-le-Strand
James Gibbs
6th August '05

The presence of the past is subtly more visible in Italy than in any other

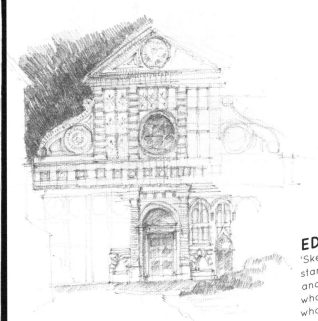

Santa Maria Novella
11th Feb 1990

ED WILLIAMS

'Sketching is an invaluable method of understanding how buildings are put together, and a very good method of remembering what I was feeling at a particular time, even what the weather was like. I have an ideas book, which I try and keep with me, just in case I think of anything or see an interesting idea.'

Simple but sound advice from serial sketcher Ed Williams of London-based practice Fletcher Priest Architects. He believes that the art of sketching is an unsurpassed tool for recording the moment. 'Sketching is the most direct method of putting down ideas—putting a mark on paper. Computers can restrict and slow down the design approach.... Beautifully computer-rendered drawings can often mask bad design. If you can sketch ideas with the client in the room, they can feel more involved in the design process and take ownership from the start.' Here we see various sketches from Williams's travels [336–37].

For Bevis Marks, an office project in London, Williams presented sketches to the city planners throughout the pre-application process. This helped develop the design, allowed a quick response to comments and clearly demonstrated that the design was still in the development stage.

'Typically, first ideas are the best ideas and these are usually in sketch form,' Williams says. 'The initial concept for Bevis Marks was much bolder than the...completed design [which] responds more sensitively to the context but is not as architecturally bold and exciting.'

337

southwark bridge road

union street ⟶

WITHERFORD WATSON MANN ARCHITECTS

Witherford Watson Mann Architects' sketch perspectives aren't conventional clean architectural drawings: they are adorned with street clutter, trees, the clues of life. 'We see it as a kind of empathy for how people use and see spaces,' says William Mann. 'They don't go round looking at the precise detail of architecture; they see cities through a blur of textual communication, of physical and social clues.'

The drawings also include a lot of context. The specific area or building considered might only be 25% of the image. The practice believes that this way you address things as they are, including the problems life sets you—not just the ones you set yourself. The images featured here are all part of a study into the potential redevelopment of a large area of London, south of the River Thames [338–41].

'An abstract diagram is all very well, but how you come to understand whatever order or clarity there is, is crucial,' says Mann. He brings the same argument to the computer versus hand drawing debate. 'On an A1 drawing your eye can zoom seamlessly between overview and detail. On a 17 inch screen you can zoom in to the detail, but you lose the overview, or zoom out, and you get the overview but lose the detail.

'Obviously we use CAD,' he continues, 'but the way we work is to print out and then mark up or draw over the print. This is probably very conventional, but when someone starts to work with us we have to make the point that we won't have a discussion pointing at coloured lines on a computer screen.'

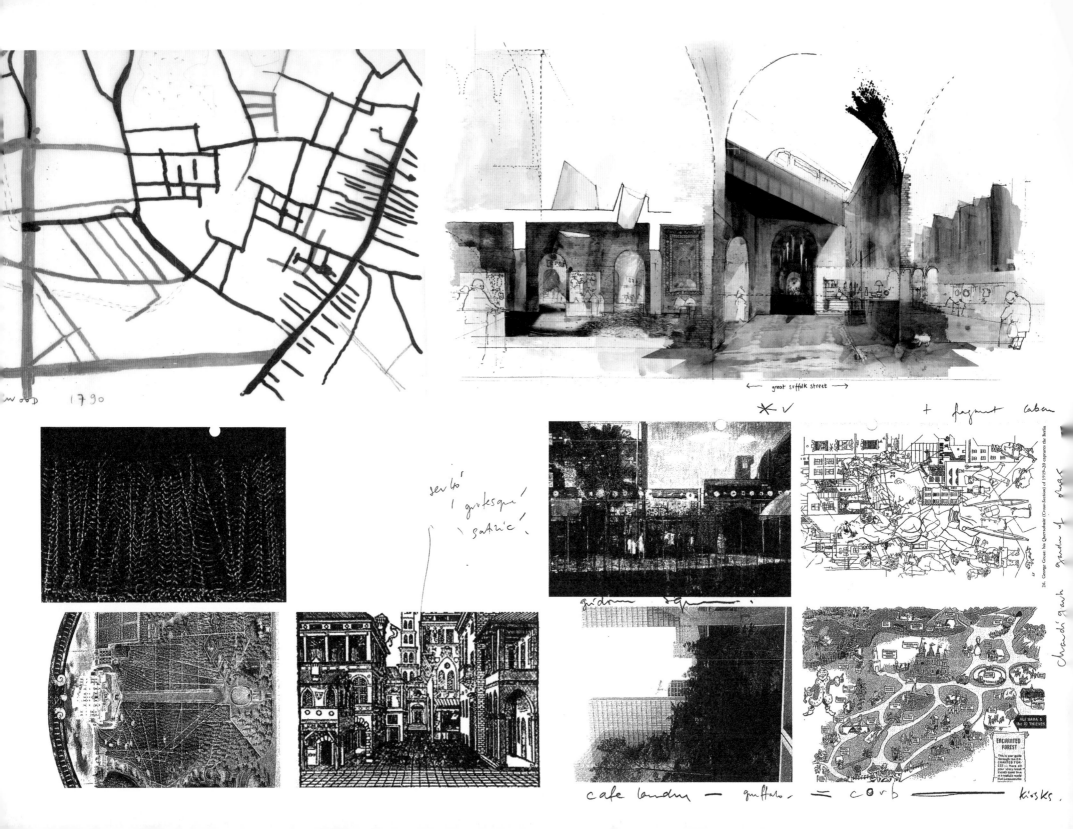

wood   1790

←— great suffolk street —→

serlio'
'grotesque'
'satiric'

cafe landing —— gruffalo — corb ————— kiosks.

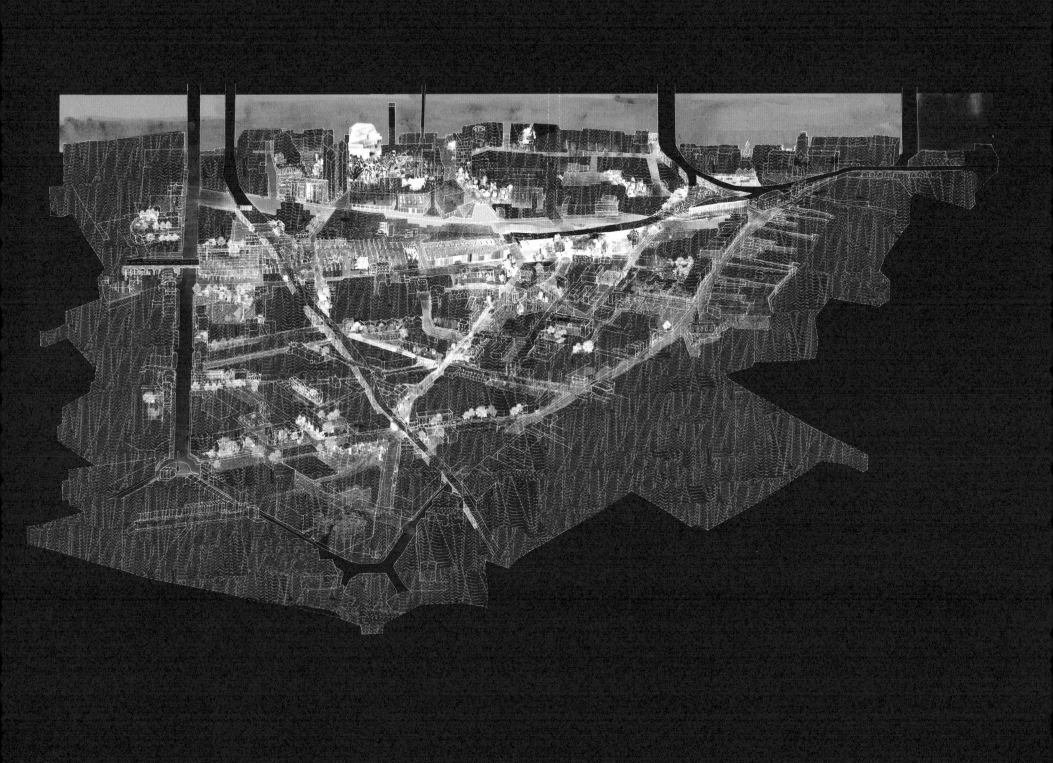

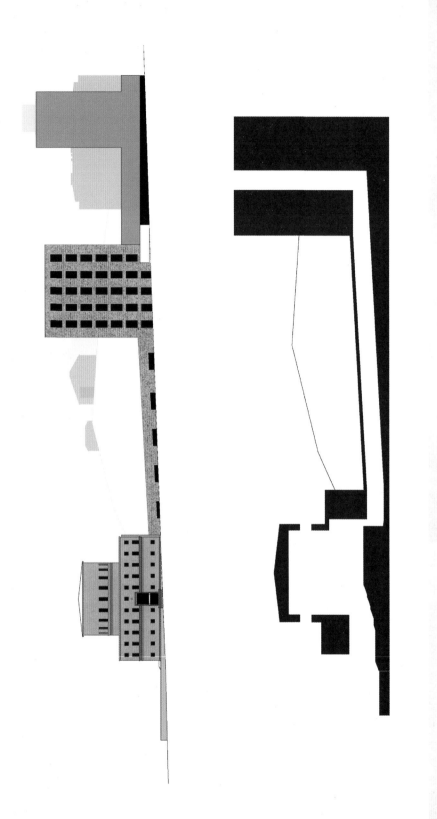

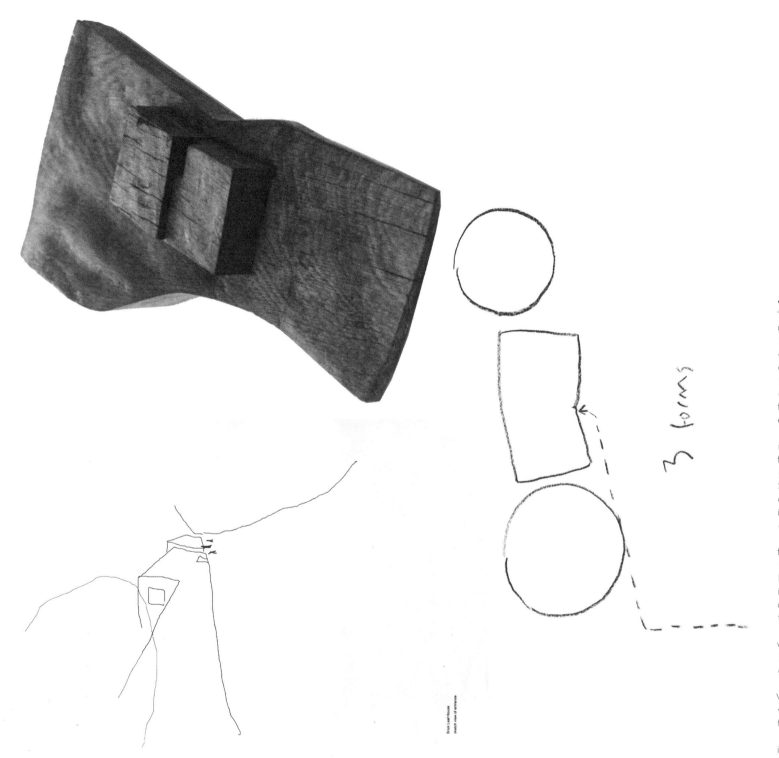

Brick Leaf House
sketch view of entrance

3 forms

JONATHAN WOOLF

'Ideas do not always arrive before what you term the "illustration", in fact often it is quite the opposite,' says Jonathan Woolf of Jonathan Woolf Architects, London. 'I don't believe we can really explain how the project finds its most responsive idea, but only accept that often the best idea comes to the surface through persistent study. It's an empirical process.'

Woolf works with a combination of models, sketches and scale drawings in order to build up a picture of the project. This allows any idea to be 'tabled for consideration'. Scale diagrams are used to analyse and question hierarchies of spatial relationships in the programme, as are physical models and precedent studies.

'Usually we can generate a series of testing ideas and play with them until we rest on one that emerges as the winner. Physical models are much more useful to us, in particular representational models, which abstract key aspects...to give a clear view of the design concept.

'We use hand sketches after we have verified the fundamental sizes of things. This is important since hand sketches are often deceptive about the actuality,' says Woolf.

Once the dimensional issues are solved Woolf uses sketches to build up the core values of the project—what he thinks of as the 'genetic code of the form'.

Woolf says: 'For me the iconic sketch is the result of the project. It "proves" the work and is often made after the model, as if drawing a still life.'

343

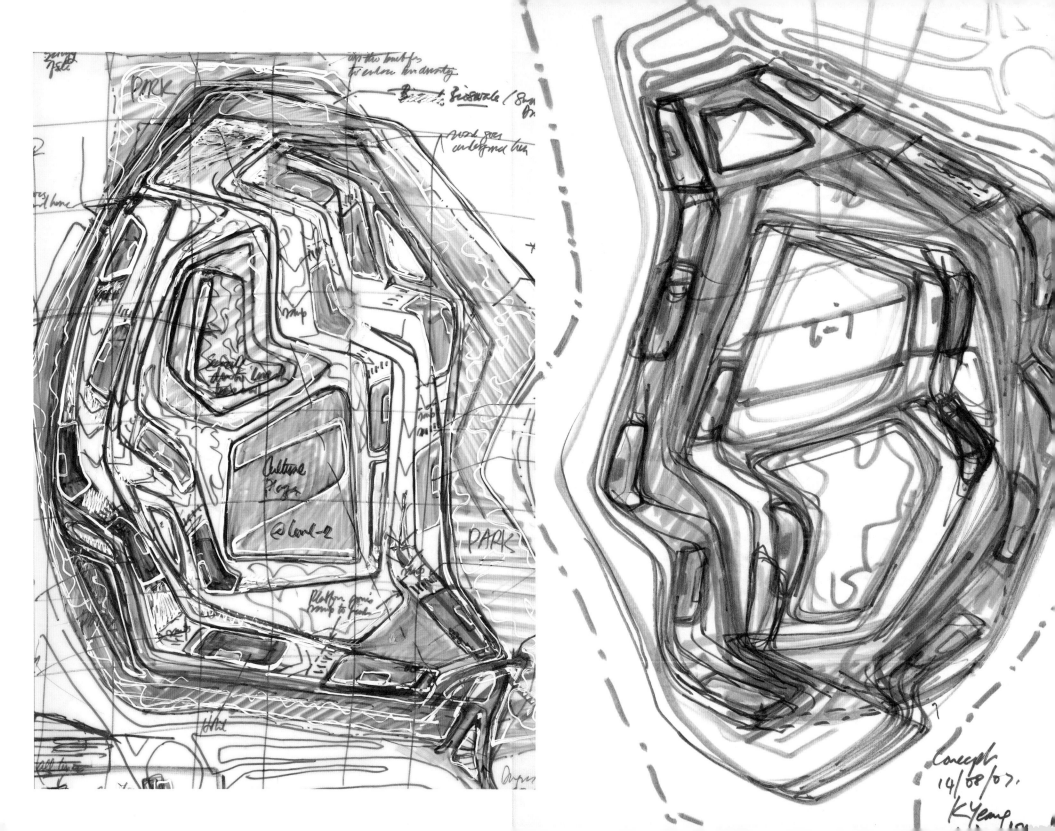

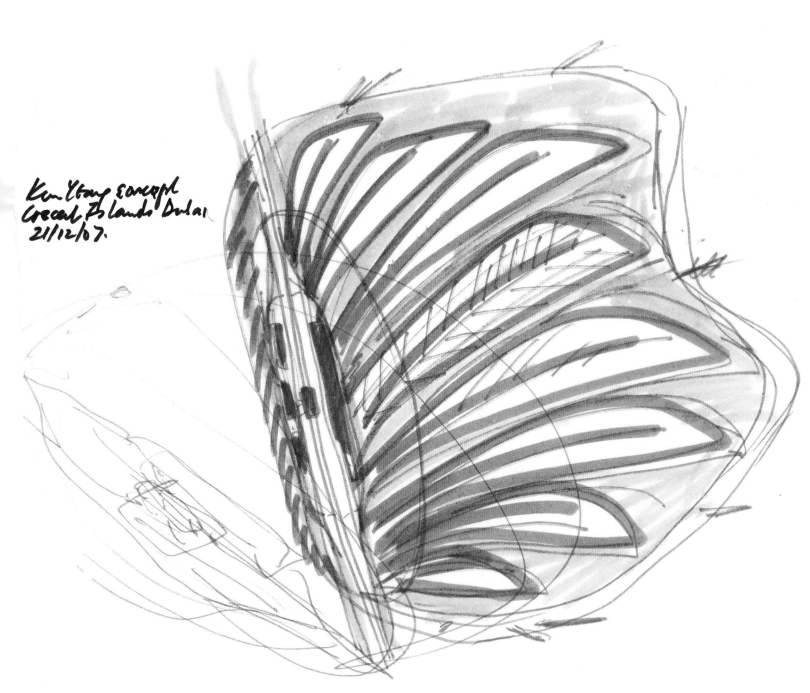

Ken Yeng concept
Crecal Islands Dubai
21/12/07.

KEN YEANG

Ken Yeang, a world-famous architect, and partner at Llewelyn Davies Yeang and T. R. Hamzah and Yeang, is renowned for his environmental design of both buildings and much larger masterplans. However, when conceiving projects, big or small, he begins with hand-drawn sketches. 'Usually I begin with a plan or idea of the spatial relationships and configuration of a scheme, but often draw it again and again until the aesthetic of the project feels OK,' says Yeang.

'Everything centres around the greening concept [the need to ensure all projects are environmentally friendly] and responses to site; and so sometimes I get an assistant to do the range of built-form options or the set of site and environmental analyses that I use as a springboard.'

The results of these embryonic ideas are 'templates' for the designs that Yeang and his team model in 3D to test shapes and aesthetics. If they don't work he starts all over again, though this isn't often necessary. 'About 80% of my designs get carried through to completion,' says Yeang. It is often the first sketch, based on a gut feeling, that ends up being the best solution.

Here, Yeang's trademark fluid style depicts designs for Zorlu Ecocity, Istanbul [345] and the Dubai Crescent Islands [344]. 'While the concurrent theoretical and technical aspects of green design, plus the constant pursuit of...innovation drive our work, we are also seeking to derive a green or ecological aesthetic, trying to define what a green building or a green masterplan should look like,' says Yeang. This is achieved through a combination of technology and sketches.

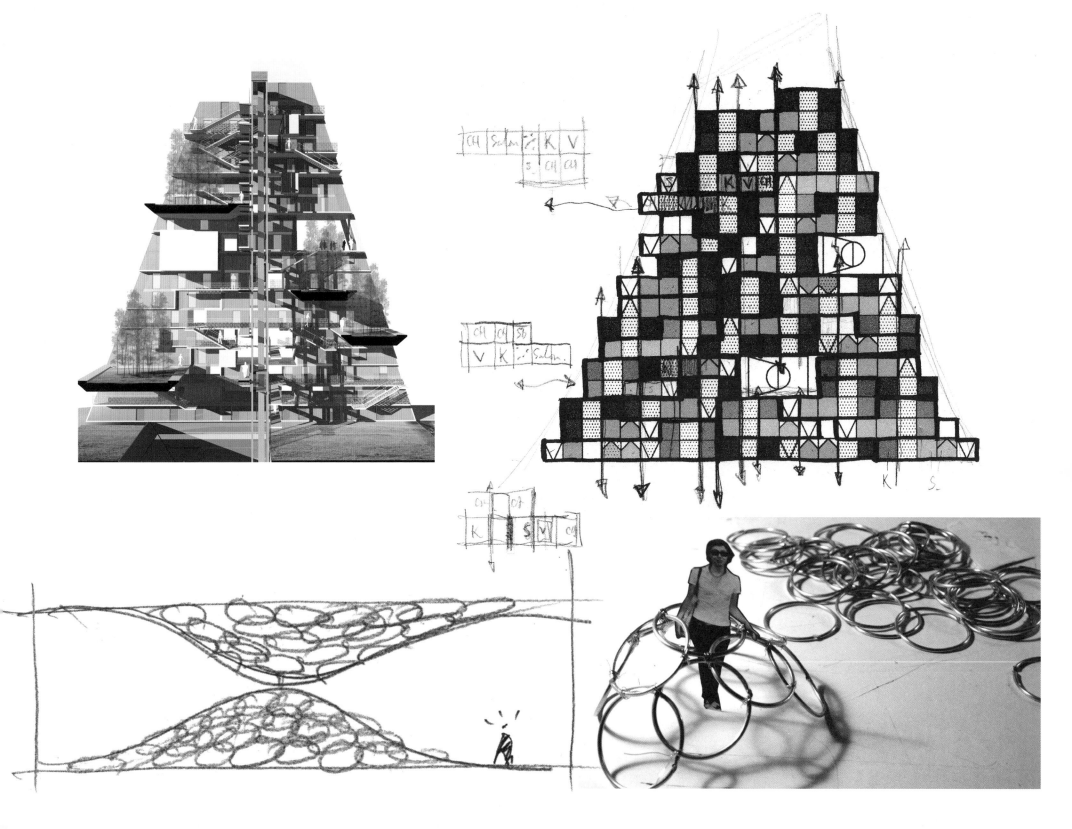

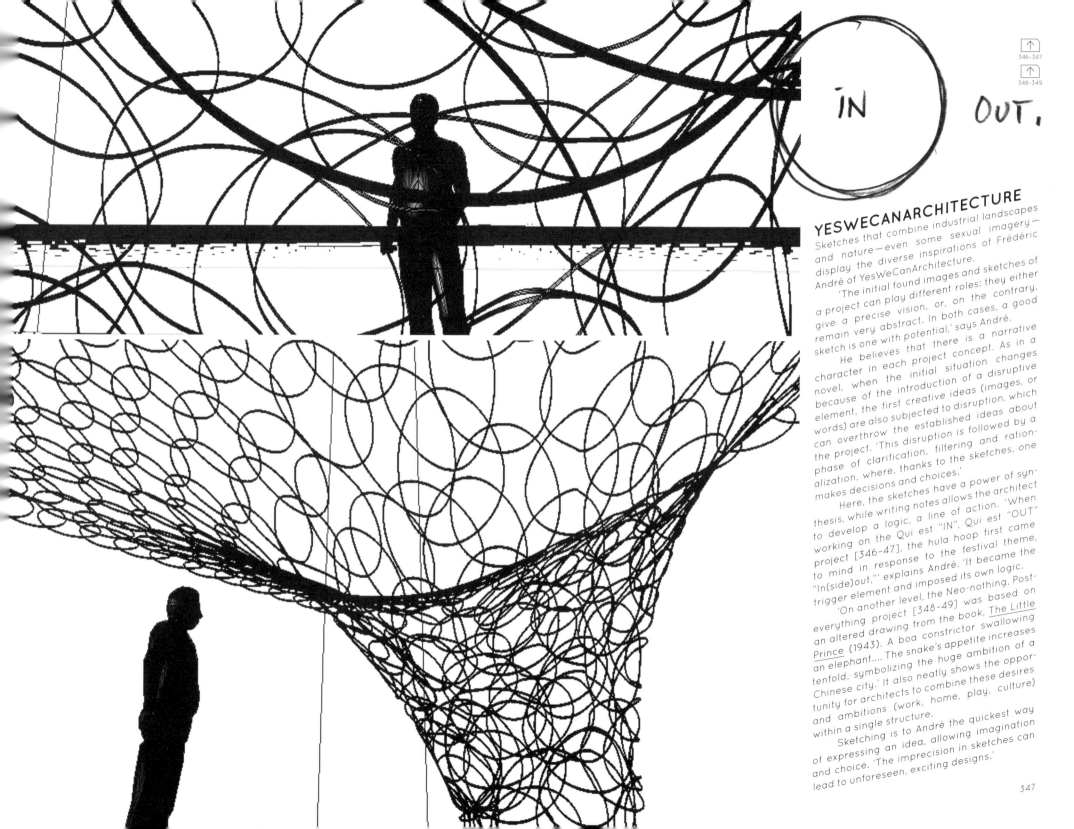

IN ◯ OUT.

YESWECANARCHITECTURE

Sketches that combine industrial landscapes—
and nature—even some sexual imagery—
display the diverse inspirations of Frédéric
André of YesWeCanArchitecture.

'The initial found images and sketches of
a project can play different roles: they either
give a precise vision, or, on the contrary,
remain very abstract. In both cases, a good
sketch is one with potential,' says André.

He believes that there is a narrative
character in each project concept. As in a
novel, when the initial situation changes
because of the introduction of a disruptive
element, the first creative ideas (images, or
words) are also subjected to disruption, which
can overthrow the established ideas about
the project. 'This disruption is followed by a
phase of clarification, filtering and ration-
alization, where, thanks to the sketches, one
makes decisions and choices.'

Here, the sketches have a power of synthesis, while writing notes allows the architect
to develop a logic, a line of action. 'When
working on the Qui est "IN", Qui est "OUT"
project [346–47], the hula hoop first came
to mind in response to the festival theme,
"In(side)out,"' explains André. 'It became the
trigger element and imposed its own logic.

'On another level, the Neo-nothing, Post-
everything project [348–49] was based on
an altered drawing from the book, The Little
Prince (1943). A boa constrictor swallowing
an elephant.... The snake's appetite increases
tenfold,' symbolizing the huge ambition of a
Chinese city.' It also neatly shows the opportunity for architects to combine these desires
and ambitions (work, home, play, culture)
within a single structure.

Sketching is to André the quickest way
of expressing an idea, allowing imagination
and choice. 'The imprecision in sketches can
lead to unforeseen, exciting designs.'

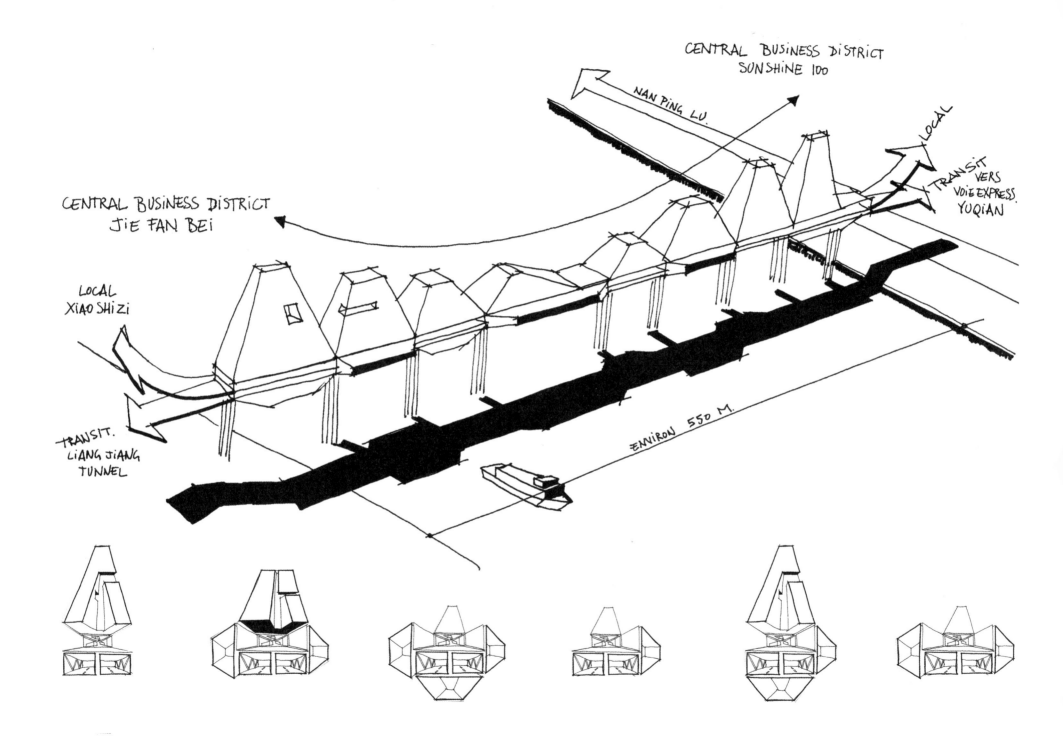

CENTRAL BUSINESS DISTRICT
SUNSHINE 100

NAN PING LU.

CENTRAL BUSINESS DISTRICT
JIE FAN BEI

LOCAL
XIAO SHIZI

LOCAL

TRANSIT VERS
VOIE EXPRESS.
YUQIAN

TRANSIT.
LIANG JIANG
TUNNEL

ENVIRON 550 M.

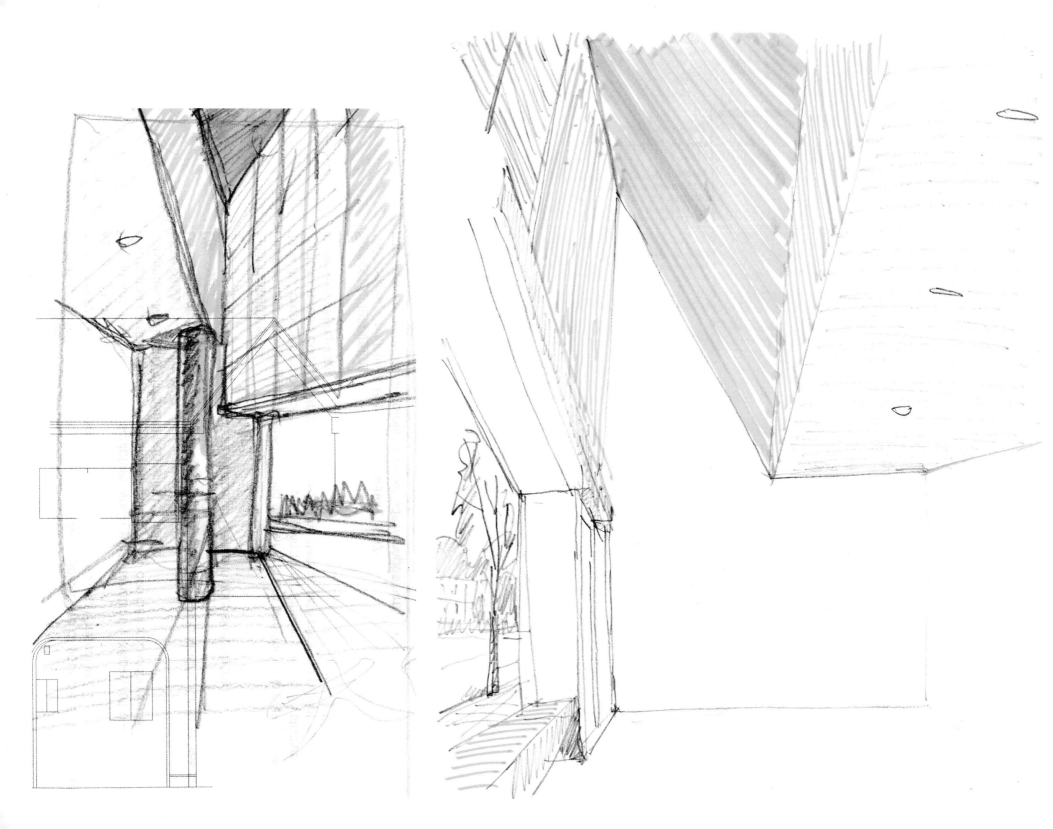

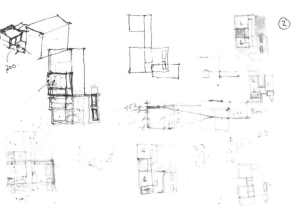

YOSHIHARA McKEE ARCHITECTS

Yoshihara McKee Architects was established in 1996 with offices in New York and Tokyo. Sandra McKee is an adjunct professor at Fordham University, New York, while Hiroki Yoshihara obtained a PhD in physics at Nagoya University, Japan, before going on to study architecture.

'We usually embark on the design process with almost illegible scribbles on the back of recycled paper, ideas that are too elusive to make a full drawing. Then, we move to tracing paper and sketchbooks,' say the architects. 'Tracing paper allows us to quickly add to ideas made in our sketchbooks, almost in a stream of consciousness.'

Yoshihara McKee combines models and sketches, taking a photograph and sketching over it, or sketching over a computer drawing. They use models to study spatial implications, starting with massing studies and working up to detailed models at a larger scale. 'The initial scribbles allow you to be totally free with your idea, and they get layered with more and more ideas,' McKee explains. 'The results are a tumble of things that all have equal importance. It is a good way to vet the meandering thoughts that you have.'

The architects' models then enforce more discipline, demanding that they think how the space will be assembled, and giving a bird's-eye view of aspects of the design that cannot be communicated on paper.

'The process of sketching is a way of thinking, a way to focus; it is not the end result,' says McKee. 'Sometimes the page is completely covered, layered with thoughts, and you must reconnect the lines to get back to the original idea. Our final drawings are not over-elaborate; they are direct and to the point.'

For Stephanie, my picture perfect —W.J.

First published in the USA in 2011 by
Metropolis Books, a joint publishing program of:

D.A.P./Distributed Art Publishers
155 Sixth Avenue, 2nd floor
New York, NY 10013
tel 212 627 1999 / fax 212 627 9484
www.artbook.com

and

Metropolis Magazine
61 West 23rd Street, 4th floor
New York, NY 10010
tel 212 627 9977 / fax 212 627 9988
www.metropolismag.com

Available through D.A.P./Distributed Art Publishers,
Inc., New York.

Library of Congress Cataloging-in-Publication Data
is available upon request

ISBN 978-1-935202-46-2

First published in the United Kingdom in 2011
by Thames & Hudson Ltd, 181A High Holborn,
London WC1V 7QX

Copyright © 2011 Will Jones

Illustrations copyright © 2011 the individual
architects, unless otherwise noted.

Printed and bound in China by Toppan Leefung

Picture credits

*All images supplied by the individual architects,
unless otherwise noted. Page numbers in bold.*

18–23 All images copyright © www.3deluxe.de **24–29**
A4 Studio—Kendik Géza **34–37** Agathom Co. (photos
Paul Orenstein) **48–51** Shigeru Ban Architects Europe
(CGI); Shigeru Ban (sketches) **116–19** copyright
© Dorell.Ghotmeh.Tane/Architects **126–29** Images
copyright © Rand Elliott **168–71** Model photos: John
Pass; Sketches: Seth Rutt, Hawkins\Brown; All other
visuals Hawkins\Brown **280–83** carlorattiassociati—
Walter Nicolino & Carlo Ratti **306–09** SMAQ—
Architecture Urbanism Research: Sabine Müller,
Andreas Quednau **338–41** William Mann and Freddie
Phillipson **342–43** Sketches: Jonathan Woolf; Other
material: Jonathan Woolf Architects

Websites

3deluxe
www.3deluxe.de

A4 Studio
www.a4studio.hu

Ben Addy
www.moxonarchitects.com

Agathom Co.
www.agathom.com

Will Alsop
www.alsopsparch.com

Architects Atelier Ryo Abe
www.aberyo.com

Shigeru Ban
www.shigerubanarchitects.com

Julio Barreno
www.juliobarreno.com

C. Errol Barron
www.errolbarron.com

Bercy Chen Studio LP
www.bcarc.com

Boidot Robin Architects
www.j-b-a.eu

BPR
www.birdsportchmouthrussum.com

Brent Buck
www.twbta.com

Casagrande Laboratory
www.clab.fi

Laurie Chetwood
www.chetwoods.com

Prue Chiles
www.pruechilesarchitects.co.uk

Cindy Rendely Architexture
www.crarchitexture.com

Peter Clash
www.clasharchitects.co.uk

Frank Clementi
www.rchstudios.com

Jeanne Dekkers
www.jeannedekkers.nl

DMAA
www.deluganmeissl.at

Dorell.Ghotmeh.Tane
www.dgtarchitects.com

East
www.east.uk.com

Elemental
www.elementalchile.cl

Elliott + Associates Architects
www.e-a-a.com

Mathew Emmett
www.mathewemmett.com

Fantastic Norway
www.fantasticnorway.com

Thom Faulders
www.faulders-studio.com

Norman Foster
www.fosterandpartners.com

Tony Fretton
www.tonyfretton.com

Glowacka Rennie
www.glowacka-rennie.com

Sean Godsell
www.seangodsell.com

Ivan Harbour
www.richardrogers.co.uk

Hawkins\Brown
www.hawkinsbrown.co.uk

Carlos Jiménez
www.carlosjimenezstudio.com

Eva Jiricna
www.ejal.com

Steven Johnson
www.thearchitectureensemble.com

Junya Ishigami & Associates
www.jnyi.jp

kennedytwaddle
www.kennedytwaddle.com

Michael Lehrer
www.lehrerarchitects.com

Alistair Lillystone
www.hok.com

CJ Lim
www.cjlim-studio8.com

Liquidfactory
www.liquidfactory.co.uk

John Lyall
www.johnlyallarchitects.com

Mackenzie Wheeler
www.mackenziewheeler.co.uk

Barrie Marshall
www.dentoncorkermarshall.com

Stephen McGrath
www.squireandpartners.com

Alessandro Mendini
www.ateliermendini.it

Mi5 Arquitectos
www.mi5arquitectos.com

Nagan Johnson
www.naganjohnson.co.uk

O+A
www.oplusa.nl

O'Donnell + Tuomey
www.odonnell-tuomey.ie

Office dA
www.officeda.com

Chad Oppenheim
www.oppenoffice.com

Terry Pawson
www.terrypawson.com

Point Supreme Architects
www.pointsupreme.com

Paul Raff
www.paulraffstudio.com

Carlo Ratti
www.carloratti.com

Rocha Tombal
www.rocha.tombal.nl

Marc Rolinet
www.rolinet.fr

Narinder Sagoo
www.fosterandpartners.com

Ken Shuttleworth
www.makearchitects.com

sixteen*(makers)
www.sixteenmakers.com

SMAQ
www.smaq.net

Smout Allen
www.smoutallen.com

Toh Shimazaki
www.t-sa.co.uk

Rafael Viñoly
www.rvapc.com

Walker Bushe Architects
www.walkerbushe.co.uk

Mark West
www.umanitoba.ca/cast_building

Ed Williams
www.fletcherpriest.com

Witherford Watson Mann Architects
www.wwmarchitects.co.uk

Jonathan Woolf
www.contemporaryarchitecture.com

Ken Yeang
www.llewelyn-davies-ltd.com

YesWeCanArchitecture
www.yeswecanarchitecture.com

Yoshihara McKee Architects
www.yoshiharamckee.com